Straining at the Anchor

NBER Series on Long-term Factors in Economic Development

A National Bureau of Economic Research Series
Edited by Claudia Goldin

Also in the series

Claudia Goldin
Understanding the Gender Gap: An Economic History of American Women (Oxford University Press, 1990)

Roderick Floud, Kenneth Wachter, and Annabel Gregory
Height, Health and History: Nutritional Status in the United Kingdom, 1750-1980 (Cambridge University Press, 1990)

Robert A. Margo
Race and Schooling in the South, 1880-1950: An Economic History (University of Chicago Press, 1990)

Samuel H. Preston and Michael R. Haines
Fatal Years: Child Mortality in Late Nineteenth-Century America (Princeton University Press, 1991)

Barry Eichengreen
Golden Fetters: The Gold Standard and the Great Depression, 1919-1939 (Oxford University Press, 1992)

Ronald N. Johnson and Gary D. Libecap
The Federal Civil Service System and the Problem of Bureaucracy: The Economics and Politics of Institutional Change (University of Chicago Press, 1994)

Naomi R. Lamoreaux
Insider Lending: Banks, Personal Connections, and Economic Development in Industrial New England, 1784–1912 (Cambridge University Press, 1994)

Lance E. Davis, Robert E. Gallman, and Karin Gleiter
In Pursuit of Leviathan: Technology, Institutions, Productivity, and Profits in American Whaling, 1816-1906 (University of Chicago Press, 1997)

Dora L. Costa
The Evolution of Retirement: An American Economic History, 1880-1990 (University of Chicago Press, 1998)

Joseph P. Ferrie
Yankeys Now: Immigrants in the Antebellum U.S., 1840-1860 (Oxford University Press, 1999)

Robert A. Margo
Wages and Labor Markets in the United States, 1820-1860 (University of Chicago Press, 2000)

Price V. Fishback and Shawn Everett Kantor
A Prelude to the Welfare State: The Origins of Workers' Compensation (University of Chicago Press, 2000)

Straining at the Anchor

The Argentine Currency Board and the Search for Macroeconomic Stability, 1880–1935

Gerardo della Paolera
and Alan M. Taylor

The University of Chicago Press

Chicago and London

GERARDO DELLA PAOLERA is rector and professor of economics at the Universidad Torcuato Di Tella in Buenos Aires.

ALAN M. TAYLOR is associate professor of economics at the University of California at Davis and a research associate of the National Bureau of Economic Research.

Excerpts from "Finance and Development in an Emerging Market: Argentina in the Interwar Period," in *Latin America and the World Economy Since 1800*, edited by John H. Coatsworth and Alan M. Taylor (1999), by kind permission of Harvard University Press.
Excerpts from "Economic Recovery from the Argentine Great Depression: Institutions, Expectations, and the Change of Macroeconomic Regime," *Journal of Economic History* 59 (September 1999), pp. 567–99, by kind permission of the Economic History Association.

The University of Chicago Press, Chicago 60637
The University of Chicago Press, Ltd., London

Printed in the United States of America
10 09 08 07 06 05 04 03 02 01   1 2 3 4 5
ISBN: 0-226-64556-8 (cloth)

Library of Congress Cataloging-in-Publication Data

della Paolera, Gerardo, 1959–
Straining at the anchor : the Argentine currency board and the search for macroeconomic stability, 1880–1935 / Gerardo della Paolera and Alan M. Taylor
p. cm. — (NBER series on long-term factors in economic development)
Includes bibliographical references and index.
ISBN 0-226-64556-8 (cloth : alk. paper)
1. Monetary policy—Argentina—History. 2. Currency question—Argentina—History. 3. Currency boards—Argentina—History. 4. Argentina. Caja de Conversión. I. Title: Argentine currency board and the search for macroeconomic stability, 1880–1935. II. Taylor, Alan M., 1964– III. Title.

HG1464 .D45 2001
339.5′3′0982–dc21

2001027898

⊗ The paper used in this publication meets the minimum requirements of the American National Standard for Information Sciences—Permanence of Paper for Printed Library Materials, ANSI Z39.48-1992.

Relation of the Directors to the Work and Publications of the National Bureau of Economic Research

1. The object of the National Bureau of Economic Research is to ascertain and to present to the public important economic facts and their interpretation in a scientific and impartial manner. The Board of Directors is charged with the responsibility of ensuring that the work of the National Bureau is carried on in strict conformity with this object.
2. The President of the National Bureau shall submit to the Board of Directors, or to its Executive Committee, for their formal adoption all specific proposals for research to be instituted.
3. No research report shall be published by the National Bureau until the President has sent each member of the Board a notice that a manuscript is recommended for publication and that in the President's opinion it is suitable for publication in accordance with the principles of the National Bureau. Such notification will include an abstract or summary of the manuscript's content and a response form for use by those Directors who desire a copy of the manuscript for review. Each manuscript shall contain a summary drawing attention to the nature and treatment of the problem studied, the character of the data and their utilization in the report, and the main conclusions reached.
4. For each manuscript so submitted, a special committee of the Directors (including Directors Emeriti) shall be appointed by majority agreement of the President and Vice Presidents (or by the Executive Committee in case of inability to decide on the part of the President and Vice Presidents), consisting of three Directors selected as nearly as may be one from each general division of the Board. The names of the special manuscript committee shall be stated to each Director when notice of the proposed publication is submitted to him. It shall be the duty of each member of the special manuscript committee to read the manuscript. If each member of the manuscript committee signifies his approval within thirty days of the transmittal of the manuscript, the report may be published. If at the end of that period any member of the manuscript committee withholds his approval, the President shall then notify each member of the Board, requesting approval or disapproval of publication, and thirty days additional shall be granted for this purpose. The manuscript shall then not be published unless at least a majority of the entire Board who shall have voted on the proposal within the time fixed for the receipt of votes shall have approved.
5. No manuscript may be published, though approved by each member of the special manuscript committee, until forty-five days have elapsed from the transmittal of the report in manuscript form. The interval is allowed for the receipt of any memorandum of dissent or reservation, together with a brief statement of his reasons, that any member may wish to express; and such memorandum of dissent or reservation shall be published with the manuscript if he so desires. Publication does not, however, imply that each member of the Board has read the manuscript, or that either members of the Board in general or the special committee have passed on its validity in every detail.
6. Publications of the National Bureau issued for informational purposes concerning the work of the Bureau and its staff, or issued to inform the public of activities of Bureau staff, and volumes issued as a result of various conferences involving the National Bureau shall contain a specific disclaimer noting that such publication has not passed through the normal review procedures required in this resolution. The Executive Committee of the Board is charged with review of all such publications from time to time to ensure that they do not take on the character of formal research reports of the National Bureau, requiring formal Board approval.
7. Unless otherwise determined by the Board or exempted by the terms of paragraph 6, a copy of this resolution shall be printed in each National Bureau publication.

(Resolution adopted October 25, 1926, as revised through September 30, 1974)

To Verónica, Marina, Carola, and Martín
G. d. P.

To Claire
A. M. T.

Contents

Acknowledgments *page* xvii

Part One: The Historical and Methodological Context

1 Introduction 3

2 Anchors Aweigh: The Drift toward Crisis in the 1880s 37

Part Two: The Baring Crisis and Its Origins

3 A Monetary and Financial Wreck: The Baring Crisis, 1890–91 67

4 Collision Course: Macroeconomic Policies and the Crash 80

Part Three: The Making of the Belle Époque

5 Relaunching the Gold Standard: From Monetary "Anemia" to "Plethora" and the Political Economy of Resumption, 1891–99 99

6 Calm Before a Storm: The Gold Standard During the Belle Époque, 1899–1914 118

Part Four: The Travails of the Interwar Years

7 Distress Signals: Financial Fragility in the Interwar Period 139

8 Bailing Out: Internal versus External Convertibility 165

9 Steering through the Great Depression: Institutions, Expectations, and the Change of Macroeconomic Regime 188

Part Five: Postscript

10 Postscript 221

Appendix 1 Historical Statistics 236

Appendix 2 The Law of National Guaranteed Banks 240

Appendix 3 Money Supply Periodization, 1884–1913 244

Appendix 4 Money and Exchange Rates, 1884–1913 247

Appendix 5 Instituto Movilizador de Inversiones Bancarias 253

Appendix 6 Humor, Politics, and the Economy 255

References 257

Name Index 267

Subject Index 271

List of Tables

1.1 Argentine Inflation, 1820–1935 14
1.2 Monetary Policy Chronology 23
2.1 Real Activity, Monetary Variables, and Interest Rates, 1861–82 40
2.2 Argentine Specie Stock, 1883–99 53
2.3 Statistical Summary, 1884–1913 56
2.4 Money Supply, 1884–1913 57
3.1 The Baring Crisis, 1889–91 71
3.2 Solvency-Liquidity Indicators, Banco de la Provincia, 1886–91 76
4.1 Fiscal Revenues, Expenditures, and Public Debt, 1884–1913 81
4.2 Federal Budget, 1885–93 88
4.3 Fiscal Deficits, Inflation, and Public Debt, 1885–93 89
4.4 Conjectural Short-term Interest Rates, 1890–91 93
5.1 Key Fiscal Indicators, 1891–99 102
5.2 The Burdensome Funding Loan Agreement 110
5.3 Selected Statistics, 1891–99 111
5.4 Monetary Ratios, 1891–99 112
5.5 Urban-Rural Welfare Measures and Interest Rates, 1891–99 115
6.1 Monetary and Fiscal Indicators, 1900–1913 122
6.2 Effects of Gold Reserves on Money Supply, 1904–13 125
6.3 Financial Crisis Indicators, 1913–14 131
7.1 Finance and Development, 1900–1939 147
7.2 Anatomy of Three Financial Crises 156
7.3 Model of Banks with "Twin Risk" 157
8.1 Banco de la Nación, 1892–1934 170
8.2 Selected Banking Ratios, 1892–1934 173
8.3 Dynamics of Internal and External Convertibility, 1908–13 182
9.1 Contours of the Argentine Great Depression 191
9.2 Changes in Gold Stocks and the Money Base, 1900–1935 197
9.3 Model of Prices, Exchange Rates, and Interest Rates 208
A2.1 Provisions of the Law of National Guaranteed Banks 241
A2.2 Balance Sheet of a Guaranteed Bank 242
A2.3 Average Bank Profits, 1885–87 242

A2.4 Balance Sheet of a Government-related Wildcat Bank 243
A4.1 Money Supply Estimation, 1884–1913 248
A4.2 Exchange Rate Determinants, 1884–1913 249
A4.3 Money Demand Estimation, 1884–1913 250
A4.4 Money Demand Estimation, 1884–1913 251
A5.1 Actions of the Instituto Movilizador de Inversiones Bancarias 254
A6.1 Presidents and their Parties, 1862–1938 256

List of Figures

1.1	Comparative Economic Development	8
1.2	Prices and Exchange Rates, 1880–1996	11
1.3	Prices and Exchange Rates, 1820–80	13
1.4	Country Risk in Argentina, Core, and Periphery, 1870–1940	27
2.1	The First Convertibility Experiment	44
2.2	Prices and the Paper-Gold Exchange Rate, 1884–1914	49
2.3	Public Hoarding of Specie, 1883–1914	54
2.4	Proximate Determinants of the Money Multiplier, 1884–1914	61
2.5	Currency, Bank Money, and Specie Hoarding, 1884–1914	62
4.1	Federal Funded Debt, 1884–1914	84
5.1	Paper-Gold Exchange Rate, 1883–1902	104
6.1	Bond Spreads, External Bonds, 1883–1913	123
6.2	Bond Yields, External and Internal Bonds, 1883–1913	123
7.1	International Comparisons of Financial Deepening, 1913–39	151
7.2	Financial Deepening and Economic Performance, 1900–1940	153
7.3	Loans by Bank Type, 1910–35	159
7.4	Capital by Bank Type, 1910–35	160
7.5	Leverage by Bank Type, 1910–35	161
7.6	Response of Bank Loans to a Shock to Gold Stock	163
8.1	Banco de la Nación Balance Sheet, 1892–1934	171
8.2	Reserve-Deposit Ratios, Actual and Counterfactual, 1892–1934	172
8.3	Phase Diagram for the Dynamic Model	180
8.4	Reserve Ratios and Gold Stocks in Two Convertible Regimes	183
9.1	Fiscal Structure, 1910–40	196
9.2	Changes in Gold Stocks and the Money Base, 1900–1935	198
9.3	Nominal Exchange Rate Versus Parity, 1900–1940	199
9.4	Composition of the Money Base, 1900–1940	201
9.5	Prices, Exchange Rates, and Interest Rates, 1929–41	210
9.6	Real Interest Rates, Consumption, and Investment, 1929–41	212

List of Cartoons

2.1	*Nuestra feliz situación*	45
2.2	*Los unos chupan*	51
3.1	*John Bull ordena*	69
3.2	*Con sus amores arteros*	78
4.1	*La crisis del progreso*	91
5.1	*Gloria á los Gobernadores*	101
5.2	*Hacer un mate sin yerba*	107
6.1	*Lo mano cerrada*	132
6.2	*Los cirujanos socialistas*	135
7.1	*Con las manos en los bolsillos*	145
8.1	*El puchero salvador*	175
8.2	*El miedo no es zonzo*	185
9.1	*En casa del oculista*	194
9.2	*El fenómeno de la Casa Rosada*	206
10.1	*Muy bien adobados*	233

A Note on the Cover

La barbaridad

The various moods of Argentine political economy are succinctly captured by the satires of cartoonists in contemporary newspapers. A smattering of these illustrations enliven the text, and a particularly piquant example is shown in its original full color on the cover. It depicts the pivotal event in Argentine macroeconomic history, the creation of a discretionary monetary authority, the central bank *(Banco Central),* and the abolition of the former currency board *(Caja de Conversión)* in 1935. The Economy Minister Federico Pinedo appears as a magician converting the gold from the vaults of the *Caja* into paper notes issuing from the *Banco Central,* to the rapturous applause of the crowd of ministers in the box seats, prominent among them the President of the Republic, Agustín Justo, seated at the front. This institutional change opened the way for inflationary money printing for the first time since the nationalization of the currency in 1891 under gold standard rules. Thus was the nominal anchor of the Argentine economy broken. Our account frames this turn of events, and the inability to escape the backward economic tendencies evident in the fiscal use of money by the provincial authorities of the nineteenth century, as an enduring economic dimension of the battle between the *civilizaciòn* (civilization) and *barbaridad* (barbarity), the rival forces in Argentine history highlighted by the former President and man of letters Domingo Sarmiento (1868–74) in his famous work *Facundo*. That this cartoon was entitled *El fenómeno de la Casa Rosada* (The Phenomenon of the Casa Rosada) shows that contemporaries had long enough memories to know well the dangers of restoring political control over money, the Casa Rosada being the executive mansion. Ironically, Pinedo had originally opposed the idea of a central bank and, in heated argument with the leading economic policymaker Raúl Prebisch (see page 204), he reacted to the plan by exclaiming «*¿Que barbaridad van a hacer?*» ("what barbarity are you about to do?"). Was his choice of adjective a coincidence or a subconscious echo from the past? We will never know, but the smiling figure seen here on the stage seems to be no longer perturbed by such concerns.

Source: Caras y caretas, vol. 38, no. 1901, March 9, 1935.

Acknowledgments

This book contains the fruits of research conducted over a span of more than fifteen years. Inevitably we have amassed many debts along the way.

The most significant material support for our research has come from the National Science Foundation's Economics and International programs, through grants administered by the National Bureau of Economic Research. We thank the NSF for its generosity in giving and the NBER for its efficiency in managing.

Other institutions have also helped us directly or indirectly, with hospitality, library access and other scholarly resources, smaller grants, and other forms of support, and these we also thank: Universidad Torcuato Di Tella; University of California at Davis; National Fellow and Visiting Fellow programs, Hoover Institution, Stanford University; Social Science History Institute, Stanford University; Northwestern University; University of Chicago; St. Antony's College, Oxford; International Monetary Fund; Centro de Estudios Macroeconómicos de Argentina; and Banco Rio de la Plata. On a personal level we must also thank certain people who helped us obtain archival resources that we would not have otherwise found: Pablo Galvan at the Library of Congress; Alejandro Costas, former Head Librarian at the Biblioteca Tornquist; Roque Maccarone, former Chairman of the Banco Rio de la Plata; and Luis María Otero Monsegur, former Chairman of the Banco Frances y Rio de la Plata.

Over the years we have presented our work at a number of workshops and conferences, and we are grateful for the critical feedback we have received from these audiences at Universidad Torcuato Di Tella; University of California at Davis; National Bureau of Economic Research; Stanford University; Northwestern University; University of Chicago; St. Antony's College, Oxford; Harvard University; Yale University; University of California at Berkeley; University of California-Los Angeles; University of Delaware; University of Michigan; University of Notre Dame; California Institute of Technology; London School of Economics; University of Warwick; Institute for Latin American Studies, University of London; Universitat Pompeu Fabra; Fundação Getulio Vargas; Doshisha University; Tokyo Foundation; Federal Reserve Banks of St.

Louis, Dallas, and San Francisco, and the Board of Governors; Latin American and Caribbean Economic Association meetings in Buenos Aires and Santiago; Latin American Cliometric Society meetings in Cartagena; Twelfth International Economic History Congress in Madrid; and the conference on Latin America and the World Economy in Bellagio.

None of these audiences bears responsibility for any remaining errors, and nor do any of the individuals who gave us helpful comments and encouragement: Pablo Martín Aceña; Michael Bordo; Guillermo Bozzoli; Charles Calomiris; Forrest Capie; John Coatsworth; Roberto Cortés Conde; Nicholas Crafts; Bradford De Long; Guido Di Tella; Rudiger Dornbusch; Barry Eichengreen; Robert Fogel; David Galenson; Ezequiel Gallo; Pablo Gerchunoff; Pablo Guidotti; Tulio Halperín Donghi; Colin Lewis; David Lorey; Daniel Marx; Deirdre McCloskey; Carlos Newland; Juan Pablo Nicolini; Maurice Obstfeld; Javier Ortiz; Norberto Peruzzotti; Leandro Prados de la Escosura; Andrés Regalsky; Christina Romer; Ricardo Salvatore; Fernando de Santibañes; Anna Schwartz; Larry Sjaastad; Carlos Végh; Eugene White; and Carlos Zarazaga. We owe special thanks to series editor Claudia Goldin; executive editor Geoffrey Huck; two anonymous referees; and the indefatigable Peter Lindert—all of whom read the entire manuscript and offered constructive criticism.

In the same spirit we must acknowledge our considerable intellectual debts to three pioneers in the study of Argentine monetary, financial, and macroeconomic history: John Williams, Alec Ford, and Carlos Díaz Alejandro. It was they who shaped this field of study in the twentieth century, and we stand on their considerable shoulders.

The work of economic history is often an arduous process of collecting obscure material, making data fit for use, tracking down sources, and constantly updating a large library of files and records. In this we would have been lost without the outstanding research assistance given by Silvana Reale, Sandra Amuso, Marcela Harriague, and Laura Ivanier. They have our deepest thanks for their efforts. We also thank Andrea Matallana, whose inspired selection of cartoon illustrations beautifully complements the text; her commentary, translated by Emily Stern, appears in Appendix 6, which we consider recommended reading for those unfamiliar with the contours of Argentine political history. The final co-ordination of production efforts at the press went smoothly thanks to editorial assistant Rodney Powell, NBER volume editor Mark Bennett, promotions manager Cristina Henriquez, and indexer Shirley Kessel.

Lastly we would like to thank our families for their forbearance and encouragement throughout this project. To them this book is dedicated.

G. d. P. and A. M. T.
Buenos Aires and Berkeley, November 2000

Part One

The Historical and Methodological Context

1
Introduction

Melancholy as it may be to dwell on old splendors when the present is uninspiring, the task of examining the past for clues about recent difficulties is indispensable in the Argentine case.
— *Carlos F. Díaz Alejandro*

In a short span of a few golden years, with their peak from around 1900 to 1913, Argentines enjoyed a Belle Époque. A visitor to Buenos Aires then would have marveled at the splendors of the city and, beyond it, the economic vitality of its hinterland: the gleaming opera house, the graceful architecture, the expansive and efficient railway system, and a vibrant agricultural economy on the pampas linked to a sophisticated urban and industrial center. Today, the visitor sees the same elegant façades, but decadence has long set in after decades of stagnant economic performance; society struggles with an economy and an infrastructure that appear, in places at least, to have seen little renewal since the remarkable efflorescence of those distant glory days.

Knowing that their ancestors once lived in one of the richest countries in the world is, naturally, of little comfort to today's Argentines as they come to terms with their country's descent into the middle or lower echelons of the global economic rankings. Unable to hide from the past, confronted with reminders of the gilded age on every street corner, Argentines display a widespread curiosity about their own economic history and a near-obsession with that epic malaise may have contributed, in no small measure, to the popular angst that gives Buenos Aires its reputation as the therapy capital of the world.

Argentine economic history is, in short, the story of a decline unparalleled in modern times. The country was fortunate to have begun the twentieth century as one of the most prosperous countries in the world; to quote the legendary economic historian Díaz Alejandro again, "to have called Argentina 'underdeveloped' in the sense that word has today would have been considered laughable. Not only was per capita income high, but its growth rate was one of the highest in the world."[1]

1. Díaz Alejandro (1970, p. 1).

The basis for those high incomes was a fortuitous mix of now well-known ingredients: a relatively literate and skilled population of immigrant stock, a seamless integration of domestic and world economies in trade through rail and shipping connections on land and sea, eventual success in the adoption of the gold standard that brought stability and credibility, and, last but not least, an unbelievably high resource-per-worker ratio in the form of a vast expanse of fertile agricultural land on the thinly populated pampas. What could possibly derail that successful combination of institutions, endowments, and global economic conditions?

Well, for a start, what had prevented success from coming sooner? In fact, prosperity had not been a foregone conclusion. After the 1810 revolution brought independence from Spain, the former Viceroyalty of the River Plate, like the rest of Latin America, hoped for peace and progress. Instead, as elsewhere, decades were lost to war: first for independence, then over territory with newly created neighboring states, and even within the borders themselves. Internal conflicts simmered longest, as Buenos Aires argued with rival provinces over the political and economic contours of a slow-to-emerge federal compact. The ongoing belligerence put a brake on economic development, due to the fiscal costs of military action and the uncertainty that affected all long-term economic decisions in such a fissiparous political environment. Not until fifty years later was a unified national government firmly established under President Bartolomé Mitre (1862–68), who was succeeded in mostly orderly transitions by the elected administrations of Presidents Domingo Sarmiento (1868–74), Nicolás Avellaneda (1874–80), and Julio Roca (1880–86).[2]

All four presidents were modernizers. Their ability to serve full terms in a somewhat democratic system stood in stark contrast to the often tenuous and volatile shifts of power that had previously obtained under the rule of various factions and their strongmen, the *caudillos*. It was this old order of "barbarism" *(barbarie)* that Sarmiento, in particular, aspired to replace with "civilization" *(civilizacion)*—as explained in his passionate and trenchant critique of Argentine society and its institutions, *Civilizacion i barbarie,* commonly known as *Facundo*. By civilization, he meant a European type of society, one centered on learning, good government, institution building, and economic stability. Beyond just importing new habits, customs, dress, and sensibility, he knew that the possibilities for development depended most of all on economic integration with Europe and the wider world, on attracting foreign migrants and capital, and engaging the world in trade so as to exploit the comparative advantage of Argentina to the full. It was an ambitious program perhaps, but in retrospect one can only be impressed by what was accomplished in the years between

2. For the historical background of the period see Botana (1986), Rock (1987), and Gallo (1997). For a less detailed view see Luna (2000). A comprehensive treatment of economic and social ideas in the period is to be found in Halperín Donghi (1977) and Botana and Gallo (1997).

the Republic's fiftieth and one hundredth anniversaries. Albeit with some false starts, the modernizers' vision of the future did take shape in the late nineteenth century and the country rose to new heights of economic achievement.

A century later the optimism has long dissipated. Argentines wonder if they will ever unleash the economic potential that once seemed to promise them a bright future as one of the most advanced countries in the world. Will this remain a longing, a yearning, an unfulfilled hope? History can be our guide as we examine the crucial transition from growth to relative retardation in the early twentieth century, an era that sheds light on the origins of Argentina's mysterious slide into economic underdevelopment. In this book we do not claim to offer cures for melancholy and nostalgia, nor treatment for any forms of depression (at least of the noneconomic kind). Still—in economics as in therapy—the first step is to understand the source of the ailment, even if the remaining eleven steps are a matter for other professionals.

For those with a personal or historical interest in Argentina, our book will try to provide some answers to a question we often hear from people in various walks of life: "given its past success, how did Argentina end up like this today?" That is the puzzle. It is a simple question, without a simple answer, but it resonates all the way from our conversations with nonspecialists to controversies at the cutting edge of academic research. In recent years, theoretical and empirical work in the study of economic growth has focused heavily on concepts of long-run convergence in per capita income. Argentina offers a different lesson, an example *par excellence* of big-time divergence. Hence, for scholars, our study informs a continuing debate on growth, its essential economic sources and its institutional preconditions.

Before us we have a rare and curious specimen: a once relatively rich country that has become relatively poor, as we shall see next in a section that looks at the cross-country evidence. In accounting for this, we do not seek to offer a monocausal explanation or even a deterministic line. Much of what has happened to Argentina's economy properly falls under the rubric of politics, and unpredictable internal and external shocks have surely left their mark too. Our account seeks to be sensitive to political-economy forces and cognizant of the occasionally random and exogenous events that have disturbed the economy. But we do aim to expose the particularly important role of macroeconomic stability, and to that end we explore in a moment the record of price and exchange-rate volatility in Argentina, also in comparative perspective. These initial forays into the statistical evidence expose the central theme of the book while sketching the major, but possibly unfamiliar, contours of Argentine economic history.

The Long-run Context: Economic Growth in Two Centuries

The puzzle of Argentine economic growth in the long run can be neatly encapsulated by looking at its level of economic development around four benchmark dates: the year 1820, a date in the early nineteenth century shortly after independence; the year 1870, a date in the middle of the "long nineteenth century"; the year 1913, a date at the end of the "long nineteenth century" and at the zenith of the Belle Époque; and the present, where we can use the latest cross-country evidence available. Studies of historical income allow us to address a central question in world history: whether the income divergence between developing economies (the "periphery") and the developed world (the "core") is a "new" phenomenon, a legacy of the industrial and postindustrial twentieth century, or whether it dates back to 1800 or even earlier.

Around 1800, according to Coatsworth's pioneering attempt to put together comparative historical estimates of per capita incomes in Latin America, Argentina, or at least that part of it occupied by Europeans, had an income level well above that of its neighbors in the region, and similar to the levels seen in Europe or the United States at that time. More precisely, Coatsworth estimates Argentine per capita income at 102 percent of the U.S. level in 1800, compared to 66 percent for the region as a whole. For a broader comparison, Maddison places U.S. per capita income at $1,287 in 1820 (in 1992 international dollars, used henceforth in this section), compared to $1,228 in Western Europe, and $1,236 in the "Western Offshoots" (meaning Australia, Canada, New Zealand, and the United States). This would place Argentina at about $1,300 per capita if it were still at 102 percent of the U.S level in 1820, the region as a whole at roughly $900. Essentially, Argentina was then a relatively rich country, but others in the region were poor—or poorer, if 66 percent of the U.S. level cannot be called poor, as is the case today.[3]

Did Argentina maintain this superiority in incomes? Despite early evidence of "Argentine exceptionalism" a new trend emerged in the mid-nineteenth century. The core economies' growth accelerated as the industrial revolution spread; but Latin America, beset by wars and economic chaos, stood still, or even fell backward. By 1870 Western European incomes had risen to $1,986 per capita, and the offshoots to $2,748. But Argentine per capita income still stood at $1,300 per capita five decades later, and the region as a whole at about $800. Argentina was still richer than its neighbors, by roughly the same amount, but it had not kept up with the core. It was at around this time, of course, that the postindependence wars ended, and aspirations for economic development that

3. Maddison (1995), Coatsworth (1999). In 1800 Coatsworth found Cuba had a per capita income of 112 percent of the U.S. level, but we exclude this island economy, so dependent on slave-produced sugar, from the comparison of mainland countries. In 1820 Maddison found that the world leader was Britain, the first industrial nation, with an income of $1,756 per capita, with the Netherlands second at $1,561, and Australia third at $1,528.

would close this gap took shape. Remarkably, the dreams started to come true: in several Latin American countries, including Mexico and Chile, but most noticeably in Argentina, there was an acceleration in economic growth rates after 1870 that implied a convergence on the core economies. For example, from the 1880s to 1913, Argentina had an average growth rate of 5 percent per annum in output, or about half that in per capita terms. This was a stunning performance by the standards of the time and sparked a flourishing of Argentine confidence at the height of its golden age. Maddison's data suggest that by 1900 Argentina's income per capita had risen from about 67 percent of developed-country levels in 1870, to 90 percent in 1900, and 100 percent in 1913. In Figure 1.1 we get a more complete picture by comparing Argentine performance to a wide sample of countries from 1820 to the present. By 1913 it must have seemed that the process of convergence was almost complete and Argentina had established a clear lead in income levels over the rest of the region.[4]

These trends surely fostered the idea that Argentina had become an "advanced" economy, differentiating herself from its "backward" neighbors. How advanced? Though historical data give some margin for error, there is little doubt that the 1913 income level was inferior to those of the richest "countries of recent settlement" such as the United States, Canada, and Australia, and also below that of the first industrializer, Great Britain. But the Argentine level of $3,797 in 1913 slightly surpassed the levels in many middle-income European economies at the time, such as France ($3,452), Germany ($3,134), and Netherlands ($3,533), and was eclipsed only by the United Kingdom ($5,032) and the four Western Offshoots, notably the United States ($5,307) and Australia ($5,505); and it was well above the levels in poorer Southern European countries such as Italy ($2,507) and Spain ($2,255)—as would be expected, since these were the very countries supplying Argentina with so many of its immigrants. All things considered, and given the vagaries of historical data, some scholars have placed Argentina's 1913 income level clearly in the world Top 10, even the Top 5. Whatever its exact status in 1913, for all practical purposes Argentina was an advanced country.[5]

The stage was then set for the *dénouement* and a dramatic reversal of fortune in the twentieth century. Economic growth in Latin America lagged behind the core OECD countries, and the performance of Argentina was worse still. A regression of disturbing proportions is clearly visible in Figure 1.1. Argentina's ratio of 80 percent of OECD income levels in 1913 accords this date great historical significance as the time when Argentina was as close as it ever came

4. In the text and in the figure we use a weighted average of Western Europe plus Western Offshoots plus Japan (a pseudo-OECD subset) as a measure of developed-country levels of income per capita.
5. Our modern-day perspective comes from the data of Maddison (1995), but those witness to events in this period were not unaware of Argentina's elevated status, as we know from sources such as Mulhall (1903).

Figure 1.1. Comparative Economic Development

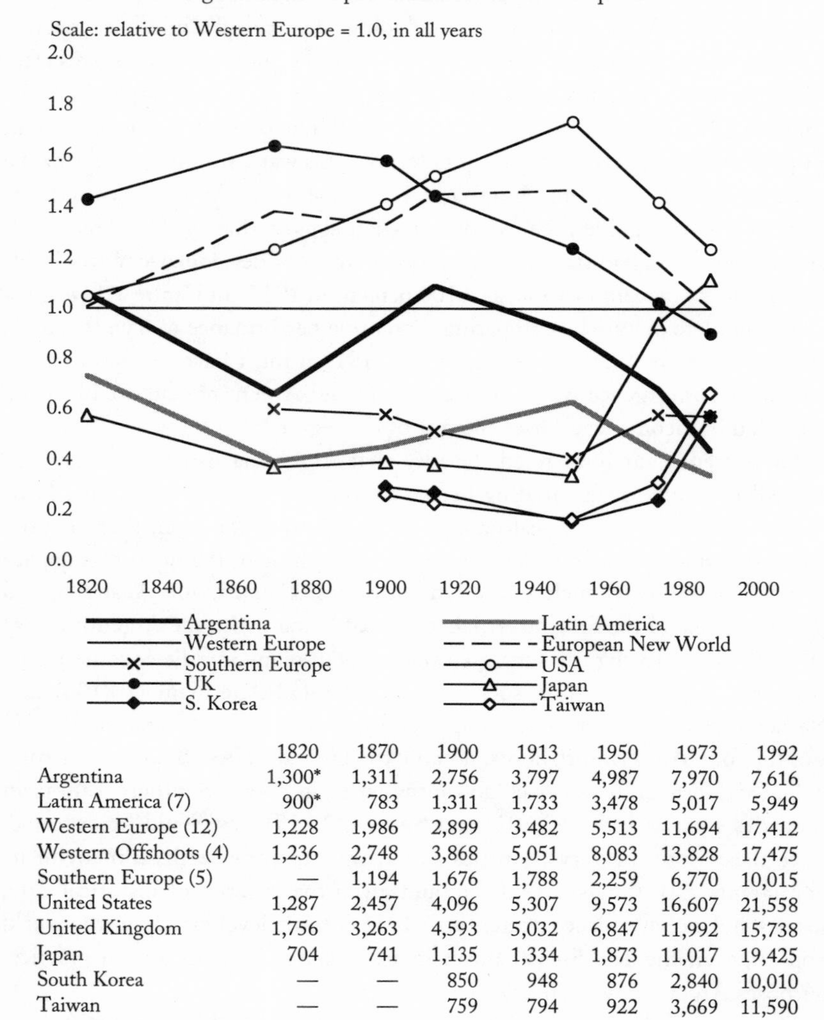

	1820	1870	1900	1913	1950	1973	1992
Argentina	1,300*	1,311	2,756	3,797	4,987	7,970	7,616
Latin America (7)	900*	783	1,311	1,733	3,478	5,017	5,949
Western Europe (12)	1,228	1,986	2,899	3,482	5,513	11,694	17,412
Western Offshoots (4)	1,236	2,748	3,868	5,051	8,083	13,828	17,475
Southern Europe (5)	—	1,194	1,676	1,788	2,259	6,770	10,015
United States	1,287	2,457	4,096	5,307	9,573	16,607	21,558
United Kingdom	1,756	3,263	4,593	5,032	6,847	11,992	15,738
Japan	704	741	1,135	1,334	1,873	11,017	19,425
South Korea	—	—	850	948	876	2,840	10,010
Taiwan	—	—	759	794	922	3,669	11,590

Western Europe (12): Austria, Belgium, Denmark, Finland, France, Germany, Italy, Netherlands, Norway, Sweden, Switzerland, United Kingdom.
Southern Europe (5): Greece, Ireland, Portugal, Spain, Turkey.
European New World (4, called "Western Offshoots" by Maddison): Australia, Canada, New Zealand, United States.
Latin America (7): Argentina, Brazil, Chile, Colombia, Mexico, Peru, Venezuela.
Notes and sources: Data in the table from Maddison (1995) in 1992 PPP-adjusted international dollars, except for the 1820 entries for Argentina and Latin America from the estimates in the text. Figure shows incomes relative to a Western Europe arithmetic average equal to 1.0. *The figure shows relative rather than absolute economic performance.*

to joining the "club" of core economies. Ever since, the income trend has been down and away from the OECD level, with a reversion back toward the average of Latin America as a whole. Argentina's ratio to OECD income fell to 84 percent in 1950, 65 percent in 1973, and to a mere 43 percent in 1987, not so far above the regional average of 34 percent. By then, any old notions of Argentine exceptionalism had been thoroughly and painfully debunked, at least for those willing to confront this uncomfortable reality and examine the statistical record.

Argentina makes a fascinating subject for historical scrutiny precisely because it experienced such a unique and pronounced rise and fall in its long-run economic status. In this respect, it has little in common with the legions of less-developed countries that have always been relatively poor and never managed to make a transition to sustained modern economic growth, for no one denies that Argentina was a very rich economy in 1900–1913. It also has little in common here with that much smaller group of poor and peripheral economies that have made a transition to developed-country status and have not, as yet, relinquished that gain; by taking a long view, we may include here such once-peripheral European countries as Norway, Sweden, Italy, Spain, Portugal, and Ireland, and Asian examples such as the striking case of Japan, as well as more recent emerging market successes in South Korea and Taiwan, countries that have lately eclipsed Argentina in per capita income (Figure 1.1).

In sum, a visitor from Buenos Aires in the early- or mid-nineteenth century, transported to the present, might see nothing strange about Argentina's lowly economic position and its similarity to that of the region as a whole. Indeed, the time traveler might be astonished to hear from one of today's locals how close Argentina came to achieving economic success, if not "civilization," in the intervening period. This is not to say that the modern Argentine would enjoy telling the story: surely, more than being relatively poor, the acutest source of melancholy is the knowledge of how close you once were to having it made.

The Central Problem: Macroeconomic Stability in the Long Run

If we accept that Argentina made a fleeting jump toward a high level of development at the turn of the twentieth century, we must next ask what formed the springboard. As we have noted, there were many factors working together to promote Argentine success in this era, including an abundant resource endowments and a fortuitous position in a globalizing world. Yet, from a comparative standpoint, there is not much uniquely Argentine about these factors, and, in many cases, little that is specific to the period 1880–1913. Other economies, like the countries of recent settlement, also had great resources and could exploit their comparative advantage in global markets. But they fared better, sooner, and even when the world economy went into temporary convulsion, as in the interwar period, it was still the case, in the long run, that they recovered and prospered more. Many comparison countries did not wait so long to grow rich in the late nineteenth century, and none has since seen its economy fizzle out.

Accordingly, we must seek some peculiarly Argentinean characteristics that mark the period 1880–1913 as particularly auspicious for economic growth, focusing on factors that have been conspicuously absent before or since. It is our thesis that such factors—explicitly, shifts in economic policies directly under the control of the authorities—set the stage for the fleeting years of success. A cursory look at the historical statistics of Argentina should, we argue, point a finger of suspicion at the record of macroeconomic instability as a crucial detriment to sustained economic growth and long-run convergence.

In the long run, a key macroeconomic challenge for a small open economy is the task of building institutions and commitments to support stable monetary and fiscal policies. If such actions are successful, an economy can gain price stability for the long run—in other words, a firm *nominal anchor*—and all of the benefits that go with it in terms of reputation and expectation effects that enhance efficiency in financial markets, contracting, and so forth. If such actions fail, an economy risks a volatile inflation rate, financial instability, and an increased exposure to banking and currency crises.

A goal of the book is to explore the causes of success and failure in this realm, but for initial motivation we discuss some of the problems encountered. It would be desirable here to examine detailed measures of the government's actions in fiscal and monetary affairs, looking at the record of budgets and money supplies and other key variables. For succinctness, and since few consistent data series exist for two centuries, we confine our introduction on this topic to two important statistical measures of stability that are relevant in a small open economy: the price level and the exchange rate.[6]

It is worth taking a moment first to reflect on the remarkable stability of the period 1880–1913 by looking at events in subsequent history, from 1914 to the present. We see from Figure 1.2 that Argentina's capacity to generate inflation has remained high in the twentieth century, as compared with selected OECD countries. The evolution of both the price level and the exchange rate tell the same story: after 1940, the end point of our study, the capacity of the economy to hold a stable level of any nominal variable—that is, to have a nominal anchor—was lost. The purpose of our book is to explain the origins of that state of macroeconomic drift by examining policy tensions in the years prior—at a time when the anchor was not yet lost, but was under considerable strain.

Some more detailed figures drive home the change of regime. Median inflation for 1940–97 in Argentina was 28 percent per annum with a maximum of

6. These two variables are potentially related, as in the purchasing-power parity (PPP) theory of exchange rates. We explore that topic for Argentina in Appendix 4.

Figure 1.2. Prices and Exchange Rates, 1880–1996

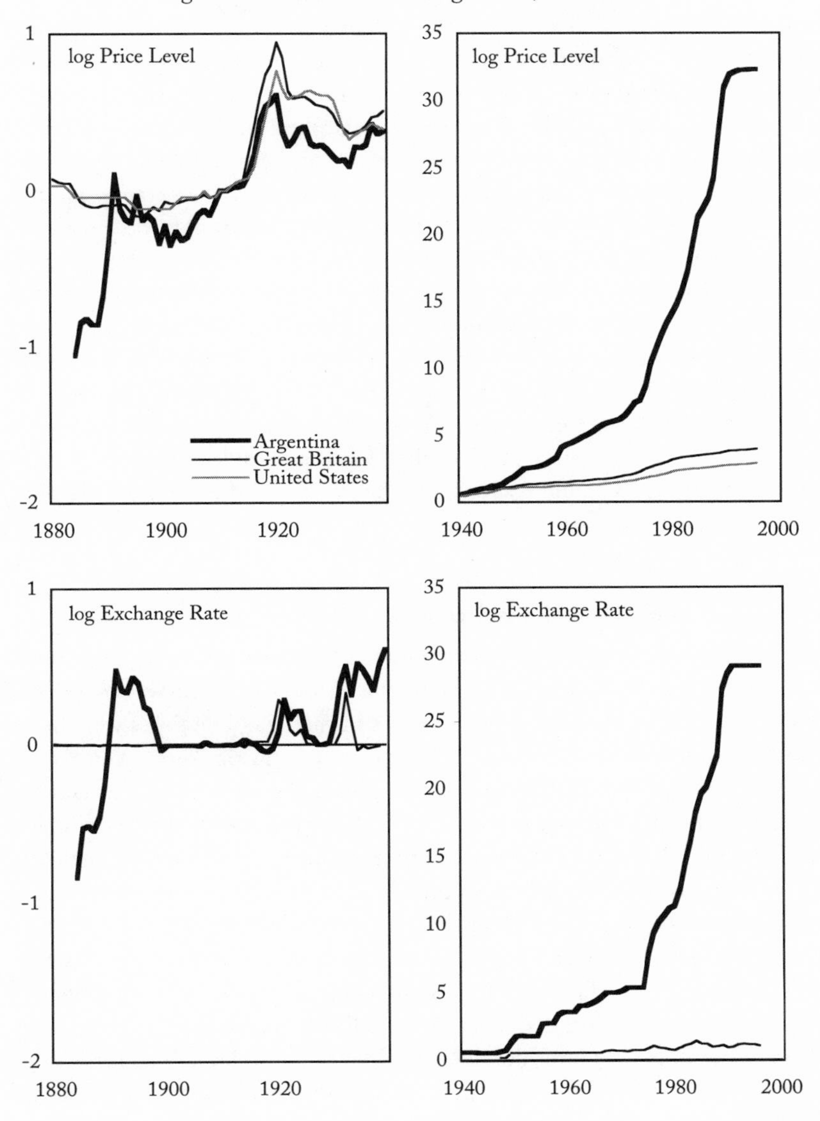

Notes: The natural log of the price level (CPI) and exchange rate (currency units per U.S. dollar) are shown, with a normalization such that 1913 log level equals zero.
Sources: Obstfeld and Taylor (2002).

3,084 percent (during the 1989–90 hyperinflation). The exchange rate moved similarly. The same statistics are 3 and 14 percent, respectively, in the United States. But as is clear from the figure, from around 1900 until 1939, the Argentine economy moved very much in synchronization with leading core economies in terms of its price level and exchange rate stability. In the decade before the First World War prices were almost perfectly stable, with a mild inflation in all countries on the gold standard due to new gold discoveries injecting liquidity into the world economy at a faster rate than output growth. After the outbreak of war Argentina kept its exchange rate at least as steady as the other countries with respect to the U.S. dollar and experienced slightly better inflation performance than some: a 1.8 percent average 1914–39 versus 1.6 percent in the United States, and 2.2 percent in Britain (for further comparison, the figures were 1.3 percent in Australia, and 1.2 percent in Canada). Only after 1940 did the real trouble begin, and Argentina's postwar inflation problem endured, at least until the "convertibility plan" of the 1990s was implemented by Finance Minister Domingo Cavallo—and, as the figure shows, this event finally put a halt to the instability.

Initial Conditions: Postcolonial Economic Disarray

Argentine history from independence until the 1860s was punctuated by a series of wars between a barely unified set of provinces, and there is no way to speak of a coherent set of national economic policies in that era. The times were heavy with economic chaos, political uncertainty, and fiscal pressure. With weak government structures at all levels, and a well-functioning bureaucracy taking a back seat to a well-functioning army, all the authorities resorted to the simplest and most reliable form of revenue creation: money printing. Seigniorage, or the inflation tax, was their key fiscal tool in times of crisis and, worse still, each province had its own money. As a result, price and exchange rate stability could never be credibly established. We see evidence of this in Figure 1.3, which shows some data for the most important province, administration, monetary system, and economic unit: Buenos Aires. During major wars and blockades, the local currency regularly devalued by several multiples. A series of high inflation episodes left the paper currency seriously suspect as a store of value, a precursor of the twentieth century experience.

It is illustrative to compare this inflation record with the stability seen in other economies under different monetary arrangements. Take, for example, the United States and the United Kingdom. Both were committed to the gold standard throughout this period: the British resuming in 1821 shortly after the end of the Napoleonic Wars and remaining on the standard until the First World War began in 1914; the United States over roughly the same period absent one major break during the Civil War, when convertibility was

Figure 1.3. Prices and Exchange Rates, 1820–80

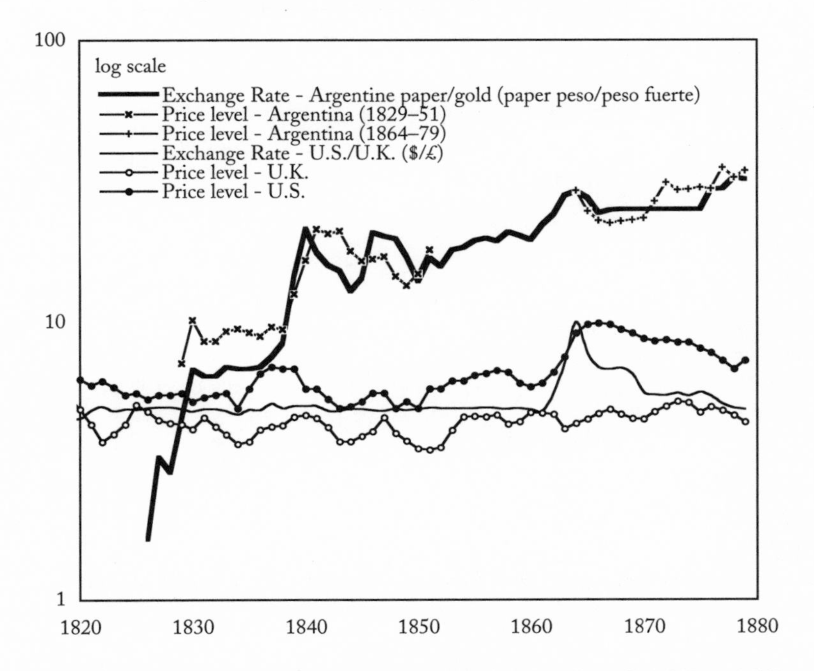

Notes and sources: Series for U.S. and U.K. price levels are taken from Global Financial Data http://www.globalfindata.com; the primary sources are Lindert-Williamson and Bowley for United Kingdom, and Warren-Pearson for United States; these are index numbers on an arbitrary scale. The series for the U.S.-U.K. exchange rate (dollars per pound) is from Officer (2001). The series for Argentine exchange rate (paper pesos per *pesos fuerte*) and price level (price index for hides 1829–51, implicit price of exports 1864–79) are from Diéguez (1972), Irigoin (2000a), and della Paolera (1983). The two disjoint Argentine price level series are *not* commensurate, and each is on an arbitrary scale.

suspended from 1861 to 1878.[7] In the United Kingdom the gold value of the currency never wavered from its legal mint value; in the United States, except for the years of suspension, the price level was stable and the dollar-pound exchange rate remained very close to par at $4.86 (Figure 1.3). The result in both countries was an extended period of price stability, excluding the U.S. Civil War, with low average levels of inflation, and low volatility. The contrast with the Argentine case is dramatic, and graphically illustrates the macroeconomic benefits of peace, political order, and institutional stability.

In the 1860s and 1870s, some stability came to Argentina in terms of the political solutions developed and also in terms of economic outcomes. Once the wars were at an end, the first three national administrations presided over years of low and stable inflation, as can be seen from Table 1.1. The later Mitre

7. See Officer (1996).

Table 1.1. *Argentine Inflation, 1820–1935*

Period	Events	Inflation Rate (percent per annum)
1820–30	war	20–22
1830–38		0
1838–42	war	25–45
1842–45		-11
1845–48	war	14
1848–61		4
1861–64	war	9
1864–67		-15
1867–75	gold standard	0
1875–78		9
1878–84	gold standard	-4
1884–89		8
1889–91		48
1891–99		6
1899–1913	gold standard	3
1914–18		13
1918–27		-3
1927–29	gold standard	-1
1929–34		0

Sources: Amaral (1988); Irigoin (1995); Bordo and Végh (1998); della Paolera (1988, 1994).

years, 1864–67, were even notable for a sharp *deflation*, when a credible effort to end inflation led to a boost in money demand even as the money supply remained more or less fixed—a textbook illustration of one of the pitfalls of stabilization. Efforts to attain a respectable and stable monetary regime in this period aimed at the single, preferred model that was sweeping the globe at the time, namely the gold standard. The Argentine authorities were enthusiastically aiming to embrace a particular set of policy choices that required discipline of a kind that had not been seen before, and central here were the commitments to fixed exchange rates and internationally open capital markets that were the *sine qua non* of the gold standard. They felt that it was only under this kind of commitment that price stability could be guaranteed over the long run.

Disappointingly, the first two attempts to set up a gold standard soon came a cropper, as can be seen from the table. We argue that, despite some success in keeping inflation low in the 1860s and 1870s, an agreement in theory on the ideal monetary arrangement could not produce lasting success until adequate reforms introduced more robustness and consistency in the underlying monetary, fiscal, and banking institutions. In boom times it proved easy to paper over the cracks, and such issues as nonexistent bank regulation or the absence of central control over money issues could be viewed in a relaxed way.

As our story opens, we spend some time discussing the ill omens of this period of ad hoc policies and the spectacular macroeconomic disaster that followed from them. When the relatively stable price record of the 1860s and 1870s gave way to a resurgence of inflation and instability in the late 1880s, a major crisis unfolded whose aftereffects took many years to die down. It was a shock that threatened to put Argentina on a different track than the group of advanced economies, with a return to high inflation and questions over its ability to run a responsible gold-standard monetary policy (see Figure 1.2 and Table 1.1). When inflation peaked in 1890–91 at around 50 percent per annum a stable future looked in grave doubt.

Faced with a make-or-break scenario, the policy reaction to the 1890 crisis succeeded in averting a meltdown and provides a pivotal event for our narrative, a decisive step that changed the course of Argentine economic history, and still, through its influence on the design of Cavallo's convertibility plan, is making itself felt today. The shock precipitated a deep institutional reform, a debate over optimal monetary and fiscal policies, and raised serious questions as to the soundness of the economy's financial architecture. More than a century has passed without diminishing the relevance of these considerations in any developing-country environment, as recent calamities in the global economy can attest.

This book speaks directly to present-day debates on the merits of opening capital markets, managing exchange rate regimes, and coping with the tradeoffs and constraints that are the occupational hazards of any small open economy in a globalized world. In the late 1880s, Argentina made one kind of tradeoff: it faced a tough choice as external capital markets tightened and economic growth slowed. The authorities could not simultaneously finance the budget, meet convertibility requirements, and allow free capital movements without a severe monetary contraction and the likelihood of acute financial distress. They balked at that kind of discipline, their commitment slipped, the exchange rate floated, and a crisis ensued. Not just any kind of crisis, but one that looks eerily familiar from our contemporary perspective—the very first crisis ever seen of a new and particularly dangerous kind.

A Pivotal Event: The First Emerging Market Crisis?

The foundation for the crisis was deep. The fiscal use of money creation was the norm in postindependence Argentina from the 1820s to the 1880s, when crises and wars exhausted the limited tax take and domestic and foreign credit was unavailable. State and provincial banks acted as money printers to their respective governments, and in this period of "monetary anarchy" multiple banks of issue constantly wrestled with pressures to overissue notes.

To try to stabilize the price level, a convertibility commitment was made in 1881, but it proved short-lived because the government never decisively limited note issues. The government held back from regulating the banks and, perhaps not coincidentally, did not escape from its own fiscal dependence on the banks' generous issues of credit. The banks of issue continued to print money to finance government deficits and engaged in falsification of balance sheets, loans to politicians, and other dubious practices. Gold reserve losses soon mounted. After 1884 a temporary "dirty float" of the paper-gold exchange rate was announced, but the gold drain continued because there had been no reforms in the underlying fiscal and monetary policy "fundamentals." Attempts to fix the banking laws were ineffective, even counterproductive, since without fundamental reform the practice of making loans based on political expediency would continue.

Contemporary parallels cannot be avoided here. Foreign investors were not unaware of the seamy side of Argentine finance, and what in Asia today has been dubbed "crony capitalism" was in the Argentina of yesteryear disparagingly referred to as "Gaucho banking" by the horrified Anglo-Saxon observers of that time:

> [The Argentine banks] were free banks in the freest sense of the term, for any Gaucho who had the political open sesame to them could ask for almost anything he pleased, and it would be given him so long as there was a piastre left in the till.[8]

Given such common underpinnings then and now we should not be surprised to see a common outcome, and the Argentine fiasco ended in a classic speculative attack with no gold left in the vaults whatsoever.

By 1890 an infamous macroeconomic and financial downturn, the so-called Baring Crisis, was underway. It involved some very familiar ingredients that we have seen so often in recent collapses: a fiscal gap, an unsustainable commitment to a fixed exchange rate peg, and poorly regulated banks that borrowed short abroad in gold and lent long domestically in pesos.[9] We now know that these ingredients form a dangerous mix: an incipient violation of the intertemporal budget constraint by the government triggers an inconsistency in the three-way compromise between a fixed exchange rate, capital mobility, and policy activism—the "trilemma," a topic we explore below. This was, in essence, the first modern emerging market crisis, and fits well with the textbook theoretical descriptions of such crises.

How did the public react to these events? External and internal credit markets virtually shut down. Furthermore, there was a dramatic internal shift away from holding the rapidly depreciating domestic paper money, and a shift to holding gold as currency. In the early 1880s currency in the hands of the public was almost 100 percent paper pesos; in the thick of the crisis it was about 80 percent gold. Such a phenomenon of currency substitution is now very familiar

8. These words from the English financial correspondent W. R. Lawson in his article "Gaucho banking" in the *Banker's Magazine* of 1891 (p. 38), quoted in Ford (1962, p. 100).

9. The principal foreign creditor was Baring Brothers, a major London bank, hence the name.

to macroeconomists working in Latin America, given the frequent postwar dollarization of the regions' economies during hyperinflation crises. The 1890 experience of Argentina stands out in history as one of the earliest and most dramatic of such episodes, one that was echoed again in Argentina's 1989–90 hyperinflationary crisis almost exactly a century later. As the flight to hard currency took place the banking sector was devastated by widespread failures, and inflation surged. The currency devalued rapidly and economic activity contracted sharply.

In both decades of the nineties, Argentina was emerging from long periods of macroeconomic instability. Monetary and fiscal policies had been brought into disrepute by years of inconsistency. The domestic currency had been devalued more times than anyone could remember. A rapidly globalizing world stood by, ready to offer the benefits of open goods and capital markets, but unsure of the trustworthiness of the local economic policy regime. Then and now, new order was imposed on the country by a radical restructuring of the money and banking system, and a preference for fiscal rectitude. The problem of inflationary monetary policy was solved by a rigid convertibility commitment, specifically via a currency board arrangement.

An Institution as an Anchor: The Currency Board

We have seen that the twentieth-century Argentine inflation record looks like a throwback to the worst moments of the nineteenth century—only much worse, with some severe spikes as in the hyperinflations of the 1980s and early 1990s that boost the averages. The eventual cure also came as a blast from the past: facing similar monetary problems, Cavallo's plan was explicitly modeled on the rigid and credible monetary institution that had been the foundation for the only episode of monetary stability in the history of Argentina: a currency board, or as it was called then, the *Caja de Conversión,* or Conversion Office, that operated from 1890 until 1935. The Conversion Office had a simple and easily monitored task: to exchange gold in its reserves for paper currency, and vice versa, at a fixed exchange rate, and to otherwise exercise no independent or autonomous monetary policy functions. Currency boards, particularly as the ratio of gold reserves to paper issues approaches 100 percent, become fail-safe methods to guarantee the convertibility of the paper currency in circulation (also known as the monetary base, high-powered money, or outside money).

It is this institution, the world's first full-fledged currency board in an independent country, that forms the centerpiece of our book.[10] Argentina stands

10. In the nineteenth century, currency boards were otherwise employed only in a few small and isolated island economies, all of them within the British Empire, namely Mauritius in 1849, Ceylon in 1884, the Straits Settlements in 1889, and the Falkland Islands *(Islas Malvinas)* in 1899. For a look at the fascinating early history of currency boards see Schwartz (1993).

as the leading historical exemplar of this particular form of monetary experiment, both in the past and in the present. In both eras, the new regime helped to solve reputational problems, both at home and abroad, to the extent that it "tied the hands" of the government. Given the current success of the Argentine economic plan since 1990, the country stands as a prototype for other would-be reformers around the world, especially those enamored of rules over discretion in monetary policy, for whom the currency board, or even complete dollarization, looks like an attractive regime choice.

The difficulty here is that the present Argentine currency board tells only one story, and an unfinished one at that. Questions are left unanswered: Will this institution endure? Can it fulfill all its promises? Have we seen it at its best or at its worst so far? Under what circumstances might it face difficulties or even collapse? These are vital questions, and, short of peering into a crystal ball, they can only be answered by peering into the murkier depths of the past to get a glimpse of how similar institutions have succeeded and failed. In the historical laboratory we can ask questions that inform our present situation: Was Argentina's search for macroeconomic stability successful in the late nineteenth and early twentieth century? How did changing domestic and international conditions affect the outcome? What political economy obstacles stood in the way and how were they surmounted, if at all? How do these events speak to the current challenges facing developing countries in a similar environment today? In this context, our book is not just about Argentina, not just about the period 1880 to 1935. It is concerned with one of the essential problems of economic development, and asks what history can teach us about how to solve that problem through particular economic policy choices.

The Major Themes: An Overview of the Book

The approach we adopt is that of a case study, blending empirical, historical, and theoretical styles in the tradition of quantitative economic and institutional history, to explore the macroeconomic history of Argentina from 1880 to 1935. These years marked the rise and fall of the country's first great convertibility experiment.[11] The outline that follows considers several factors that influenced this trajectory and introduces the major themes of the book.

11. The systematic study of Argentine monetary and financial history is a phenomenon of recent and growing interest. Among the most prominent new historical works are those by Fishlow (1985); Amaral (1988); Cortés Conde (1989); Regalsky (1994); della Paolera and Ortiz (1995); Bordo and Végh (1998); Irigoin (1999, 2000a, 2000b); and Nakamura and Zarazaga (1999). We might also add our own articles on which parts of the present book are based (della Paolera 1988, 1994; della Paolera and Taylor 1999a, 1999b, 1999c). These studies, in their more formal examination of the behavior of monetary and financial institutions in an open peripheral economy, build on the earlier classic works by Williams (1920), Prebisch (1922), and Ford (1962).

Political Economy Dynamics

An overarching aim of our study is to understand the key economic and political actors, their objectives and constraints. We will focus on several types of agent in the economy and their interaction: the government authorities, both fiscal and monetary, and the potential conflicts between the two; the banks, both public and private; the general public; and the external sector, the rest of the world, especially the international capital market. What conditioned the behavior of these various parties? Here we have a second aim, to map the contours of the institutional landscape. But this landscape, as we shall see, was constantly changing.

The government, in some sense, was the first to move by setting the "rules of the game"—that is, the monetary regime and its objective, banking regulations, and the more general institutional framework in the economy. However, the government also faced constraints on these choices, notably the intertemporal, or long-run, government budget constraint. Fiscal strength or weakness can interact with the monetary regime via the need for seigniorage, that is, the inflation tax. This was an important feature of postindependence Argentina and derived from poor tax capabilities and the inability to issue debt domestically to the public, or globally to the world capital market. The choice of monetary regime determined the path of exchange rates and prices via the constraints (or lack thereof) on monetary policy. This in turn shaped banking behavior, and, along with bank regulations (or lack thereof) determined when credit would be easy or tight, how boom and bust cycles would evolve.

Given the actions of the state, how did other agents react? The public plays a key role through their willingness to hold money, both currency ("outside money") and bank deposits ("inside money"). Too much bad credit from banks would lead the public to substitute cash for banking deposits and, in an extreme case, set off a run on banks. Too much inflation would encourage currency substitution—the public would substitute gold or other "hard" assets for paper money and, in an extreme case, set off a run on the currency. There was clearly feedback on the fiscal position here: a run from paper money dented seigniorage revenue, and bank weaknesses would impinge on fiscal expenditure if Lender-of-Last-Resort responsibilities were, implicitly or explicitly, a part of the "rules of the game."

Finally, while all of these forces could operate within a closed economy, an external sector provided additional sources of feedback. Banks (when extending credit) and the government (when bridging a fiscal gap) might also have access to foreign capital—but equally might not if a general economic and financial crisis were perceived, setting the stage for a typical emerging market type of crisis. Foreign lenders, sensing a default risk, or country risk, both in the banks and government balance sheets, could refuse to roll over credit, leaving both institutions scrambling for funds. Besides adding directly to fiscal problems, this would further raise the probability of bank runs and failures and thus indirectly worsen the fiscal tension. The positive feedback allows expectations of such crises to be self-fulfilling. Seen as a structural feature of the monetary regime, the possibility of such events could be built into world capital markets' expectations ex ante, limiting the country's access to credit. In addition to this feedback from endogenous variables, the external sector frequently imposed very severe shocks on this small open economy of an entirely exogenous character, shocks that were to be especially large and adverse after 1914, adding another layer to the story.

This is not quite the whole picture. Given the above reactions by agents within and beyond the domestic economy, one can then explore how the state, in turn, reacts and searches for improvements to the institutional structure. How do state objectives change and what are the political economy forces at work? Is inertia such as to allow a functional but inefficient institutional structure to persist? When an institutional structure fails, when a regime crumbles or is severely tested by a crisis, what gives? This sets up a kind of "institutional search" process that can roam far and wide, and our book is about exactly this kind of search in Argentina from the 1880s to the 1930s. We will see how episodes of bold experiment with new institutions can transform the landscape for better or worse; how conservative adherence to old structures can assure stability or pose problems as economic conditions change. Sticking to the right path is an enduring challenge, as we know from the similar and recurrent problems faced by so many developing countries today.

The Budget Constraint and the Trilemma

Our discussion of the Baring Crisis sets the scene for our study by putting the spotlight on one of the major historical events of the period and drawing attention to the significance of macroeconomic policy and outcomes. How will we approach the task of fitting this and other events into an analytical framework? Our methodological approach builds on several major strands of open-economy macroeconomic theory that deal with intertemporal policy choices, budget constraints, and consistency.

One major element in our study is public debt theory.[12] The theory shows that if a government wants a good reputation in its two major liabilities, money and bonds, then the solvency of the government should never be in doubt. In detail, the monetary and fiscal authorities have an intertemporal budget constraint that needs to be respected. Attempts to violate this constraint, even in the short run, imply an inconsistency between monetary and fiscal policies and, hence, that

12. Sargent (1986); Calvo (1988).

at some point the government will have to default—either to money holders (by printing more money), or to bond holders (by reneging on debts), or both. This offers an easy route to bad macroeconomic outcomes, such as inflation, exchange-rate crises, default on public debts, loss of credit-worthiness, and even financial crashes. Since these symptoms are so widely seen in the annals of Argentine history, this theory is highly relevant.

Another major element in our book is the choice of a monetary regime as a nominal anchor. Since money is a government liability and a source of revenues, the public debt problem is obviously closely related to price and exchange-rate stability. But the precise form of anchoring matters a great deal for what policymakers can and cannot do: the policy may target a price or an exchange rate and the commitment might be via a rigid rule or may allow considerable discretion. The exact form of the policy will determine whether there is any exchange-rate flexibility and whether the country has any independent monetary policy at all. The macroeconomic policy trilemma summarizes the main tradeoffs in this sphere. Policymakers can only choose two out of three objectives from the list of fixed exchange rates, capital mobility, and activist monetary policy.[13] Clearly, as Argentina struggled with its nominal anchor choice and its commitment to the gold standard during our period of study, these tradeoffs were of central concern.

Still, history shows that, despite all of the external volatility of the period, by and large Argentina remained committed to open markets before the 1930s. If openness is assumed, the trilemma reduces to a dilemma: a choice between fixed exchange rates and activist monetary policy. Both were tried at various times, despite the existence of the Conversion Office, a currency board with a seemingly very hard rule. The tensions were at their highest during times of financial stress for the simple reason that the dilemma then took on a particularly threatening form. Argentina had a fractional-reserve banking system, but, given the currency board rules, no Lender of Last Resort. The monetary (and fiscal) flexibility required to provide liquidity to banks in distress simply did not exist as a result of this institutional design.

The dilemma was thus all about the conflict between goals of "internal convertibility" (of bank deposits into currency) and "external convertibility" (of currency into gold at a fixed par). In a floating rate system, the tension can be solved since the monetary authority can use discretion to inject money as a way to stave off an incipient banking crisis. Adjustment comes via the price of outside money, via the external value of the currency, or the exchange rate; note that—as is usually, but not necessarily, the case—there was no scope for pricing inside money, the bank deposits. But in a fixed rate system, there is no easy way out since there is no such discretion available.

13. On the trilemma, and its historical manifestations, see Obstfeld and Taylor (1998).

This set of contradictions, we argue, eventually compromised the whole system. But, as we will discuss in our concluding chapter, the experience is more than just a historical curiosity. The challenges faced by Argentina raise questions about the choice of monetary standards and the institutional design of traditional banking systems. They throw light on contemporary debates such as the benefits of currency boards and dollarization, and may prompt careful consideration of neglected alternatives such as the narrow banking model. All of the same technical problems challenge monetary and financial stability around the global economy today.

The Search for a Monetary Authority and the Global Context

A monetary standard can be defined as a set of transparent monetary rules designed to govern the evolution of key nominal variables such as price levels, nominal exchange rates, and nominal interest rates. Rules can then be chosen to govern monetary expansions and provide a credible framework which guarantees a minimum of inflation. Early Argentine monetary history reveals considerable instability in the type of monetary regime adopted. A search was under way for a credible monetary regime, with several attempts to adopt the gold standard, as we saw in Table 1.1. Here, Table 1.2 sets out in more detail the major institutional developments during our period of study.

It is important to see the Argentine record in comparative perspective. Prior to the First World War, most core countries, and an increasing number of countries at the periphery, adopted the gold standard—a monetary rule that, if credible, offered some promise of committing monetary authorities to a price-stability objective.[14] The gold standard required three basic policies to function adequately: a fixed value for the domestic currency in terms of gold set by the monetary authority; the free mobility of convertible foreign exchange or specie; and the establishment of rules relating the quantity of money in circulation with the stock of specie.

The ramifications of nominal exchange-rate stability for domestic price stability depended on the operation of the forces of purchasing power parity and price stability in the rest of the world, and on the real and monetary adjustment mechanisms that mediated these forces at home. For a small country, open to the movement of goods and capital as Argentina was at the time, a fixed exchange rate anchored the domestic price level of internationally tradable goods to world levels.[15]

The alternative to such a convertible regime is an inconvertible regime. Under an inconvertible monetary standard, the bills and coins issued by the monetary

14. On the adoption of the gold standard in this period see Eichengreen (1996, ch. 1).
15. On the workings of purchasing power parity (PPP) in the gold standard era see McCloskey and Zecher (1976). On PPP in a longer run context see Taylor (2001).

Table 1.2. *Monetary Policy Chronology*

Period Before Our Study	
1810–67	Floating exchange rate. Period of "monetary anarchy" after independence. Rival provinces fail to unify; a single federal structure is postponed. Each province issues its own money through state banks, no central authority. Frequent foreign and civil wars lead to seigniorage abuse, chronic inflation.
1862-67	First national administration of Bartolomé Mitre. Stable monetary policy causes deflation, with aim of gold convertibility.
1867–75	Fixed exchange rate. Convertibility under the auspices of an Exchange Office within the Banco de la Provinicia de Buenos Aires, but other banks maintain independence. System fails after adverse external shock in 1873 leads to gold drain and exposes contradictions in the system.
1875–83	Floating exchange rate.
Period Covered in Our Study	
ca. 1880	Government begins discussion of monetary reform.
1881	Law 1130 proposes a metallic regime to end the "monetary anarchy" that had occurred under the auspices of multiple banks issuing paper money.
1883	Law 1130 implemented, gold standard established.
1883–85	Gold standard; par is 1 gold peso = 1 paper peso.
1886–91	Baring Crisis; fiscal use of money; inflation; collapse of convertibility; exchange rate begins to float and depreciates markedly.
1890	Law 2741 creates Conversion Office (Caja de Conversión), with a monopoly over the emission of a new currency.
1891–99	Inconvertible paper currency. Floating exchange rate of paper to gold pesos. Macroeconomic reforms bring about stability and currency appreciation.
1899	Law 3871 (Convertibility Law) orders the Conversion Office to act as a currency board, and exchange gold pesos for paper pesos at a new par (2.27) for all transactions. Though initially having zero gold backing for the currency in its vaults, Conversion Office accumulates gold rapidly after 1902.
1899–1914	Gold standard; 1 gold peso = 2.27 paper pesos.
1914–27	Inconvertible paper currency. Floating exchange rate of paper to gold pesos. Gold flows at the Conversion Office limited to occasional government uses. Conversion Office continues to exchange gold pesos for paper pesos at new par (2.27) for these transactions. Laws 9479 and 9577 are passed in 1914, granting the Conversion Office and the Banco de la Nación permission to employ rediscounts for reasons of wartime emergency. Suspension occurs. Briefly, in 1925, the rediscounting facility is employed by the Conversion Office. The Banco de la Nación makes extensive use of this facility.
1927–29	Gold standard resumes; 1 gold peso = 2.27 paper pesos.
1929–31	Inconvertible paper currency. Floating exchange rate of paper to gold pesos. Gold flows at the Conversion Office limited to fiscal uses (payment of government foreign debt). Conversion Office continues to exchange gold pesos for paper pesos at new par (2.27) for these transactions.
1931	Conversion Office deviates from its previous mechanical money creation rule and starts to rediscount commercial paper. An independent Argentine monetary policy resumes.
1935	Creation of the Central Bank (Banco Central). Takes over all assets and liabilities of the Conversion Office. Revalues gold stock according to prevailing market rate of exchange (new par is 4.96 versus 2.27). Uses proceeds to increase backing of money base, and to bail out financial system.
Period After Our Study	
1935–90	Discretionary monetary policy managed by Central Bank. Return of chronic inflation, with hyperinflations in 1980s.
1991–2000	Return of currency board system: Cavallo's convertibility plan. Price and exchange rate stability achieved.

authority have no intrinsic value, nor are they backed or guaranteed by any external real object. They are, however, legal tender and must be accepted by the public in economic transactions.[16] Under inconvertibility, the monetary authority has total discretionary powers over the nominal amount of money, and thus, in principle, over the price or exchange rate at which this money would be exchanged for gold, for foreign currencies, and for domestic goods.

Inconvertible regimes (that is, noncommodity monies) are now the norm. Almost all countries issue fiduciary money, with the world divided into countries that have a fixed exchange rate relative to some base currency and countries that have a flexible or floating rate of exchange. In contrast, from around 1880 until the Second World War, the use of an inconvertible regime was a matter of some disrepute. Though floating was often useful as an emergency measure, convertibility was prized as a policymaking goal and the gold standard was its accepted and preferred form. In just a moment, when we examine the reputational benefits of a credible convertible regime, we will see why.

First, we pause to note how even supposedly unrestrained discretionary monetary policy can limit its own effectiveness in times of abuse, providing another motive for the embrace of a rule-based policy. Though couched in terms of a specific historical choice for Argentina, the same decision faces many developing countries today as they weigh up the pros and cons of fixing their exchange rates or, going further, adopting a currency board or joining a currency union.

Currency Substitution as a Policy Restraint

Without a rule-based monetary regime there are, nonetheless, some market-based limits to the discretion of policymakers and the extent to which they can abuse fiscal and monetary policy. Still, these limits appear only when the economy labors under very stressful conditions, and when the reaction of the public is such as to preclude further abuse. The Argentine government was to discover these limits in the crisis of 1890, a time when policy inconsistencies brought the use of paper money almost to a standstill and one of the world's earliest episodes of capital flight taught an important lesson.

The crisis had its origin in an ill-conceived domestic monetary and fiscal experiment: the Law of National Guaranteed Banks. In 1887, the federal government launched a new banking law in which any banking organization with a minimum required capital could issue paper notes backed by government gold bonds. The majority of these banks were national and mixed provincial-private banks, and to take part in the plan they floated foreign loans in Europe to purchase the national bonds with gold. The scheme was thus a leveraged

16. These standards were named by the Latin word *fiat,* which means "let it be done"—referring to the fact that such inconvertible monies are created by government command or decree.

arbitrage operation by which foreign investors were implicitly partners in the business of issuing government guaranteed paper-money.

Like so many schemes of that ilk, it appeared workable so long as foreign creditors were happy to go along—and, critically, so long as all the supplementary note issues were backed with 100 percent marginal bullion reserves. But in the late 1880s capital inflows began to reverse and, as conditions tightened in early 1889, the government broke the rules of the game and decided to pay off in paper money part of the internal debt denominated in gold. The decision was tantamount to a partial default, and both foreign and domestic investors became reluctant to absorb more Argentine government debt.

In Buenos Aires the public started to attack the paper peso. The government decided to intervene with gold to support the paper peso so as to calm the expectations of devaluation, but it soon proved to be a futile defense and by 1889 the government had lost almost 90 percent of its specie stock. The lack of coordination in monetary and fiscal policies resulted in an almost complete reallocation of specie from the banking system to the public and ultimately provoked the Baring Crisis. In this historical instance, the currency substitution phenomenon could be defined, in modern terminology, as capital flight—not in the sense that specie fled the country, but in the sense that the specie pocketed by the public was financed with government external debt.

Having tested the limits of seigniorage and discretionary monetary policy and found them wanting, the government absorbed an important lesson. Ironically, once all the gold reserves had been spent, the currency question was definitively settled with the creation in 1890 of the Conversion Office, a currency board, as the sole monetary authority of Argentina, and the search for a centralized monetary authority ended, one might say, by default.[17]

Monetary Credibility and the Capital Market

We have seen that periods of convertibility were successful in bringing down inflation (Table 1.1). Later on, we will present typical tests of purchasing power parity and confirm that during periods of convertibility Argentina was firmly anchored to the world price level. But the adherence of Argentina to an internationally approved monetary regime like the Gold Standard was also

17. The Conversion Office was created by Law 2741 of October 7, 1890, which took the note issue privileges away from the banks and effected the gradual conversion and amortization of the legal tender currency. This law was promulgated by the Executive and later approved by Congress (in November 1891). However, there was no convertibility of notes into gold in 1890, that is, external convertibility; though this was announced as the ultimate goal, it was not formally established until the Law of Convertibility, Law 3871 of October 31, 1899. The differences between the two laws should be kept in mind: the first law established the Conversion Office with its note issue prerogatives; the second was a law about how to conduct monetary and exchange policy within the already existing Conversion Office. See Table 1.2.

a more subtle political-economy decision that had implications beyond just tethering domestic prices.[18]

For a borrower country such as Argentina, a very important aspect of an efficient monetary standard is its ability to facilitate the integration of the local economy into world capital markets. In this way a capital-scarce domestic economy can take advantage of capital inflows, and foreign savings can contribute to long-run accumulation and economic growth. A transparent set of monetary rules designed to insure macroeconomic stability can limit the future discretion of the authorities to deviate from their precommitted policy.

The credibility so generated should be reflected in the reduction of so-called country risk. This is the interest-rate premium charged by foreign borrowers, expanding the choice set of the domestic economy through lower costs of finance and, via a reduction of credit rationing, through higher debt ceilings. In that sense too, the adoption of a metallic regime can be a welfare-improving strategy. One might ask if such welfare gains were realized.

Contemporary emerging market analysts use bond spreads as a critical measure of country risk, and we apply the same yardstick. We would like to know where Argentina's spread stood in relation to the range seen in other markets, so we use the standard statistical method of the confidence interval, the mean plus or minus 2 standard deviations. Figure 1.4 suggests that a sound reputation did pay off in terms of reduced country risk in global capital markets.

The figure is based on the spread between a long-term external government bond yield and the yield on the international benchmark bond of that era, the British consol, using data for those countries that had continuous quotations in London noted in *The Economist* newspaper. The "core and empire" group consists of putatively safe bonds from eleven countries: Australia, Canada, France, Germany, India, Netherlands, New Zealand, Norway, South Africa, Sweden, and the United States. The "periphery" group (on the same scale) consists of bonds issued by potentially more risky borrowers: Chile, Greece, Hungary, Italy, Japan, Mexico, Portugal, Spain, and Uruguay. In the 1860s and 1870s, the modernizing Argentina aspired to be treated like the borrowers in the first group, not like the emerging markets in the second group, and sought to reform policies to that end. Did this plan succeed?[19]

The two figures show that Argentina was treated like a member of the core during periods of convertibility, or around such periods when the exchange rate

18. This section on reputational effects, and the gold standard as a commitment device, draws on della Paolera (1994), Bordo and Kydland (1995), and Bordo and Rockoff (1996).

19. Note that core and periphery status was not necessarily clear cut, and there were shifting boundaries between these two groups. We chose a fixed set of countries, for simplicity, but even these groups present a moving target. The core saw its spreads narrow as the gold standard coalesced after 1880 and ushered in the globalization of the capital market centered on London. The periphery saw convergence, but volatility too. Its bond spreads waxed and waned, growing large during global downturns, notably in the market tightenings of 1873 and 1890.

Figure 1.4. Country Risk in Argentina, Core, and Periphery, 1870–1940

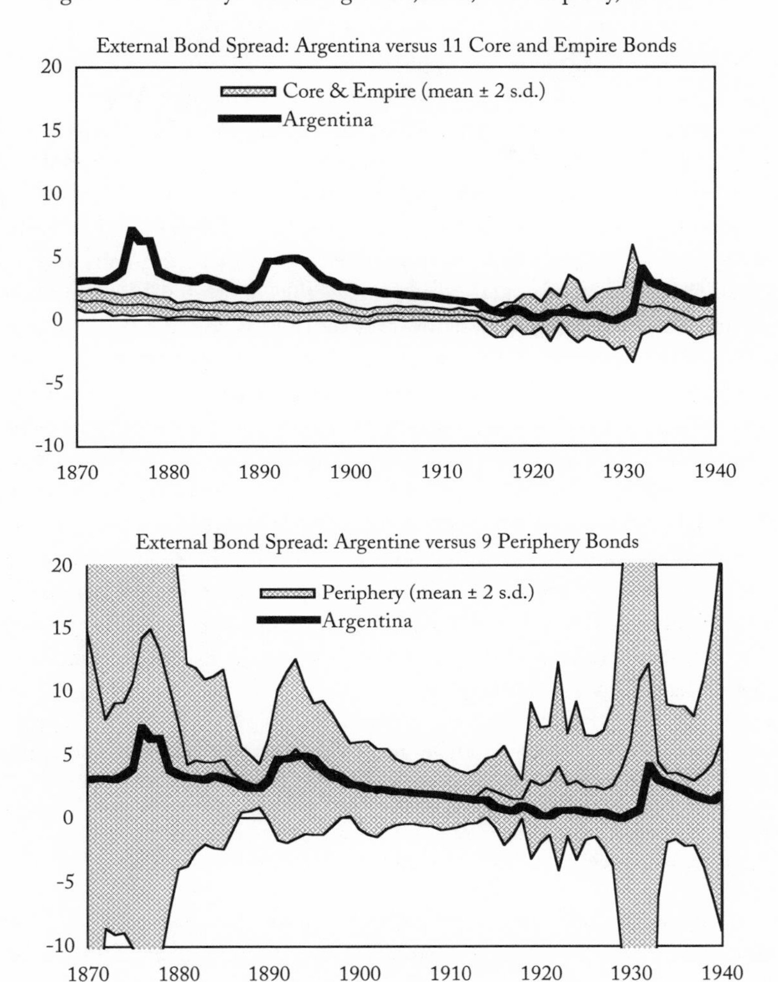

Units: percentage point spread over U.K. consol yield.
Notation: Heavy line = Argentina; Solid line with shaded area = mean plus or minus two standard deviations for comparison group of bonds; Core and Empire = Australia, Canada, France, Germany, India, Netherlands, New Zealand, Norway, South Africa, Sweden, and the United States. Periphery = Chile , Greece, Hungary, Italy, Japan, Mexico, Portugal, Spain, and Uruguay.
Notes and sources: Country risk is spread between a government external long bond yield and yield on British consols. Yields are based on the sterling coupon to price ratio in London. From Global Financial Data <http://www.globalfindata.com>, except Argentina 1884–1913 from Appendix 1 (unlike the Global Financial Data we include here only federal bonds not in default). Primary data from *The Economist*. It is to be understood that bonds exhibiting a discount of 50 percent or more, roughly corresponding to yield spreads in excess of 10 percentage points, were almost always in default.

was close enough to parity to indicate credibility (1868–75, 1880–89, 1900–1931); but when its commitments were in doubt it faced much higher bond spreads, like many other members of the periphery (1876–79, 1890–99, post-1932). When the convertibility experiment collapsed in 1875 Argentina's bond spread roughly doubled, from about 4 percent to 8 percent. The spread narrowed again in the 1880s when a new convertibility plan was announced, but when the spectacular Baring Crisis erupted all those efforts went up in smoke as the bond spread doubled again. Moreover, this is not to say that foreign loans were available at that rate after 1890—there were no new loans for many years–but it reveals the secondary market's perception of the country's solvency problems.

It can be seen in the lower figure that in 1890 Argentina was starting to look like an extreme point even by the standards of the periphery, rising more than 2 standard deviations above the mean bond spread in this reference group. This was just the kind of shameful position that the modernizers explicitly wanted to avoid. Those left to clean up the mess after the Baring Crisis, particularly the interim President Carlos Pellegrini (1890–92), had the repair of this sullied reputation at the top of their list of priorities. They had a long and arduous task ahead of them. Even by 1899, with the economy stable and the resumption of convertibility at hand, foreign observers remained skeptical that just by dint of some new monetary regime Argentina could rise above the bad habits of nineteenth-century Latin America, a world where political and economic instability seemed to go hand in hand:

> [South Americans] are always in trouble about their currency. Either it is too good for home use, or, as frequently happens, it is too bad for foreign exchange. Generally they have too much of it, but their own idea is that they never have enough...the Argentines alter their currency almost as frequently as they change their presidents.... No people in the world take a keener interest in currency experiments than the Argentines.[20]

As the upper part of Figure 1.4 shows, regaining the trust of world capital markets was a slow business of rebuilding confidence. After 1890 the bond spread slowly converged down and into the 90 percent confidence interval (the mean plus 2 standard deviations) for the core and empire group. Finally, in 1913, a date that here takes on yet more historical significance, Argentina was a member of the club, a core economy, as measured on the risk dimension.

The interwar period also offers an interesting picture, since here the core itself started to become a riskier place, as a result of war, uncertainty, and economic fluctuations before and especially during the Great Depression. By then Argentina was looking like a very good risk indeed—a somewhat Pyrrhic triumph, we would say, since global capital markets had imploded and credit rationing obstructed new bond issues in almost every year after 1913, except for a few

20. This quote comes from the English correspondent W. R. Lawson again, in the *Banker's Magazine* of 1899 (p. 691), quoted in Ford (1962, p. 90).

successful forays into the New York market in the late 1920s and late 1930s. It is also striking that all bond spreads widened as the Great Depression rolled in during the early 1930s. For Argentina the major shock was a big jump in the bond spread after 1931, a date to keep in mind since it was the occasion of another major change in macroeconomic policy, the effective demise of the currency board system, a pivotal event at the conclusion of our study.

Overall, it is fair to say that the adoption of a credible monetary regime represented a positive institutional innovation as measured by country risk, at least so long as global capital markets functioned smoothly. This was the case at least before 1913. At the cost of building up of a huge stock of international reserves to foster the credibility of the regime, Argentina obtained cheaper and better access to world capital markets, easing the constraints on investment and growth. But when capital markets seized up after 1913, this particular cost-benefit calculation changed markedly: a low bond spread was of little use if no new bonds could be issued.

Public Debt Credibility and the Capital Market

Of course, monetary regime credibility could only obtain if the underlying fiscal position was also credible. In order to maintain fiscal credibility, the government had to back all of its liabilities *and not just the country's money* with a combination of specie *and a solvent fiscal position.* Thus, for present-day market watchers monitoring a fixed exchange-rate regime, some of the key indicators to be watched are the evolution of the exchange rate, the backing in specie (or international reserves) of the monetary base, and measures of fiscal performance, ideally the evolution of deficits and the stock of public debt. Similarly, our understanding of the tensions of the Argentine fiscal-monetary nexus is not complete without some discussion of the overall policies relating to public debt management.

In the 1880s boom the term "debt management" would be, perhaps, too kind, given the way fiscal gaps caused public sector borrowing to spiral quickly out of control. From 1881 to 1889 the funded public debt of the provinces, mainly held by foreign investors, grew 746 percent in real terms.[21] Over the same period the federal funded public debt grew 95 percent, an indication in and of itself of the extremely expansionary fiscal policy adopted by the administration of President Miguel Juárez Celman (1886–90). It is hard to overemphasize the extent to which foreign investors began lending to all manner of new borrowers within this emerging market in a short space of time. The Province of Buenos Aires was the only province that, before the euphoria of the eighties, had had genuine access to international capital markets. It was in 1883 that the bandwagon

21. *Memorias de Hacienda* (Treasury Reports; 1892, 1893).

started to roll: ten other provinces and ten municipalities floated their first long-term bonds in the London market. By year's end, the consolidated provincial external amounted to 35 percent of consolidated federal debt. On the eve of the Baring Crisis in 1891, this proportion had climbed to 114 percent.

By 1891 almost all municipal and provincial foreign debts were technically in default. Only through the extraordinary leadership of Pellegrini did the national government avoid an across-the-board default on its foreign debt. To be fair, he was given some help in the form of a "bailout." In January 1891 the Bank of England acted in ways akin to the IMF's interventions in recent crises, advancing to the federal government a three-year bridge loan of £15 million to cover the service and amortization of external debt. This did give Argentina a breathing space in which to work out an orderly set of rescheduling arrangements with its creditors, a diverse array of banks and other private bondholders; but it did not help that much and no new external credit was available for years in the private or public sectors.

The costs were serious and illustrate the importance of public debt credibility. From 1891 to 1902 Argentina suffered stringent credit rationing and financial isolation. The sudden collapse of foreign capital flows required drastic adjustments in the structure of the domestic economy, as was well understood at the time.[22] Argentina had to endure austerity conditions so as to generate sizeable trade surpluses. But the impact went far beyond mere consumption effects: a decade of economic growth was effectively lost due to the sharp contraction of investment, a direct consequence of the withdrawal of foreign investment. The parallels with contemporary emerging market crises are striking: we are reminded that all aspects of domestic economic activity are compromised by such shocks. The standard of living may need to fall, and investment for the future may need to be halted too, all in order to solve this particular kind of "transfer problem."

Deflation, Expectations, and Investment

The trauma of the Baring Crisis was to leave its mark on the design of new macroeconomic policies in the remainder of the decade. The political-economy constraints of the moment produced an original, effective, but very costly economic phenomenon: deflation under a pure paper standard with a fixed money base.

22. José Terry, one of the government's leading financial experts, wrote shortly after the Baring Crisis that: "It is true that, after all, products must be settled with products; but it is also the case that a country can have a number of years in which it settles products with credit; the credit in that case represents the product to be exported in the future...here we can observe that, after any crisis in which the country loses external credit and capital, imports diminish considerably—because Say's law must then apply exactly, for in those moments there is neither money nor credit that could replace it." (Terry 1893, pp. 64–68, our translation).

In the Baring Crisis, the paper peso *(peso moneda naciónal),* nominally equivalent to one gold dollar by virtue of the 1881 convertibility law, suffered a depreciation of 274 percent. Despite this very severe misalignment, in 1893—and in the middle of delicate negotiations with international creditors to resolve the default—Argentine monetary authorities assured investors that convertibility would be resumed at par. The Conversion Office had no backing to issue new money, so the stock of high-powered money was held fixed at its pre-crisis level for a decade. Once the inflation inertia of the crisis subsided a rapid deflation and appreciation ensued as money demand recovered.

The deleterious effects of the deflation were soon felt, a direct result of this extraordinarily restrictive monetary policy. In 1897 a political-economy debate began as to whether a return to a convertible monetary regime would be advisable or not. The debate centered on whether the paper peso should be restored to convertibility at the original par or else at the then-prevailing market exchange rate, thus accommodating the devaluation. Predictable divisions arose. Urban sectors and commercial interests favored a convertibility plan fixed at par while politically powerful rural interests were keen to see an end to the deflation and appreciation that squeezed their profits on exported agricultural and pastoral goods.[23]

Yet, if we can put distributional conflict aside, the most important arguments for devaluation centered on the damaging *economy-wide* effects of deflation for investment and economic growth. These concerns originated from the now-obscure Argentine political economist Silvio Gesell (1862–1930), whose works anticipated Fisher's ideas on tight money, interest rates, and the problem of the debt-deflation trap, and even the ideas of later scholars such as Mundell and Sargent on the importance of regime changes, expectations, and the impact of monetary policy via the real interest rate. Real interest rates were quite high in Argentina, averaging 10.4 percent in the 1892–99 period. In this sense, a looser monetary policy that accommodated the devaluation seemed, in principle, the appropriate course of action. At the resumption in 1899, this was in fact the final outcome.

Given the rigid monetary policy implemented in the early 1890s, we might ask what the tradeoffs were for policymakers. Here a comparative perspective can be informative, and in one thread running through the book we are careful to examine choices and outcomes in the 1890s crisis relative to later slumps in 1913–19 and 1929–33. For example, when we analyze how Argentina overcame the Great Depression, we emphasize a change in macroeconomic regime in 1931 that destroyed prevailing deflationary expectations—but also destroyed the nominal anchor and the years of investment in monetary regime credibility.

23. Ford (1962). Such intersectoral conflicts were common in all countries already on, or attempting to join, the gold standard. The political divisions in the 1890s United States offer a well-known, but not the only, example. See Eichengreen (1992a; 1992b) and Frieden (1988; 1997).

Convertibility and the Financial System: Walking a Tightrope?

The loss of financial intermediation in the 1890s imposed serious real costs on the Argentine economy in the short run. The poorly designed banking system was left in tatters following the abortive boom and bust of the 1880s. In the longer run, however, we need to know what institutional and economic impediments hindered the growth of a resilient financial system that could rekindle and sustain the process of domestically financed capital formation.

The postcrisis reconstruction was not smooth. In spite of a diversified branch-banking system, and even when macroeconomic policy seemed under control, financial crises were still recurrent in Argentina. To explore this problem, we invoke the idea of the intertwined monetary and financial macroeconomic "twin risk" that confronts a small open economy under a fixed exchange-rate standard.

Until 1935 the Argentine monetary and financial regime operated without a central bank. The modern conception of a central bank envisages an official bank with the monopoly right to issue money and the capacity to rediscount the financial system's portfolio of commercial obligations in order to act as the system's Lender of Last Resort. Thus, a possible cause of a suboptimal financial structure was the existence of a less powerful (that is, less discretionary) monetary authority. The Conversion Office, as a currency board, had a single, exclusive macroeconomic responsibility of guaranteeing the external value of the domestic currency. Certainly, it had no mandate to guarantee the internal convertibility of banking deposits into cash in the event of general bank runs. Simply put, the Conversion Office could not act as a Lender of Last Resort by providing unbacked currency to the financial system—at least, not without breaking its own rules.

A common characteristic of real financial crises is that a fall in bank money (or in the ratio of inside to outside money, due to a persistent run on bank deposits) coincides with a severe loss of output. The story for 1913–14 is compelling and exposes the weakness of the "one size fits all" monetary policy that the currency board had introduced. Unlike the 1890–91 crisis, on this occasion Argentina did not need protection from its own economic policy mistakes; instead it was volatility in external markets that disrupted local conditions, as war and uncertainty gripped the core. But the nature of the adverse shock, the reason for a reversal of capital flows, was not a contingency that the monetary rule took into consideration. The authorities had tied their hands, and watched from the sidelines as a massive gold drain imposed a large monetary contraction on the economy. True, a major devaluation of the currency was avoided, as had happened during the Baring Crisis, but the price was very high. The banking industry, which had by now got back on its feet, was again devastated. Bank stock prices fell by 38 percent in one year, and there was a severe capital crunch felt by all banks.

The dilemma is clear. If such an external shock were to hit the economy, a financial crisis could start if economic agents began to panic and, doubting internal convertibility, tried to convert all their deposits into currency. If the Conversion Office were to act as a Lender of Last Resort to stave off the liquidity problem, this could feed a new run on bank deposits, but this time under doubts about external convertibility, with the public now rushing to convert peso deposits into specie. Thus, under this kind of "twin risk" scenario, the institutional design was quite unforgiving and (deliberately) inflexible.[24] Without a safety net, the Argentine monetary authorities were walking a most dangerous tightrope given the prevailing monetary and financial architecture. Would the currency board stand on the sidelines in any banking collapse of any magnitude? The 1913–14 crisis seemed to indicate they had the will to do exactly that. History soon presented a tougher test of their nerve when the world economy offered up its biggest external shock to date in the crisis of the 1930s.

Toward Central Banking: Evolutionary Enhancements or Malign Mutations?

Historically, many central banks around the world have emerged organically from large banks—bankers' banks—or from specially privileged banks established by states as their fiscal agents with some monopoly rights in their charter.[25] Certainly, the Argentine landscape had some potential in this regard, given the early establishment of state banks in the nineteenth century. But these banks were provincial, not national, in their scope, and their capability to operate as prudent financial institutions was repeatedly compromised by the provinces' desire to use them as agents for levying seigniorage. No truly national bank was chartered until after a federal system came into being.

In our period of study the only state bank of any consequence was the Banco de la Nación Argentina, which began life as the Banco Nacional in 1872. It was the major state bank and the fiscal agent of the federal government. After playing a key role in the abortive banking experiment of the late 1880s, it was liquidated during the Baring Crisis and refounded as the Banco de la Nación in 1891. It remained the government's principal fiscal agent and, having been cleaned up after the Baring Crisis, it emerged as Argentina's most important commercial bank in the 1890s, a time when the financial crash had put almost every other bank was in dire straits.

24. This is not to say that having a central bank can prevent all financial crises, as recent experience shows, and as the United States experience showed in the Great Depression. The central bank must have a clear mission to assist banks in distress and it must discharge its responsibilities in that area, conditions that the 1930s Federal Reserve failed to satisfy, plunging the U.S. banking system into collapse. A Central Bank is not a sufficient condition for the prevention of banking crises. But absent an alternative fiscal source of banking insurance resources or a reliable private-sector insurance system—both being elusive solutions in reality—it is certainly a necessary condition.

25. For more on the evolution of central banks, see Goodhart (1988).

After the crisis, the government took great care and instituted strict policies to restrain the Banco de la Nación by governing its level of reserves and limiting its rediscounting capacity with the government itself. Moreover, the Banco de la Nación and the Conversion Office were kept at arm's length in an attempt to isolate two important functions. The responsibilities for note issues and their eventual convertibility—that is, outside money and the problem of external convertibility—were assigned to the Conversion Office. The state and commercial banking activities—that is, inside money and the problem of internal convertibility—were to be the domain of the Banco de la Nación. It was hoped that this separation of powers would constitute a more robust regime by keeping banking activity out of the purview of the institution that was ultimately responsible for the currency, with the goal of creating sufficient credibility to rejoin the gold standard.

The clean separation was essentially maintained until the crisis of 1913–14 when an emergency rediscount law was enacted, admitting much more flexibility into the system. The Banco de la Nación was authorized to rediscount the commercial obligations of other private banks, which at the same time could be rediscounted at the Conversion Office for cash. In other words, the state bank now had the ability to act as Lender of Last Resort to the financial system, and the monetary authority had the power to finance such activity with money printing unbacked by gold. In practice, what happened? The Banco de la Nación immediately began putting its new powers to use and started to extend rediscounts to other banks. But the Conversion Office shunned its new prerogative and kept money and gold synchronized on the margin for a long time. In fact, as we shall see, the Conversion Office only put the rediscount provision into practice in the 1931 crisis to offset a severe gold drain.[26]

This institutional path could not be described as the coherent evolution of a money and banking system toward a mature design built around a central bank. In Argentina the idea of a central bank, and the concept of regulating and supervising the financial system, were foreign to the thinking of monetary authorities, as well as the banking community itself, at least until after the First World War.[27] Yet from these conditions a central bank did emerge. In April 1931 the critical mutation of the monetary system occurred. The provisional

26. At the provincial level, the Banco de la Provincia de Buenos Aires had had certain currency board features in earlier years, from 1867 to 1876, with the operation of its own internal Exchange Office (Oficina de Cambios). Note that this was a matter of provincial, not federal, money and banking policy at the time, and no national money then existed. See our discussion in the next chapter.

27. For example, until 1935 there was no official policy regarding the level of reserves—the relationship between cash and deposits—that should be maintained by the private banks in the financial system. No institution acted as a Comptroller of the Currency, as in the United States, to supervise banking institutions. Transparency and the dissemination of economic information were rare: before 1900, the *Memorias de Hacienda* did not systematically include any consolidated monetary and banking statistics showing the condition of the banking system.

government started to use the rediscount mechanism at the Conversion Office, allowing the currency board to finance the Banco de la Nación's Lender-of-Last-Resort activities by rediscounting commercial paper. The administration eventually convinced Congress to pass a law that gave the government the power to place state bonds—an issue called the "Patriotic Loan"—directly at the Conversion Office in exchange for cash.

Beyond the Belle Époque

While a tacit spirit of laissez faire had guided the financial system for many years, the rise of central banking elsewhere in the world only added fuel to animated debates that soon sprang up over the best monetary policy regime for the country. The Conversion Office did not survive the Great Depression: its functions were reorganized within a central bank proper in 1935 and along the way a massive bank bailout was engineered using the vast seigniorage receipts. The printing press, long quiescent, was humming again.

After the fateful event of April 1931, the genie was out of the bottle. With the ink barely dry on the freshly printed notes as they left the monetary authority on their way to the state bank, and later the finance ministry, discretion had decisively replaced rules in monetary policy. The pretense of maintaining a metallic regime was over, credibility was soon spent, and a fiduciary regime had crept back in place. While perhaps understandable at the time, this reaction to a crisis had disastrous ramifications for subsequent Argentine economic history.

What lessons does history have for us as we look back with the benefit of hindsight and what implications for present-day concerns? The importance of consistent macroeconomic policies cannot be overstated. Fundamental economic contradictions appeared in the Argentine system and were allowed to grow by a curious financial architecture which looked sound on the surface but was in poor shape at deeper levels. Here, the importance of institutional design is clear. Macroeconomic policy and bank behavior do not happen in a vacuum.

One institutional contrast stands out at the center of our study. The Conversion Office succeeded in its mission for a very long time, thanks to an elegant and robust design. The Banco de la Nación, on the other hand, was subject to weak oversight, and was repeatedly modifying its objectives and expanding its scope until it had bailed out almost the entire financial system and reduced its own balance sheet to a shambles. To save the bank, in the end, the convertibility plan had to be sacrificed. It was a case, we might say, of bad institutions driving out good. Or, as is often asserted but rarely demonstrated in practice, it really does matter how your complete financial architecture is designed, from top to bottom: getting one element right, like the currency board, is no guarantee that flaws elsewhere will not bring the whole structure down sooner or later. Given the institutions it built, and their inability to withstand certain kinds of shocks, Argentina was eventually due for some kind of serious macroeconomic setback.

In this case it took a while, but slow declines sometimes offer more drama than instant collapses: a process of gradual decay is seen for a while, only to be punctuated by a loud crash when a massive piece of the edifice cracks and falls apart. Such a process invites the thicker descriptions and layers of analysis that the tools of modern economic history put at our disposal, and so our study employs formal econometrics and economic theory, exploits new quantitative data, evinces a sensitivity to institutional context, and explores a range of narrative sources.

It is only with attention to the relationship between institutional structure, policy choices, and economic conditions that we can begin to offer an explanation of Argentina's puzzling decline after the golden years at the turn of the twentieth century. It was then one of the richest countries in the world, but its potential went to waste in the long run as a growing incoherence in policies emerged. It is a sad but valuable story, a cautionary tale with much to say about today's challenges for economic reform in developing countries. Argentine economic history demonstrates that prosperity in incomes and prosperity in institutions are two very different things. A failure in the second can be the undoing of the first.

2

Anchors Aweigh: The Drift toward Crisis in the 1880s

As we have just seen in the last chapter, the predominant economic problem facing Argentina in the decades after independence was sporadic runaway inflation. Or perhaps, more accurately, we can say that inflation was the most serious symptom of deeper institutional and political problems that forestalled the creation of a stable macroeconomic regime.

Frequent bouts of inflation in the Province of Buenos Aires coincided with economic crises—commonly during wars and the fiscal consequences associated with sudden bursts of government expenditure. The inflation experience was quite similar in other jurisdictions. All provincial governments lacked the fiscal tools to perform "tax smoothing." They had no significant access to international bond markets and no capacity to float debt on a domestic bond market. They had weak powers of taxation except in trade taxes—the very source likely to fail in times of war or crisis.[1] Consequently, until alternatives could be found, the authorities resorted all too often to the only tax device left: the inflation tax, or seigniorage.

Of course, a coordinated solution to these problems was hindered by sectional divisions among the provinces. Each province has its own monetary system and banking structure, but all suffered from similar difficulties. This epoch has been characterized as one in which national money did not exist:

> Each province had its own money, and the same money had a different value between one province and another, and even between cities in the same province. In Buenos Aires there were four varieties of paper, as well as foreign coins. In the other provinces, Chilean, Bolivian, Peruvian, and other gold, silver, and copper coins circulated side by side with provincial paper, with the notes of the Banco Nacional, the notes of private bankers, and even of ordinary houses. There was convertible and inconvertible paper. Of the silver coins, many were from Chile, Bolivia and Peru; and of these many were underweight.[2]

1. See Amaral (1988), della Paolera (1988), Cortés Conde (1989), Bordo and Végh (1998), and Irigoin (1999).
2. Williams (1920, p. 31).

The fledgling banking system had to cope with monetary instability and bank failures were common in times of crisis. The only banks sure to survive were the banks owned and operated by the provincial governments. For economic agents acting in this environment such volatility confounded any solid expectations of stability and any long-term forecasts of prices and economic conditions. The various monies in circulation hindered exchange and prevented the smooth operation of domestic commerce within the national free-trade area comprising the Province of Buenos Aires and the other provinces that were united in the Argentine Confederation. The payments system and banking channels were weak and unreliable in hard times and the circulating paper currency could not be counted on as a useful store of value.

This period has often been referred to as one of "monetary anarchy." Yet, once the wars subsided, and political union was achieved and consolidated in the 1860s and 1870s, political leaders turned their attention away from matters of security, territorial expansion, and internecine conflict. Instead, they began to focus on the welfare of the nation state and sought to put Argentina on a path toward civilization through modernization, education, economic growth, and stability.

Economic reforms were a key element of this agenda. If Argentina were to modernize it was readily appreciated that a stable economic environment would be needed, so as to facilitate the activities of commerce and finance, both domestically and with the rest of the world. All sides appreciated the need for institutional reforms to achieve that result, and as more and more countries in the rest of the world began to adopt metallic standards as their monetary system, an obvious path forward seemed to open up.

A Failed Convertibility Experiment

In 1862 the recently inaugurated first national administration, led by President Bartolomé Mitre (1862–68), began the process of monetary reform when it decreed that only paper money issued by the Banco de la Provincia de Buenos Aires was to be accepted as legal tender by the Customs Office. The parity was set at 20 paper pesos per *peso fuerte,* the latter (the "hard peso") being the specie *numéraire* of the economy. This was clearly an attempt to force a financial innovation to encourage the use of paper money as a means of payment. The plan also aspired to increase confidence in the paper money because on the foreign exchanges the market rate at that time stood at 24 paper pesos per *peso fuerte*. Institutional innovations would be needed to make the regime more credible in the wake of a period of profligate monetary and fiscal activity. The Banco de la Provincia, the single bank of issue, was still under provincial jurisdiction and operated under a charter that specified neither a limit on paper note issues nor the type of assets to be held against its note issue liabilities.

Thus, to redress the expectations of devaluation in the foreign exchange market was not an easy task. As shown in Table 2.1, paper money had depreciated rapidly from 22 paper pesos per *peso fuerte* in 1861 to 29 in 1864. Memories of reckless paper printing were fresh. The Banco de la Provincia had expanded the quantity of paper money by 88 percent to permit the Province of Buenos Aires to finance military expenditures in 1859 and 1861, notably for the decisive civil war battles of Cepeda and Pavón fought against the other provinces of the Argentine Confederation. A commitment was made to buy back the notes at the end of the conflict. Still, once the wars ended, the commitment was in doubt when the national administration of the new Argentine Republic failed to negotiate with the Province of Buenos Aires a plan to amortize the paper notes consistent with the targeted exchange rate of 20 paper pesos per *peso fuerte*.

At the national level, the government announced in 1863 that consolidated budget deficits would be covered with issues of convertible bonds and presented a plan with two alternatives for the future operations of the Banco de la Provincia. Under Plan A, the state would take over the privilege of issuing paper notes from the Banco de la Provincia. Under Plan B, the government would establish a regime of competitive banks of issue for issuing bond-backed convertible notes.[3] However, neither plan was approved by Congress and so the Banco de la Provincia formally retained its independent control of monetary policy. As we shall see, the nation would have to wait thirty years until a crisis led to the issue of fiduciary currency being centralized in a decisive reform.

In the meantime, a piecemeal evolution of the monetary and financial institutions was underway. In 1864 the government agreed with the Banco de la Provincia to establish a Conversion Law to take effect on July 1, 1865. This deadline was not met. It turned out that nobody had thought to figure out where to find the real resources needed to fund the necessary specie reserves. The starting date for the convertibility plan was put back to 1867. While the plan had failed in the short run, it sent a clear signal of the new direction of money and banking policy. In 1864, knowing that it would have to meet the eventual limits that would be imposed by the law, the bank began to retire paper notes. As Table 2.1 shows, the tightening of credit in the money market was dramatic and loans denominated in paper pesos declined by 51 percent in the 1864–67 period. The monetary situation reached peak illiquidity in 1865. Outstanding credit in paper pesos declined by 27 percent in one year while domestic activity, as proxied by the semisum of exports and imports, increased by 21 percent.

The political economy reaction to the new policy was sharp. The export sector (the ranchers, or *hacendados*) argued with the authorities over the inconvenience

3. See Cortés Conde (1989, p. 31).

Table 2.1. *Real Activity, Monetary Variables, and Interest Rates, 1861–82*

Year	Exchange Rate	Exports	Imports	Banco de la Provincia: Money Base	Specie Reserves	Deposits	Money Supply	Loans	Deposit Interest Rate: Gold	Paper	Internal Bond Yield
1861	22.1	—	—	—	—	263	—	179	9.8	7.9	—
1862	24.0	16.1	22.1	—	—	296	—	154	8.0	6.8	—
1863	28.0	18.2	25.2	354	14	344	711	241	11.3	10.6	—
1864	29.0	18.8	21.8	342	32	334	718	252	10.0	10.0	15.0
1865	27.4	22.0	27.1	347	48	321	679	183	10.5	12.2	15.0
1866	24.3	26.7	37.4	431	112	251	762	129	9.8	14.2	14.7
1867	24.9	33.2	38.8	536	30	296	978	123	7.0	7.0	11.6
1868	25.0	29.7	42.4	588	90	324	1,045	260	7.5	8.0	12.6
1869	25.0	32.4	41.2	558	15	348	1,157	307	7.0	7.0	10.4
1870	25.0	30.2	49.1	639	45	367	1,247	372	—	—	9.2
1871	25.0	27.0	45.6	802	93	372	1,423	449	—	—	8.7
1872	25.0	47.3	61.6	964	138	486	1,824	581	6.0	6.0	8.0
1873	25.0	47.4	73.4	827	63	487	1,653	687	6.0	6.0	7.6
1874	25.0	44.5	57.8	787	110	457	1,563	569	—	—	7.8
1875	25.0	52.0	57.6	717	85	615	1,619	544	8.0	—	8.9
1876	29.4	48.1	36.1	895	4	622	1,835	546	8.0	—	12.8
1877	29.5	44.8	40.4	790	4	734	1,832	675	—	—	10.6
1878	32.4	37.5	43.8	870	4	744	1,862	704	—	—	10.7
1879	31.9	49.3	46.4	853	10	801	1,937	775	—	—	9.2
1880	28.6	58.4	45.3	864	4	814	1,836	820	—	—	7.9
1881	25.0	57.9	55.7	828	128	—	1,921	785	—	—	7.0
1882	25.0	60.4	61.2	740	22	959	2,065	1,005	—	—	6.9

Notes and sources: Exchange rate in paper pesos per *peso fuerte*. Exports and imports in millions of gold pesos. Balance sheet data in millions of paper pesos. Interest rates and bond yield in percent. From República Argentina (1916); della Paolera (1983); Cortés Conde (1989).

of a contractionary monetary policy combined with a floating exchange rate regime. At the height of the business cycle they favored a fixed exchange rate regime that would stop the appreciation of currency, since specie inflows would then have increased the quantity of money. The appreciation of currency was strongly correlated with the rise in domestic nominal interest rates as shown in Table 2.1. Even more striking was the fact that the ex post real interest rate in the economy skyrocketed: it went from 6 percent in 1864, to 18 percent in 1865, and a high of 29 percent in 1866.[4]

The behavior of real interest rates prompted the government to put an end to the appreciation of paper money. By 1867, two new monetary laws had passed. First, the Banco de la Provincia was authorized to issue metallic notes up to a maximum of 100 million paper pesos.[5] Second, an Office of Exchange *(Oficina de Cambios)* was established on January 3, 1867, *within* the most important official, albeit provincial, bank, the Banco de la Provincia de Buenos Aires. The new Office of Exchange was intended to be functionally equivalent to the Office of Exchange at the Bank of England on which it was modeled. The Law established that the Bank would stand ready to automatically exchange paper pesos for hard pesos at a rate of 25 paper pesos per *peso fuerte*.

What were the expectations surrounding this new monetary institution? The historian of the Banco de la Provincia de Buenos Aires, Osvaldo Garrigos, writing in 1873, was quite emphatic when he explained why the Office of Exchange, a precursor of the Conversion Office, was established as an entity quite separate from the other business areas of the bank:

> The name given to the Office of Exchange is due, without doubt, to its function, independent from other functions, and hence it stands as a separate division within the bank.[6]

Garrigos and his contemporaries understood very well that the Office of Exchange function dealt with variations in outside money, or the outstanding amount of money in circulation in a clean gold standard, and not with inside money or secondary money creation:

> The paper money that the Office of Exchange was putting in circulation, did not multiply money, rather it was just a public signaling of exchange. The issue was limited and had as backing an equal amount of gold.[7]

The question still remained whether this clean separation of the inside and outside money functions would be respected, a question that would pervade

4. The ex post real interest rate was calculated using the exchange rate as a proxy for domestic prices. This approach assumes purchasing power parity and stable world prices, both reasonable assumptions. See della Paolera (1983).
5. Specie reserves backing the so-called metallic notes were set at 33 percent of outstanding circulation. See Cortés Conde (1989, p. 50).
6. Own translation from Garrigos (1873, p. 147).
7. Own translation from Garrigos (1873, p. 148).

Argentine monetary history from that day forward. As we shall see next, the Office of Exchange's automatic mechanism functioned well in the first four to five years after its inception; but thereafter the Banco de la Provincia was "used" in a discretionary way by Sarmiento. The mechanical rules were no longer respected, and it evolved into what we might call a managed gold exchange standard.

To sum up the 1860s experience, we can ask how well did the disorganized regime function? The period from 1862 to 1868 can be divided in two subperiods: 1862–64, a period dominated by inflationary expectations; and 1865–68, a period characterized by the revaluation of paper money and an increase in nominal and real interest rates. This set the stage for a stable period from 1867 to 1876 when Argentina formally adhered to the international gold standard.

The years of President Domingo Sarmiento's term in office (1868–74) can certainly be characterized as an era of prosperity and economic stability. From 1868 to 1872, exports and imports increased on average by more than 50 percent. Aggregate demand was also expanding, mainly driven by public investments at the federal level: the cumulative deficit of the national administration for 1868–72 amounted to 2.5 times fiscal receipts.[8] Deficits were covered with external loans and bank advances. Interestingly enough, public expenditures seemed to have had no sizeable contemporaneous crowding-out effects. Yields on financial assets were steadily declining throughout the convertibility period. From an average level of 15 percent in 1866, domestic interest rates fell to 7.5 percent in 1872, a sign of loosening monetary policy. In 1871, commercial paper rates and yields on public bonds had started to converge toward levels observed in the U.S. economy.[9]

The adjustment was a corollary of the large role of capital imports in the economy, stimulated in part by the convertibility regime. Sizeable balance of payments surpluses increased the stock of money in the economy and, in turn, this reinforced the downward pressure on domestic interest rates. From 1868 to 1872 the monetary base increased at an average annual rate of 16 percent. The large increase in the demand for money was also met with an expansion of banking money at an average annual rate of almost 20 percent in the same period; clearly the broad money supply expansion was not solely the result of the automatic gold-standard mechanism.

Using conventional accounting procedures to perform a decomposition of the sources of money growth, one can infer that 68 percent of the increase in the money base was explained by gold inflows to the Office of Exchange.

8. The deficit is measured as fiscal receipts minus total outlays of the public sector, a concept termed *uso del credito*. Data from Cortés Conde (1989, p. 86).

9. The table shows the commercial deposit rate was 6 percent in 1872; call money rates (lending rates) in the United States stood at 8 percent in the same year. See Friedman and Schwartz (1982, p. 122).

Bank issues of metallic notes explained only 17 percent of the growth in the monetary base. While this expansionary of the fiduciary issue was not quantitatively important in 1872, it reflected a fundamental weakness in the monetary and banking institutional arrangements and showed that, on the margin, the monetary base was not fully backed as in a strict gold standard.

In this sense Argentina was on a "managed" gold standard regime, with both rules and discretion in play. The Banco de la Provincia could manage two instruments of monetary policy.[10] First, the reserve-deposit ratio, a means to control the elastic relationship between inside and outside money. Second, the supply of fractionally backed metallic notes, the elastic supply of outside money itself. The potential for conflict and collapse arose from this ill-designed system. Recall that there was still no national currency per se. The notes of the Banco de la Provincia were supposed to be the de facto convertible currency of the country, but this reputation rested on the additional presence of the Office of Exchange and its commitment to the international monetary standard.

Thus, the degree of discretion in one element of the system could pollute the clean, rule-based structures put in place elsewhere. This very primitive example of inconsistent policies in the Argentine case will set the tone for much of the history we discuss in the rest of the book; it was a case, so to speak, of bad monetary institutions driving out good.

During the 1868–72 period of economic expansion and capital inflows the level of specie reserves and the money supply moved together, and expanding credit fed into an already liquid money market. Adverse domestic and international conditions took hold in 1873. The government reacted to the contraction in the gold-backed money supply by expanding the stock of metallic notes, that is, by pursuing a policy of sterilization.

It was hoped that the expansionary monetary policy would not just prevent a fall in the domestic money stock but also replenish the exhausted banking reserves of the Banco de la Provincia. At the start of the monetary crisis the bank tried to decrease its level of reserves, but the external drain quickly became an internal drain as depositors tested the convertibility of deposits into cash. This is shown clearly in Table 2.1. The reserve-deposit ratio declined from 20 percent in 1872 to 3 percent in 1876. Only the issue of more metallic notes prevented the Banco de la Provincia from collapsing.

Predictably, the attempt to sterilize the negative effects of gold outflows failed and convertibility was abandoned in May 1876, with the state of suspension being known by the curious term *curso forzoso*. Figure 2.1 describes extremely well some of the dynamics of this period. In particular, under a credible convertible regime with a fixed exchange rate there was a fall in nominal interest

10. There were other small banks, including the newly founded Banco Nacional, but they amounted to less than 10 percent of the banking system. Hence, we focus our attention in this section solely on the Banco de la Provincia.

Figure 2.1. The First Convertibility Experiment

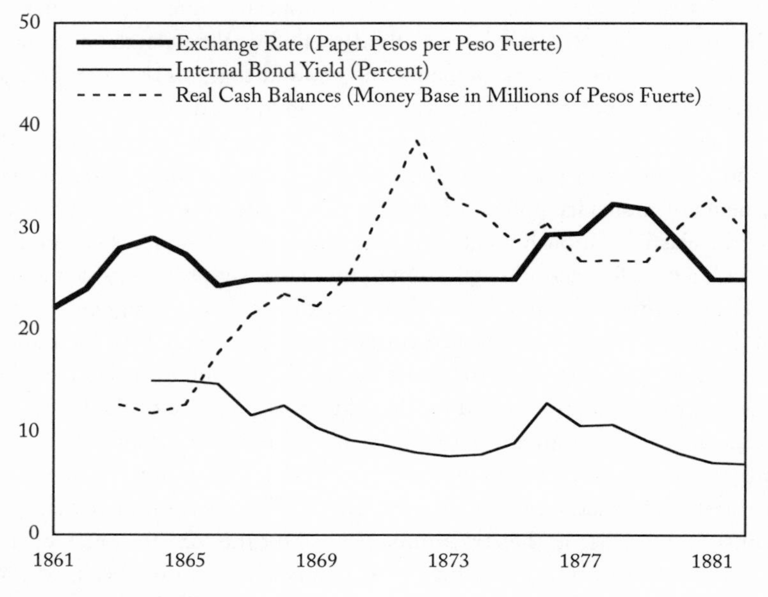

Notes and sources: See Table 2.1.

rates coupled with a rise in the real level of monetization of the economy (the period 1868–72). Subsequently, the process of monetization was halted when the economy was overheated by an expansionary fiscal policy that was inconsistent with the convertible regime (the period 1873–76). This latter episode is characterized by a decline in real cash balances as agents converted money to specie, ending in a final speculative attack à la Krugman and a collapse of the fixed exchange rate.[11]

The incoming administration of President Nicolás Avellaneda (1874–80) thus had to cope with a depreciating currency, capital outflows, and a precarious budgetary situation.[12] The real sector of the economy adjusted almost instantaneously to the credit-rationing situation. Trade deficits were reversed and sizeable surpluses emerged to cope with the burden of external debt service. The adjustment was promoted by the implementation of restrictive monetary and fiscal policies: public expenditures were reduced by 40 percent in real terms in 1877, the money base remained fixed, and the nominal exchange rate appreciated to its earlier level of 25 paper pesos per *peso fuerte*. The new economic equilibrium prepared the way for a fresh monetary experiment and yet another attempt to get the monetary and financial institutions right.

11. Krugman (1979).
12. In 1876, the budget deficit was 93 percent of fiscal receipts (Cortés Conde 1989, p. 112).

Cartoon 2.1. *¡16 de Mayo 1876! El cuadro consolador de nuestra feliz situación.* (The comforting picture of our happy situation.)
Notes: The cartoon conveys the idea that the 1876 suspension of convertibility called *curzo forzoso* (written on the guillotine) is in breach of the constitution (the already decapitated body on the scaffold). At left, President Nicolás Avellaneda, the executioner, holds the head of the constitution. *Agio* (written on the blade) is the gold premium, or, equivalently, the devaluation relative to par. Under the platform a group of masked men fill up their bags with gold. At the top of the steps, the priest administering the last rites to the next victim, public credit, is Finance Minister Santiago Cortinéz.
Source: El mosquito, no. 698, May 21, 1876.

Another False Start

We now turn to the 1880s and 1890s, focusing on institutional developments in the realms of money and banking that contributed to a major macroeconomic crisis and its eventual resolution. Serious legislative efforts to devise a new monetary system began in 1878. Congress debated the establishment of a national monetary system that would put an end to the period of monetary anarchy. Plans were drawn up and finally, in 1881, Congress voted for a currency reform law.

The Monetary Law of November 5, 1881, was intended to put Argentina on a new kind of monetary regime, a bimetallic standard. It was decreed that units of gold and silver pesos would exchange with new paper peso notes at given par values, and fixed exchange rates against key international currencies would thus be established.[13] In addition to establishing the units of the currency, the law stipulated that, after eight million gold pesos and four million silver pesos were coined, the use of foreign metallic coins as legal tender was to be prohibited. Only national minted coins and "accepted national money" could serve as legal tender for all debts, private and public. A mint was to be created and foreign metallic coins were to be accepted at their bullion value in exchange for gold and silver pesos.[14]

The transition to this new regime was not smooth, however, and the law supplied few details as to the implementation of the plan. The problem was how to replace the stock of old paper notes in circulation, 882 million inconvertible paper pesos, for new paper notes exchangeable at par with the gold peso. In 1881, the vestigial notes represented 73 percent of the total currency in circulation. The law only indicated an accounting device: banks of issue were required, within two years, to replace their paper notes with the new monetary unit based on the prevailing market rate of exchange between old paper pesos and the new gold peso.

Another provision of the law sharply curtailed "wildcat banking" tendencies by limiting the capacity for monetary expansion in the banking system as a whole. In a drastic change, the privilege of issuing the new notes was restricted to just five banks. Four of these were publicly owned (state and provincial) banks: Banco Nacional; Banco de la Provincia de Buenos Aires; Banco Provincial de Santa Fé; and Banco Provincial de Córdoba. The fifth was Otero & Co., the only private bank accorded the privilege.[15]

13. The monetary units were to be the gold peso, of 24.89 grains, 9/10 fine, and the silver peso, of 385.8 grains, 9/10 fine (Article 1). At these definitions of content, the legal ratio of gold to silver was 15.5 and the following parity rates were established with the key currencies of the major countries on the gold standard: one British pound = 5.04 gold pesos, one U.S. dollar = 1.04 gold pesos, and 5 French francs = 1 gold peso.
14. See Article 5. Agote (1882, p. 212) estimated that, by the end of 1881, foreign metallic currencies represented 27 percent of total currency in circulation including paper notes.
15. Williams (1920, p. 35).

Absent direct government control of the money supply, the behavior of the banks of issue would determine the viability of the new regime. Could they be relied upon to adhere to sound practices and so maintain convertibility of the notes they issued into specie? There was the usual problem that banks have little incentive to maintain non-interest-bearing reserves above the required level. Specie was not to be solely confined to use as backing for paper note issues. Since national minted coins were to be legal tender, banks could choose to make loans and discounts in metallic coins as long as they did not violate the monetary reserve requirements.

In short, specie holdings were to have a double purpose: first, as an asset held to ensure convertibility and, second, as an asset held to meet liabilities payable in specie; thus, profit maximization would lead banks to make the reserve requirements a binding constraint most of the time. In a crucial omission, the new law was silent with respect to the specie reserves that banks would have to hold to back their paper note issues. Thus, the only rules regulating the relationship between paper notes and specie would be the self-imposed rules laid down in the respective charters of the banks themselves.

These rules varied considerably from case to case. For example, under its 1872 charter, the issue of convertible notes by the Banco Nacional could not exceed 200 percent of bank capital, and the bank had to maintain a specie reserve of 25 percent of all notes issued. The original charter of the Banco de la Provincia de Buenos Aires was much more lax: it specified neither a limit on note issue nor the assets to be held as reserves. This lack of regulation was soon rectified, and in March 1883 the Board of Directors passed a special motion stating that "the specie held by the bank will be increased to a minimum of a third of the circulating bank notes." At the Banco Provincial de Córdoba specie reserves were to be 45 percent of the note issues. The Banco Provincial de Santa Fé was subject to a more vague requirement that "the bank could increase its emission in proportion to its capital and resources."[16] Were these reserve requirements sufficiently strict? By international comparative standards of prudent banking regulation, we think not: note issues certainly did not require anything like the 100 percent marginal bullion reserve as under the British specie standard.

The law went into effect in July 1883. From that time Argentina operated under a mixed specie and fiduciary standard where the paper peso exchanged at par with the gold peso. Yet the system was unlike many metallic standards in that it was still very decentralized. No national monetary authority existed and all control over the convertibility of notes rested with the five banks of issue.

The period of convertibility lasted only seventeen months. From late December 1884 the banks of issue refused to exchange gold at par for notes. The de facto suspension of convertibility was soon accommodated by the government,

16. Agote (1887, pp. 212–15, 218–25); Piñeiro (1921, p. 247); Cuccorese (1972, p. 297).

since, having no institutional power over the monetary system, there was little they could do to prevent it. In March 1885, the federal Government decreed *curso forzoso* again, that is, the inconvertibility into gold of paper money, with a promise that convertibility would be restored in December 1886.

Lacking any direct control over the monetary system, the government could do little more than resort to moral suasion. Banks were exhorted "to discount in gold, to take exchange with gold, or to carry out any other legal operation intended to raise the value of the currency and devoting new elements to commerce and to the industries."[17] But there was no direct intervention, and no steps were taken to repair whatever it was that had ailed the banks and left their balance sheets so fragile that they had been forced to suspend in the first place. The strategy of the government was one of hoping and waiting, trusting that an upswing in economic conditions might boost the health of the banks enough to permit a resumption of convertibility.

As one might have guessed, resumption was never achieved. When December 1886 arrived, convertibility was suspended indefinitely. What happened afterward is succinctly captured by Figure 2.2. From 1884 to 1899, the Argentine monetary regime was a de facto paper standard in which the paper peso floated against gold, and hence against the key currencies. The gold premium remained fairly stable in the first two years that followed the suspension of convertibility but, thereafter, it skyrocketed until 1891. Moreover, as one would expect in a small open economy feeling a powerful influence of purchasing-power parity, the price level moved in tandem with the exchange rate.

Toward a Working Currency Board

A major theme of this book is to show how the record of monetary instability prior to 1890 played a critical role in shaping the design of new institutions. A cursory outline of these events will set the stage for what follows. The opportunity for redesign came after a peculiar banking experiment, which is discussed in the next section, gave way to a financial crash and a major recession in 1890–91, the Baring Crisis, which is discussed at greater length in the next chapter. Argentine economic policymaking was to live in the shadow of these events for decades to come.

Following the Baring Crisis, the government sought to cast off, once and for all, the monetary anarchy of the nineteenth century by tying its hands as firmly as possible. Adopting a rigid commitment device—that is, a "hard" gold standard rule—the government stuck to a strict disinflation policy in the 1890s in an attempt to reestablish the gold standard at the old parity. In November

17. Agote (1887, p. 627).

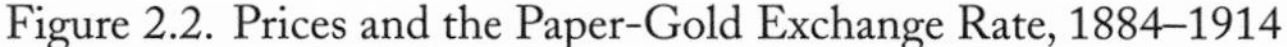

Figure 2.2. Prices and the Paper-Gold Exchange Rate, 1884–1914

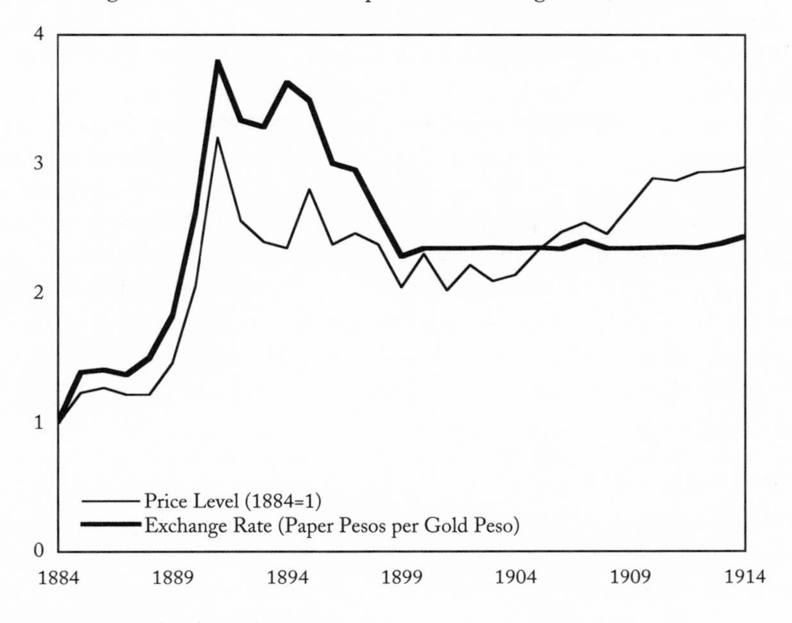

Notes and sources: See Appendix 1.

1891 Congress approved the October 1890 Conversion Office law proposed by the Executive.

The centerpiece of the law was a new national monetary authority, one under direct government control. This was to be called the Conversion Office *(Caja de Conversión)*. It would have the sole right to engage in note issues, a privilege that was to be withdrawn from the banks following their dismal record of irresponsible note issues that had left a trail of increasingly worthless paper in economy and established a pattern of chronic inflation. The Conversion Office was to function as a currency board, or redemption bureau, modeled after the issue department of the Bank of England. It would simply and mechanically exchange national paper notes for gold, or vice versa, on demand, and at a fixed exchange rate.

As is apparent from Figure 2.2, deflation took place until 1899, though it was insufficient to force prices and exchange rates back to their levels under the old parity. That being so, resumption was going to require some form of devaluation. After long and protracted arguments—to which we shall return in due course—the exchange rate was fixed at 2.27 paper pesos per gold peso. That rate, being the market rate, meant that Argentina, instead of debasing the gold peso created in 1881, opted to devalue the paper currency as a way to achieve convertibility. Under this new regime, convertibility was successfully maintained until the outbreak of the First World War, and the currency board itself operated until the 1930s.

To summarize, the institutional developments in the Argentine monetary system from the 1880s until 1913 can be briefly restated.[18] Argentina legally adopted gold and silver as the basis for its monetary system in 1881, and operationally in 1883. This metallic standard, in which specie coins would circulate side-by-side with paper notes, soon failed in 1884. An inflationary boom-and-bust cycle ensued. Following the crisis, in 1891 a completely new design brought the monetary system under the central control of a currency board. After a period of inconvertibility, in 1899 Argentina reentered the gold standard system, but under a regime very different from, and more robust than, the initial bimetallic standard envisaged in 1881.

Money, Banks, and Currency Substitution

Having surveyed the major institutional developments at the level of the monetary regime, we now seek to appraise how changes in institutional structure affected the expectations of economic agents. A useful way to attack this question is to assess the role and use of specie by the public.

The willingness of the public to hold notes rests on their confidence in convertibility. If the public ever suspects that convertibility will be suspended, or that their holdings of paper might be susceptible to devaluation, then banks might face a sudden run on gold reserves as agents seek to convert paper into specie. Such runs could cause bank failure if the reserves are insufficient to cover deposits. If a crisis looms, a government then faces the question of what it will (or can) do about it. After such crises, and even if banks resume convertibility, cautious agents may still prefer to hold the cumbersome metal rather than paper notes for fear that the same might happen again.

At the start of our period there are few quantitative measures of public holdings of gold and silver. However, contemporary scholars did report that gold and silver coins were never widely used in domestic monetary transactions: specie in hands of the public in 1881 was estimated to be 3 million gold pesos. Such a figure would correspond to about 5 percent of the total currency in circulation in that year (defined as the sum of paper notes and metallic coins).[19] Moreover, within a short span of time silver ceased to play an active monetary role. It seems that the mint ratio was set at a level that drove silver out of circulation given the (world) market price for silver, a classic case of Gresham's

18. For more details, the reader may refer back to Table 1.2.

19. Agote (1882, p. 211) estimated the currency in circulation at the end of 1881 at 56.1 million gold pesos; of this, fiduciary notes represented 41 million, specie in banks 12.1 million, and public holdings 3 million.

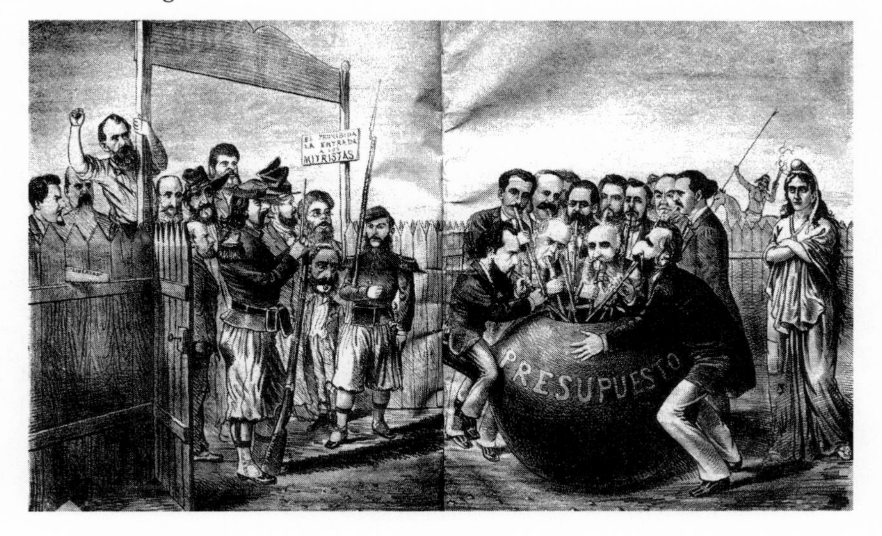

Cartoon 2.2. *Los unos chupan con una gana asombrosa, los otros se chupan los dedos, mientras tanto, nuestra pobre República, que es la que ceba el mate, espera que los chupadores se recuerden que ella esta muy enferma y espera el cuidado y el ayudo de todos.* (Some of them are sucking with great pleasure, others are sucking their fingers, while in the meantime our poor Republic, who made the *mate,* is waiting for the suckers to remember that she is very sick and needs the help of all of them.)
Notes: The *mate* is a traditional drink of Argentina brewed from hot water and herbs *(yerba),* and the term also refers to the bowl from which it is drunk through straws. This *mate* is labeled *prosupuesto* (budget), a reference to the politicians' ability to drain the public coffers. Sucking at the *mate* are many politicians, including (front row, left to right) President Nicolás Avellaneda, former President Domingo Sarmiento, Finance Minister Santiago Cortinéz, and former governor of the Province of Buenos Aires Adolfo Alsina. All those inside the stockade are of the same political party, the PAN *(Partido Autonomista Nacional).* Outside the gate, stands former President Bartolomé Mitre and his rival faction who were opposed to the PAN, behind the sign that says *es prohibida la entrada a las Mitristas* (no entry to Mitristas). Someone is forcing through the fence a saw that bears the name *libertad* (liberty). Meanwhile, an Indian rides by in the background.
Source: El mosquito, no. 682, January 30, 1876.

Law at work. Argentina was soon a de jure bimetallic country, but a de facto monometallic country, as was typically the case.[20]

Subsequently, net flows of silver with the rest of the world were insignificant; hence, silver coins may safely be excluded from the definition of the Argentine currency stock for the period under study.[21] By contrast, bank notes were issued in smaller denominations.[22] Therefore, it appears that even the five gold peso coin was inferior to the five gold peso note for transaction purposes.

What happened next? For the period after the demise of the bimetallic

20. From 1881 to 1884, silver coins worth 2.8 million gold pesos were minted. During the same period the outflow of silver was equal to 2.8 million gold pesos (Lorini 1902, p. 366).
21. For 1886–99 the cumulative net import of silver from the rest of the world amounted to 0.3 million gold pesos.
22. For example, at the most important bank of issue, the Banco de la Provincia de Buenos Aires, metallic notes up to five gold pesos were issued in eight small denominations: 8, 10, 16, 20, and 40 cents; and 1, 2, and 4 pesos. Cuccorese (1972, p. 283).

standard, recent scholarship takes the view that specie in circulation was still insignificant relative to the currency stock, and stayed that way. For example, Ford stated that "by 1896 when the coinage of gold ceased, gold coins to the value of 31.7 million gold pesos had been issued (nearly four times the original issue planned), yet in 1896 no gold coins circulated, any more than they did in 1881."[23] However, we are not satisfied with such an incomplete account. Ford does not explicitly report the evidence on which his assertion is based. Moreover, as we show below, the use of specie as a means of payment does not tell the relevant story for the interim years during the crisis.

To assess specie holding by the public we have to distinguish the use of specie as a *means of payment* and its use as a *store of value*. First, the fact that the authorities discontinued minting of coins would not have precluded domestic residents from holding specie (just as, today, the fact that the Argentine government is not empowered to issue U.S. dollars does not preclude residents from holding and hoarding U.S. dollars in significant amounts). Second, even if gold did not circulate as a generalized means of payment, one should not leap to the conclusion that its role as a store of value was insignificant.

To try to resolve the question, we now present new estimates for the specie in hands of the public for the period 1884–1914.[24] The data for 1883–99 are displayed in Table 2.2 and Figure 2.3. The evidence suggests that public hoarding was due to the failure of the monetary regime. In every year from 1884 until the financial crash of 1891 we can see that the public, as asset holders, attempted to restore their portfolio balance in the face of expected paper money depreciation, demanding gold as hedge against inflation. This trend became especially prominent after 1888.

An important issue here is that if people attempt to flee from the paper peso and into gold, and the monetary authorities do not precommit to fix the paper-gold exchange rate, then, under the assumption that the stock of gold is reasonably steady, one should expect the gold premium to rise. That the public distrusted the regime may seem all the more surprising given the spectacular economic boom that took place in the late 1880s, but subsequent events were to confirm the public's suspicions that a crisis was at hand.

23. Ford (1962, p. 93).
24. The method used is very simple. Briefly put, at each moment in time there is a given stock of specie in the country. Because Argentina is not a specie producer, this stock of specie gets increased or decreased by the net flows of specie from abroad. Hence, with data for specie flows and an initial stock of specie for the year 1883, we can generate a time series on the stock of specie for the remaining years. The specie stock may be held by three categories of holders: the monetary authorities, the banks, and the public. Elsewhere, we can obtain the holdings of specie by the domestic financial system including monetary authorities, and then, as a residual, we obtain public hoarding of specie.

Table 2.2. *Argentine Specie Stock, 1883–99*

Year	Initial Specie Stock	Net Specie Flow	Terminal Specie Stock	Specie Held by Banks	Public Hoarding of Specie
1883	—	—	22.5	19.5	3.0
1884	22.5	0.4	22.9	20.7	2.2
1885	22.9	-2.1	20.8	17.4	3.4
1886	20.8	12.3	33.1	26.5	6.6
1887	33.1	-0.1	33.0	21.9	11.1
1888	33.0	36.1	69.1	52.7	16.4
1889	69.1	-16.7	52.4	22.0	30.4
1890	52.4	1.9	54.3	10.0	44.3
1891	54.3	7.5	61.8	7.9	53.9
1892	61.8	4.5	66.3	9.1	57.2
1893	66.3	3.7	70.0	11.8	58.2
1894	70.0	2.9	72.9	10.7	62.2
1895	72.9	4.6	77.5	13.0	64.5
1896	77.5	3.9	81.4	12.9	68.5
1897	81.4	-4.3	77.1	12.3	64.8
1898	77.1	5.7	82.8	13.4	69.4
1899	82.8	1.7	84.5	18.4	66.1

Notes and sources: Units are millions of gold pesos on December 31. See Appendix 1.

Monetary and Fiscal Policy Inconsistencies

To better understand the public's reaction we must step back and survey the broader macroeconomic picture of Argentina in the 1880s and the rising role of international finance.

Even as the first attempts to reform the monetary system ran into difficulties, the new spirit of modernization in the country had been noted on a global level. Foreign investors were alert to the untapped potential of a rapidly growing economy with abundant land, an open frontier for expansion, and a seemingly more stable macroeconomic environment. Growth and investment surged in the boom years of 1884–90, a period that Williams called one of "heavy borrowing" with massive capital inflows from abroad:

> The borrowing was maintained throughout the eighties, culminating in loans of such extent as have probably never been equaled, by a country of so small a population as was that of Argentina.[25]

Argentina's rise to prominence in the London capital market was impressive. In these years the country absorbed 11 percent of the new portfolio issues of the London market; North America, with a population twenty times that of Argentina, absorbed only 30 percent of London's new issues.[26]

25. Williams (1920, p. 3).
26. London issues for Argentina from Ford (1962, p. 148); total London issues from Simon (1968, p. 38). North America includes Canada and the United States.

Figure 2.3. Public Hoarding of Specie, 1883–1914

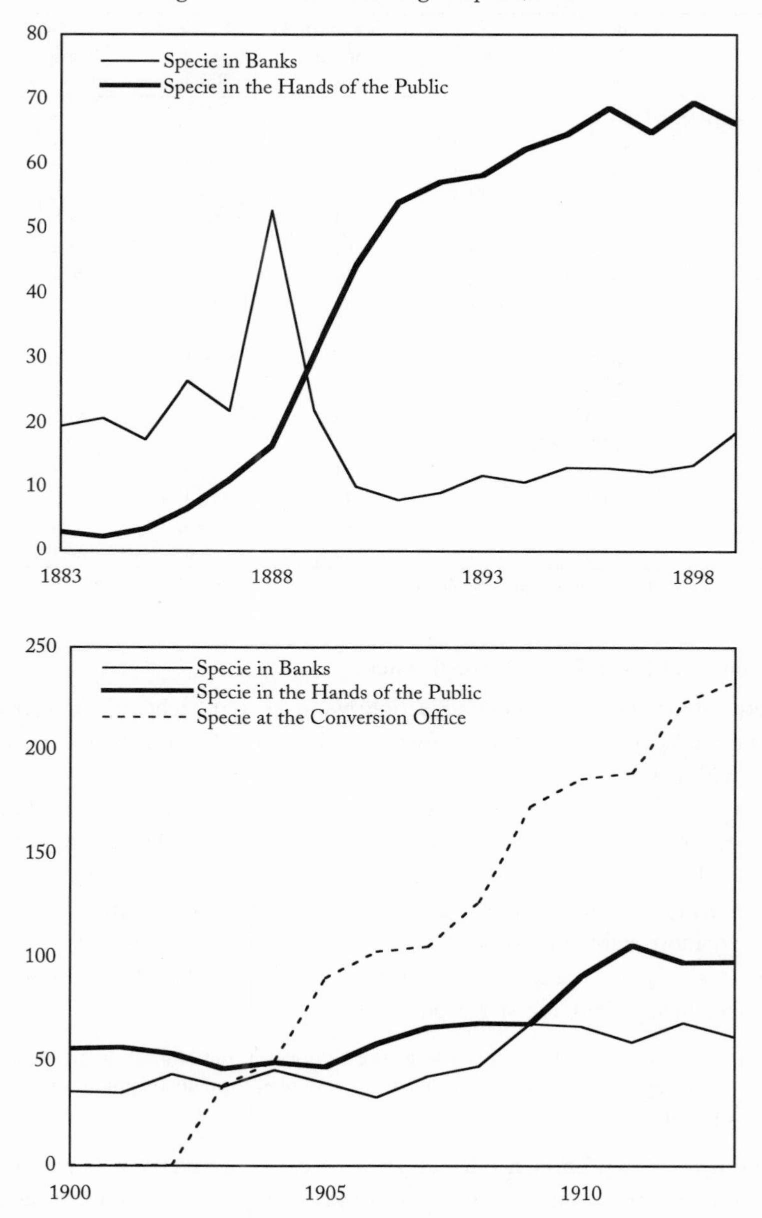

Notes and sources: Units are millions of gold pesos on December 31. See Appendix 1.

Equations (4.1) and (4.6) show that deficits are not inflationary if the authorities can finance them by borrowing or by running down specie reserves, or both. But equation (4.6) illustrates the well-known proposition that in a credible gold-standard regime governments cannot persistently use money creation as a source of revenue because specie reserves would eventually be depleted, forcing the country to adopt a fiduciary regime as in equation (4.7).[13]

Here, balance of payments crises become a public finance phenomenon once the government of a small open economy can no longer borrow from capital markets to finance a chronic primary deficit. The Argentine historical experience fits well with this description. Table 4.2 shows that the federal government did not collect enough revenues to cover its expenditures and so ran persistent flow deficits from 1885 to 1892. We should recall that immediately after the 1885 demise of the bimetallic standard the monetary authorities precommitted themselves to restore convertibility early in 1887. The conduct of fiscal policy seemed to have supported this goal since the 1886–87 budget deficits were sharply reduced relative to both expenditures and receipts. The fiscal scenario dramatically changed in 1888 when, in only one year, fiscal expenditures inclusive of debt service payments grew by 41 percent and fiscal receipts remained steady. From then on, until some fiscal adjustment took place the federal government typically had to raise additional revenues equal to almost two thirds of receipts to cover the flow deficits. Only during the 1892–93 reform years did fiscal budgets converge toward balance—expenditures were frozen in nominal terms but the gap was closed by a rise in receipts.

How did the economy respond to this set of policy choices? Table 4.3 shows the exchange rate, the budget deficit, the inflation rate, changes in the level of the public debt, and reserves during the crisis. It is true that there is no direct evidence on the flow of paper notes directly advanced to the treasury by the banks of issue; however, here, inferences can still be made and theory can substitute for facts. The counterfactual inflation rate was constructed under the assumption that, in each year, federal deficits were completely financed with issues of paper notes. In other words, if fiscal deficits had been fully monetized, yet other factors such as output and money velocity had remained approximately the same, what would have happened with the inflation rate?[14]

13. Reserves may even be exhausted in an instant by a speculative attack (Krugman 1979).

14. The counterfactual inflation rate is constructed as follows. First, assuming the deficit is fully monetized, the counterfactual growth of paper money $\widehat{MB}_{\mathrm{CF},t}$ is the deficit (column 3) divided by the outstanding stock of paper notes. Thus, following equation (4.1), let $DEF_t/DC_{t-1} = (DC_{t-1} - DC_{t-1})/DC_{t-1} = \widehat{MB}_{\mathrm{CF},t}$. Now, paper money in circulation MB_t times the velocity V_t must equal output Y_t times the price level P_t, so that $MB_t V_t = Y_t P_t$. Log differentiating, and inserting the counterfactual money growth, we obtain

$$\widehat{MB}_{\mathrm{CF},t} + \hat{V}_t = \hat{Y}_t + \hat{P}_{\mathrm{CF},t}.$$

By assuming that output and velocity behave as they did (in both actual and counterfactual scenarios), we can solve for counterfactual inflation $\hat{P}_{\mathrm{CF},t}$. The data are from Appendix 1.

Table 4.2. *Federal Budget, 1885–93*

Year	1885	1886	1887	1888	1889	1890	1891	1892	1893
Millions of Paper Pesos									
Receipts	36	42	52	52	73	73	76	111	125
Expenditure	55	56	68	76	107	96	127	128	123
Corrected Expenditure	56	58	68	86	121	115	128	128	123
Corrected Budget Deficit	19	16	16	34	48	42	52	17	-2
Millions of Gold Pesos									
Receipts	27	30	38	35	41	28	20	34	39
Expenditure	40	40	50	51	60	37	34	39	38
Corrected Expenditure	41	42	50	58	67	45	34	39	38
Corrected Budget Deficit	14	11	12	23	27	16	14	5	-1
Corrected Deficit as Percentage of:									
Receipts	53	38	32	66	66	58	69	15	-2
Corrected Expenditure	35	27	24	40	40	37	41	13	-2

Notes and sources: Corrected expenditures are reported expenditures plus the difference between the debt service realized and budgeted. See text and Appendix 1.

For 1885 the inflation rate is closely matched by the counterfactual rate, which suggests that the monetary authorities may have monetized a considerable proportion of the budget deficit. This possibility is well supported by the fact that the federal government appeared to have been credit constrained and had to amortize part of the public debt stock. In 1886 and 1887, debt played a leading role as a mean to finance the deficit; consequently, there was no clear correlation between deficits and inflation rates in those years.

Why was debt finance available? The primary deficit in Table 4.3 shows a healthier budgetary situation that may have positively influenced public perception of the government's ability to meet its service obligations without resorting to inflationary finance, making the promise of a return to parity more credible. This, in turn meant that the government could float more public bonds in the capital markets and at better prices, since there is a direct link between the market value of government debt and the market's forecast for prospective deficits. In fact, it can be shown that as a consequence of the long-run budget constraint, or solvency condition, the market value of the government's debt at any time is equal to the present value of the government's primary surpluses.[15]

15. For a detailed discussion on the links between public debt and fiscal policy see Dornbusch, Blanchard, and Buiter (1986) and Sargent (1986). For an analysis of the linkages among public finances, credit ceilings, and the market valuation of the public debt in relation with developing-country debt problems see Sjaastad (1983). Formally the link between the value of the debt and fiscal surpluses is as follows. Setting $DC_t = DC_{t-1}$ the government budget implies that $B_t = -SUR_t + (1 + i_t)B_{t-1}$, where $SUR_t = T_t - G_t$ is the nominal primary surplus at time t. Solving recursively forward in time and imposing a no-Ponzi-game condition yields

$$B(0) = SUR_0 + \frac{SUR_1}{1 + i_1} + \frac{SUR_2}{(1 + i_1)(1 + i_2)} + \dots,$$

which states that the value of the debt outstanding equals the present value of future surpluses.

Table 4.3. *Fiscal Deficits, Inflation, and Public Debt, 1885–93*

Year	Paper-Gold Exchange Rate	Total Paper Notes	Corrected Budget Deficit	Primary Deficit	Inflation Rate	Conterfactual Inflation Rate
1885	1.37	74.8	20.1	5.4	22.8	24.1
1886	1.39	89.2	15.9	-1.0	3.1	8.8
1887	1.35	97.3	16.3	0.4	-4.0	3.3
1888	1.48	129.5	34.2	15.1	0.0	7.9
1889	1.80	163.7	48.1	18.9	19.8	31.2
1890	2.58	245.1	42.2	12.8	40.9	19.7
1891	3.74	261.4	52.2	8.8	56.2	62.3
1892	3.29	281.6	17.1	-15.7	-20.6	-21.8
1893	3.24	306.7	-2.2	-38.8	-6.0	-12.1
Year	**Change in Public Debt (Variant 2)**	**Change in Specie Reserves**	**Yield Internal Bond**	**Yield External Bond**	**Spread over Rendita Italiana**	**Spread over British Consol**
1885	-12.7	-4.8	7.90	6.09	1.53	3.10
1886	23.8	9.1	7.86	5.93	1.79	2.93
1887	10.5	-5.3	8.79	5.48	1.02	2.48
1888	34.0	23.8	8.02	5.18	0.66	2.18
1889	43.1	-31.2	8.01	5.17	0.59	2.37
1890	11.8	-6.3	10.34	5.83	1.23	2.93
1891	15.7	-0.8	10.28	7.58	2.87	4.67
1892	56.7	0.4	9.15	7.51	2.85	4.71
1893	1.7	1.2	8.73	7.70	3.07	4.90

Notes and sources: Exchange rate is paper pesos per gold peso. Total notes and deficits in millions of paper pesos. Inflation and interest rates in percent. Change in public debt and change in specie reserves in millions of gold pesos. See Appendix 1.

Hence there was a positive reaction to the improved fiscal and monetary indicators. By 1888–89 bond prices had started to rise and so, ipso facto, yields were falling (Table 4.3). Another important development was a fall in "country risk" assessed by foreign investors and likely correlated with the perceptions of the government's solvency position. There was a large decline in the spread on bonds relative to both a comparable European long-term bond (the Rendita Italiana) and the British consol, evidence of the government's good credit ratings in the international capital markets.

The fiscal discipline was short lived, and it was precisely then that the public finances were derailed. In 1888, despite a clear worsening in the budget situation, we can see that the inflation and depreciation rates are not closely associated with the counterfactual inflation rate. How was this possible?

Recall that 1888 was the *only* year in which the monetary authorities respected the rules of the game established by the Law of Guaranteed Banks, laws that provided for gold-backed paper note issue. This is evidenced by the close association between the increase in paper notes and the increase in the stock of specie in Table 4.3. But we note also that specie reserves, in turn, were matched by an increase in the level of public debt.

The causation is clear given the institutional background of the previous chapters: banking reform was financed by an arbitrage operation involving loans negotiated abroad. Basically, the expansion of a gold-backed monetary base was a key component of the expansionary fiscal policy, and there were no dramatic changes in the price level or the paper-gold exchange rate.

As we have seen, the fiscal regime clearly changed early in 1889 when the Argentine government decided to pay off in paper pesos part of the debt denominated in gold. This was tantamount to a partial default by the Argentine government on its contractual obligations. As one might expect, the international financial community reacted in anger. For example, harsh judgment was passed by *The Economist* on May 25, 1889, in an article entitled "Argentine Untrustworthiness":

> That those who are now protesting against the claim of the Argentine Government to pay off the Hard Dollars Loan in paper have justice on their side is unquestionable...the claim of the Argentine Government comes as an opportune reminder that in its dealings with its creditors it is not to be trusted, and it is well that this fact should be brought home to investors, because it would appear that before long it will be attempting to raise money here...but the experience that has lately been gained of its financial untrustworthiness, exemplified both in its dealings with bondholders and its refusal to respect its own laws, ought to make investors little disposed to respond to fresh appeals.

It is hard to find an economic rationale for this abrupt change in the debt-service regime. It is even harder to understand why the government embarked on a policy that combined a partial repudiation of its debt, thus damaging its capital market reputation, with a protracted intervention in the foreign exchange market to stabilize the value of the "guaranteed" paper notes. The intervention in the foreign exchange market was a futile strategy because the public—correctly—anticipated that the "dirty float" monetary policy would soon shift from the announced convertibility-resumption objective and end up being a tool for fiscal profligacy. A massive flight from paper currency into specie, an intense currency substitution, resulted.

The monetary and fiscal inconsistency became apparent by the end of the year 1889. The government, already under a debt-ceiling constraint and with its specie reserves almost depleted, had no choice but to switch from debt finance to money creation to cover an ongoing budget deficit. For the 1889–91 period, the accumulated inflation rate (163.7 percent) and the accumulated depreciation rate (152.7 percent) are closely correlated with the accumulated counterfactual inflation rate (154.9 percent). It seems that in the midst of the crisis inconvertible paper notes were issued almost exclusively for the purpose of financing fiscal deficits. In this way, the world's first emerging-market crisis got underway.

Cartoon 4.1. *La crisis del progreso. — Tenia que suceder, Señora; cargado como lo esta, quizo ir tan arriba... que perdio el equilibrio.* (The crisis of progress. — It had to happen, Madam; burdened like that, he wanted to go so high...that he lost his balance.)
Notes: The Baring Crisis, the crash being depicted by the country *(el pais)* falling from a precarious position high atop a pile of seats. Each of the seats bears the name of a failing bank. Seat and bank are the same word in Spanish *(banco)*—a play on words. Falling from the country's arms and bag are piles of debts (*cédulas, títulos,* etc.). Finance Minister Vicente Fidel López is the one doing the explaining; listening is public opinion.
Source: El mosquito, año 27, no. 1422, April 13, 1890.

Before the curtain fell in 1891, the drama concluded with an economic policy that had finally exhausted all the available genuine means of finance and heavily relied on the inflation tax to finance the budget. The inflation tax and currency substitution interacted in unfortunate ways that exacerbated the fiscal problem. If there is a high sensitivity of velocity to inflation (a greater propensity for currency substitution) then this will imply a higher inflation rate for the same level of deficit, all else equal. Moreover, currency substitution will lower the base for the inflation tax, requiring an *even higher* inflation rate to sustain the same fiscal gap. [16]

Interest Rates in the Crisis

We cannot conclude a discussion of the crisis without giving some consideration as to its effect on the domestic credit market. As is well known from recent experience, one of the main side effects of monetary and financial crises in emerging markets can be a sudden and large increase in interest rates for short-term loans. These can result from either active policies of the central bank to restrict credit or, alternatively, from the upward revision of inflationary expectations in the market once a fixed exchange-rate peg starts to crumble and devaluation fears set in.

What can we say about short-term interest rates during the Baring crisis? Unfortunately, until 1901, there is a lack of reliable direct information on the values of the market short-term interest rates and only scattered facts could be gathered from Ricardo Pillado's biweekly report "Revista Económica" published in the newspaper *La Prensa*. In June and July reports of 1890, Pillado asserted that the official banks were still rolling over loans at a 10 to 12 percent annual rate, but he observed that there was no credit available on the margin at those rates. Several quotations suggest that money-lending activities flourished and that transactions were made at unusually high discount rates.

However, by an appeal to theory, we can move beyond anecdotes and indirectly infer the impact of the Juárez Celman's inflationary policies on domestic nominal and real interest rates. Of course, we do have data on long-term interest rates, and a perusal of Table 4.3 seems to indicate, at first glance, that inflationary expectations were not incorporated into the expected return of assets denominated in paper pesos. But such an inference could be far off the mark once it is realized that the yield reported is the yield to maturity of a *long-term* internal government bond. The yield to maturity is the interest rate that equates the discounted value of payments received from the bond with its

16. For illustration, the 1885 deficit in real terms equaled 20.7 million paper pesos in 1886 prices, and it was financed with an inflation rate of 24.6 percent. The 1891 deficit was almost exactly the same in real terms, 20.6 million 1886 pesos, but then it required a 63.2 percent inflation rate. Here, the 1885 deficit of 20.1 million is deflated by 0.97, while the 1891 deficit of 52.2 million is deflated by 2.53. See Appendix 1.

Table 4.4. *Conjectural Short-term Interest Rates, 1890–91*

If the Juárez Celman administration and the inflation were expected to last:	1 Year	2 Years	4 Years
and a 9% short rate would resume thereafter:	54.5	31.8	20.4
and an 8% short rate would resume thereafter:	88.5	48.3	28.1
with a 9% rate for 5 years, then 8% the next 5, and a 7% rate thereafter:	107.5	57.3	32.1
and expected short term rates coincided with the *ex post* historical interest rates:	120.3	63.4	35.0

Notes and sources: The approximate average maturity of the Argentine bond was 35 years; the estimated yield for 1890–91 was 10.3 percent. Rates are in percent and their calculation is a straightforward application of the formula in the text. For example, the first entry $i = 0.545$ was found by solving the expression $0.103 = (1 \times i + 34 \times 0.09)/35$. The final row of interest rates was estimated by taking, in each case, the actual bond yields for 1892–1900 and bank discount rate for 1901 onward. The bank discount rates are taken from Comité Nacional de Geografía (1941, p. 430).

market value and, as is well known, a bond's term to maturity affects its interest rate.

A link between short and long rates can be estimated based on the theory of the term structure of interest rates. The theory states that the yield on a long bond will equal the average of short-term interest rates that people expect to occur over the life span of the long bond.[17] Thus, the yield on a T-period long bond is approximately equal to

$$YIELD_t = \frac{i_t + E_t i_{t+1} + \ldots + E_t i_{t+T-1}}{T}, \qquad (4.8)$$

where T is the number of periods to maturity, i_t is the time t one period interest rate, and $E_t i_{t+j}$ is the time $t + j$ one period interest rate expected at time t. Hence, by making some controlled conjectures on the expected postcrisis short-term nominal rates (conditional on the public's expectations as to the duration of the inflationary upsurge) one can guess the likely range of short-term nominal interest rates during the Baring Crisis years.

Our guesswork is shown in Table 4.4, and it suggests that short-term nominal rates may have greatly exceeded the reported long bond yields, under the assumption that people perceived Juárez Celman's policies as likely to last only a short period of time. We think it reasonable to limit the expected duration of Juárez Celman's regime to one or two years for two reasons. First, in 1889, the Executive had lost the support of Congress when the coalition that brought Juárez Celman into power broke down. Second, the social and political unrest that erupted in 1890 increased the likelihood of a drastic change in the future

17. Mishkin (1986, pp. 140–45).

course of the economy. The revolutionary forces of 1890, headed by the newly founded Civic Union, later renamed the Radical Civic Union (Unión Cívica Radical), denounced the depreciation of the paper money, the disarray of the public finances, and the implications for the country of an open policy of debt repudiation. There were two likely scenarios at this stage: either Juárez Celman would limp along and painfully struggle to the end of his constitutional term in 1892, or he would quite possibly be overthrown well before that time.[18]

As an additional check on our guesswork, we can note that the range of values for the nominal rates of interest simulated in Table 4.4 are consistent with the impact on Argentine interest rates of arbitrage in the foreign exchange market. During the 1880s Argentina had suddenly became well integrated into the world economy and the foreign exchange market was an active margin on which domestic prices and interest rates were determined. With British annual discount rates averaging 4 to 5 percent and the paper peso expected to depreciate by 50 or 60 percent per year, short-term interest rates ought to have been, as a conservative guess, about 60 to 70 percent.

Finally, a sharp upsurge in short-term interest rates is entirely consistent with what we know about credit contraction in the banking sector. Bank created money shrank by 8 percent in 1890 and by a massive 64 percent after the demise of the official banks in 1891. Such a collapse of intermediation would be expected to drive up the price of short-term lending.

The Agenda for Reform

We conclude that the collapse of Argentine financial and monetary institutions was a direct consequence of domestic macroeconomic mismanagement. The plan for growth through financial expansion had been built on the same explosive foundations as failed schemes of the past, such as the Mississippi Bubble.[19] As before, appeals to the fundamentally flawed "needs of trade" (or "real bills") doctrine of money and banking could not disguise an uncontrolled fiscal and monetary profligacy that directly contradicted the commitment to parity.

Up to a point international capital markets accommodated the precrash developments in domestic economic policy. A boom in lending originated in the London market after the Goschen debt conversion of 1887, and this temporar-

18. The political economy issues were explicitly stated in the revolutionary manifesto of July 1890: "Al Pueblo:.... El patriotismo nos obliga a proclamar la revolución como recurso extremo y necesario para evitar la ruina del país.... Pero acatar y mantener un gobierno que representa la ilegalidad y la corrupción; ver desaparecer día por día las reglas, los principios, las garantías de toda administración pública regular, consentir los avances al tesoro, la adulteración de la moneda, el despilfarro de la renta,...esperar la hora de la bancarrota internacional que nos deshonraría ante el extranjero sería consagrar la impunidad del abuso..." (Sabsay 1975, pp. 611–14).

19. Garber (2000).

ily eased the access of the Argentine government to external bond finance.[20] During the early stages of the boom foreign investors were persuaded that the paper peso would return to par, and hence they heavily invested in assets denominated in paper pesos. Yet domestic residents, perhaps with better or, in some cases, inside information, started to bet against the paper peso.[21]

The information asymmetry could not last forever. When foreign expectations were revised, an extreme credit-rationing situation precipitated an inflationary upsurge via deficit monetization and sterilization. The chain of events discussed in this section clearly suggests that it was both the actual and perceived mismanagement of borrowed funds that ultimately caused the credit-rationing phenomenon and the subsequent balance of payments crisis—and not the other way around. International credit tightening was a natural outcome whenever financial markets perceived that a government was not adjusting its plans to avoid default.

The key question for Argentine policymakers after 1891 was how they could overcome such a crisis. Could they resolve the policy inconsistencies behind the crisis, restore macroeconomic stability to the economy, lay the ground work for a more secure financial system, and sufficiently repair Argentina's tattered reputation in global capital markets so as to regain access to foreign credit? These were the urgent tasks for the remainder of the decade that we consider in the next chapter.

20. The nominal rate of interest on British consols were reduced from 3 percent to 2.75 percent in 1887 by Governor Goschen of the Bank of England. The side effects of the debt conversion on Argentina were discussed by Kindleberger (1984, pp. 166–67): "But while the annual cost [of the debt conversion] to the Treasury is reduced, there may well be side effects. In particular, holders of retired debt may not be prepared quietly to accept a lower level of income and, in an effort to prevent this, may switch from government stock into higher-yield and riskier investments.... Another peacetime conversion under Goschen in 1887 fed the boom in securities that culminated in the Baring Crisis of 1890."

21. Williams (1920, pp. 62–63) stressed the important point that European syndicates also intervened in the foreign exchange market to keep down the value of the paper peso with the aim to influence expectations in London: "To make these securities more salable European syndicates shipped gold to Buenos Aires. The increase in the supply of gold would cause paper to appreciate for a time. The fall of the gold premium would create the impression that the paper currency was on the mend. People would take a more hopeful view of the situation in general, and Argentine securities would begin to rise in value."

Part Three

The Making of the Belle Époque

5

Relaunching the Gold Standard: From Monetary "Anemia" to "Plethora" and the Political Economy of Resumption, 1891–99

As the Baring Crisis swept over the Argentine economy uncertainty over the future course of economic policy grew. The fiscal imbalances were readily apparent but resolving them would depend on finding the political leadership and will to either raise taxes or cut spending. The financial sector continued to be a massive drain on the national coffers, and it was discovered far too late that the incentives of the Law of National Guaranteed Banks would prove unsustainable.

Had support of the banks been terminated a major banking crisis would have ensued. In addition to all this, the continued devaluation of the peso, and the lack of control over the money supply, indicated a need for an overarching monetary reform that could deliver macroeconomic stability and put an end to the decades of inflationary turmoil that had beset the republic since its inception. Clearly, there would have to be some kind of change in economic policies, but at first it was quite unclear what form this would take.

In this chapter we follow the momentous events of the 1890s, a watershed in economic policy. All these challenges were faced and a new institutional structure built that would place the Argentine economy on a firmer footing. Central to this discussion will be a continuing analysis of the conflicts at the fiscal-monetary policy nexus in a small open economy. Policymakers realized the importance of these tensions, and a resolution of the policy trilemma required hard choices.

Ultimately, a new path took shape and, perhaps unexpectedly, it eventually delivered impressive results. The choices were made with a sophisticated consideration of the tradeoffs—inflation and deflation risks, external credit market reputation, and the problem of making a credible commitment. In the end, by aiming to establish a hard convertibility commitment through a currency-board arrangement, the Argentine authorities sought to permanently lock monetary policy in a realm safely outside political control—and then throw away the key.

Tentative Reforms, 1890–91

Dr. Carlos Pellegrini took office as the new president in August 1890 in the midst of a chaotic economic and political situation. On the economic front the domestic financial system was collapsing, the inflation rate was rising to disconcerting levels, and the provincial and national governments were on the point of defaulting on their debt service obligations. On the political front, despite the suppression of the July revolutionary insurrection, there still lurked the threat of another attempted coup d'état.

President Pellegrini sought to temporize and made an important concession to the moderate wing of the Civic Union by appointing two of its most prominent affiliates to crucial positions in the Cabinet. Vicente Fidel López was given the finance ministry and Victorino de la Plaza was to serve as the middle-man for the renegotiation of the external debt.[1] On the positive side for Pellegrini, at least all of the factions in the new political coalition agreed on the diagnosis that the economy was seriously disrupted by inflation and that the public finances were in complete disarray.

On the downside, the agreement stopped there—there was no consensus among congressmen and policymakers on the right course of economic policy to address the fundamental fiscal and monetary problems, to overcome the ongoing banking crisis, and to resolve the foreign debt shambles. A graphic illustration of the political climate was provided by Pellegrini in his speech to the opening session of Congress on May 25, when he remarked that "there is great anarchy in opinion about the means to confront the difficulties in which we are immersed and this anarchy does not surprise me."[2]

A clear sense of this state of confusion and uncertainty is an important starting point in our understanding of the stabilization and disinflation experience following the Baring Crisis since these political constraints were to leave their mark in the design of macroeconomic policy in the early 1890s.

Fiscal Reforms

The fiscal inconsistencies of the old regime had been recognized relatively early, but the authorities were slow to act and the problems soon spun out of control. Some timid steps to stabilize the real (gold) value of fiscal revenues (collectible only in paper) had been taken by the Juárez Celman government. When the paper peso started to depreciate the government's revenues from trade taxes declined, because official duties *(aforos)* were levied according to their paper value. In 1889 Congress voted an additional import tax of 15 percent to alleviate

1. Ferns (1973, p. 454). Alonso (2000) writes of the composition of the cabinet that "officially, this was not a coalition government. The appointments were one of the many conciliatory gestures taken by the new government toward the opposition."
2. Mabragaña (1910).

Cartoon 5.1. *Gloria á los Gobernadores que, en medio de estos horrores, nos dejan sin dos centavos, llenos los Bancos de clavos y miles de acreedores.* (Glory to the governors that, in the middle of these horrors, left us not two cents, left us banks [seats] full of nails and thousands of creditors.)
Notes: President Carlos Pellegrini is the puppet master in control, trying to rescue the banks and provinces. The banks and provinces are depicted as full of nails *(clavos)*, a colloquial term for debts. Seat and bank are the same word in Spanish *(banco)*—a play on words.
Source: Don Quijote, año 7, no. 2, August 31, 1890.

the fall in revenues. Fiscal revenues rebounded by 16 percent, only then to fall by 30 percent in 1890 (Table 4.2).[3] In 1890 a new customs law required that half of all trade duties should be paid in gold pesos and the rest in paper pesos at par.

In January 1891 the government finally made a bold fiscal move and new tax measures were implemented. First, custom duties were to be paid in full with gold pesos or in equivalent paper pesos at the prevailing paper-gold market rate. Second, an ad valorem tax of 4 percent on exports of skins, wool, and meat was

3. See also *Memorias de Hacienda* (1890, p. 119) in "Sources of Revenue" under "Adicional de importación 15 percent"; and Martínez (1898, p. 522) under "Droit additionnel à l'importation."

Table 5.1. *Key Fiscal Indicators, 1891–99*

Year	Consumption Tax Yield (Gold)	Fiscal Receipts (Gold)	Fiscal Receipts (Paper)	Fiscal Expenditure (Paper)	Fiscal Deficit (Paper)	Corrected Fiscal Deficit (Paper)	Primary Deficit (Paper)
1891	3	20	76	128	52	52	9
1892	4	34	111	128	17	17	-16
1893	7	39	125	123	-2	-2	-31
1894	7	34	122	143	21	4	-36
1895	8	38	131	166	34	20	-17
1896	14	44	129	179	50	41	5
1897	21	52	150	178	28	16	-17
1898	21	53	137	206	70	70	39
1899	34	73	164	173	9	9	-49

Notes and sources: Units are millions of pesos, gold or paper as indicated. See Appendix 1. For the period 1894–97, the corrected service of the debt under the Romero agreement was estimated as follows. A 6 percent rate of interest plus amortization was applied to the outstanding stock of internal debt denominated in paper pesos. A 4.5 percent interest rate was applied on the internal debt denominated in hard currency not including gold bonds related to the Law of National Guaranteed Banks. The external debt service was 1.6 million British pound under the agreement plus 1 million gold pesos in payments on performing external bonds not included in the agreement.

to be imposed temporarily. Third, taxes on consumption were to be introduced, for the first time, at the federal level.[4]

Unfortunately, this effort to address the fiscal problem came a little too late. During 1891, the dramatic real depreciation caused the value of imports to fall by half. Fiscal receipts fell by 31 percent.[5] Since import duties represented 65 percent of total revenues (Table 4.1), tax receipts in gold pesos were bound to worsen in the short run. Thus, a full adjustment to a balanced budget as a step toward eliminating the inflation tax was clearly infeasible without further reforms. For example, in 1891 a balanced budget would have required a cut in expenditures, net of interest payments, of 62 percent.[6]

Moreover, the budget would continue to worsen because the value, in paper pesos, of external debt service increased with depreciation. A large part of fiscal expenditures were thus indexed to the gold premium. In 1890, debt service amounted to 11.4 million gold pesos, representing 25 percent of expenditures; in 1891, debt service payments were 11.6 million, or 34 percent. Even with approximately the same real debt service payments in gold pesos for those two years and even holding all other expenses constant in paper pesos, the 1891

4. See *Memorias de Hacienda* (1891, pp. 109–19). The report stresses that importers, anticipating that the law would pass, invoiced huge amounts of imports in December and January of 1890. Thereafter and until the end of the year, the custom revenue was nil. The custom duty reforms of 1891 established that duties should be paid in gold or their equivalent in paper pesos and that the schedule of import valuations *(tarifa de avaluos)* was to be established in gold pesos.
5. Value of total imports from Appendix 1.
6. Expenditures net of debt service, was 84 million paper pesos, and the budget deficit was 52. A balanced budget implied a reduction in net expenditures of about 62 percent. See Table 5.1.

level of expenditures would have increased by 11.2 percent due to just the paper peso depreciation alone.[7] In the event, expenditures increased in 1891 by 10.9 percent because little fiscal adjustment could be accomplished in time.

Monetary Reforms

As regards monetary policy reform, the new administration was eager to end the devaluation of the currency and impose control over the money supply. The plan was to put a stop to the uncontrolled decentralized emission of paper notes by the banks. Instead there would be a centralized authority with a national monopoly over base money issue. To that end, in October 1890 the Executive Power and Congress acted together to settle the currency situation. They created a new institution, the Conversion Office (Caja de Conversión), a body that would take the note-issue privilege away from the guaranteed banks and "effect the gradual conversion and amortization of the legal tender currency."[8]

The ambitions of the new monetary regime extended even further. Article 11 of the Conversion Office charter stated that the government would not only aim for price stability of the paper money but also, it was claimed, the paper peso would revert to convertibility at its par value with respect to gold:

> Once the amount of paper notes amortized equals the amount of paper notes issued by the Banco Nacional, or when the market value of the fiduciary currency is at par or near to par, the Board of Directors of the Bureau of Exchange, in agreement with the Executive, shall exchange paper notes for gold, or vice versa, with the aim of fixing the value of the fiduciary currency.[9]

Notwithstanding this announced commitment to revalue the currency and restore the gold anchor, there still remained the obvious question of where the real resources were to be found to finance the plan—and here, of course, the proposals were very unclear. To allow redemption of the paper currency the project contemplated the creation of a Conversion Fund. This fund was supposed to be financed from three sources: first, the metallic reserves of the guaranteed banks—which, unfortunately, were almost exhausted at the moment the law was passed; second, public funds issued to guarantee paper notes; and third, by a vague appeal to "all sums that, by virtue of other legislative acts, might be directed to the conversion of bank paper, specially those arising from economies in the general budget."[10]

Needless to say, even with all these legal and institutional gymnastics to redress the currency situation, the short run economic results in 1890 were just

7. Since debt service was almost the same in 1890 and 1891, assuming all else constant, the effect of the depreciation on expenditures is equal to the product of the 1890 debt service share (0.25) and the rate of depreciation (0.448). This equals 0.112.
8. Caja de Conversión, Ley 2741, 7 de octubre de 1890, Artículo 1. Sabsay (1975, pp. 615–16).
9. Sabsay (1975, pp. 615–16).
10. Martínez and Lewandowski (1911, p. 343).

Figure 5.1. Paper-Gold Exchange Rate, 1883–1902

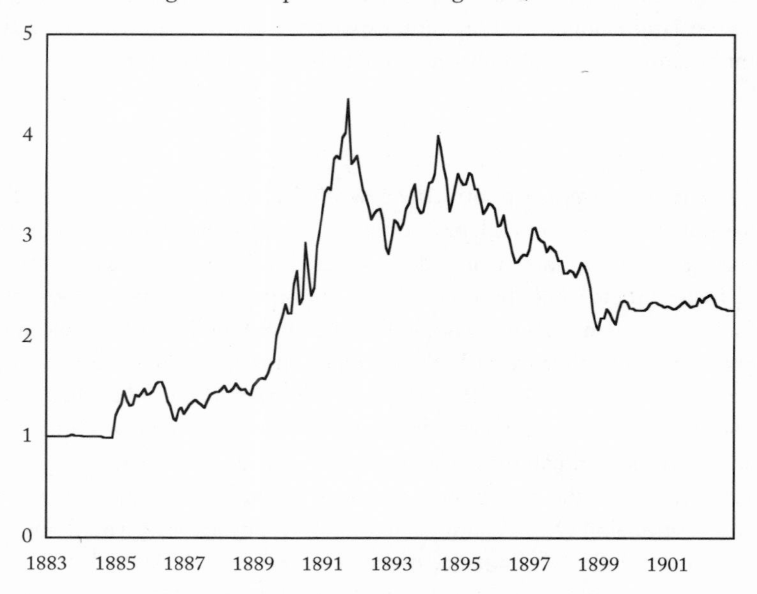

Notes: End-of-month data. Units are paper pesos per gold peso.
Source: Alvarez (1929, p. 122).

the opposite of those intended. The continued depreciation of the paper peso shown in Figure 5.1 was the market's response to a government that, by printing money to acquire real resources, turned its back on its own monetary pledge. The markets judged that the fiscal reforms did not square with an institutional reform that called for tight control of the monetary base. Why was this so?

We have found that the path of the exchange rate for the period 1885–99 can be fairly well explained by a structural model (see Appendix 4). The model includes fundamental variables such as the relative money supplies of Argentina and the rest of the world (proxied by the United Kingdom), the relative levels of real output, and the relative innovations in the long-term interest rates. However, when we look at the model's within-sample predictions, although the 1890 and 1892 predicted depreciation rates are very close to the observed rates, for 1891 the prediction of the model is extremely far off the mark. The paper peso rate of depreciation predicted by the fundamentals was only 4.9 percent whereas the observed rate was 37 percent.[11]

This result shows, first, that the proxy we used for the formation of expectations, the long-term interest rate, is inadequate. Second, it implies that when

11. Recall that the exchange rate model was fitted in first difference form. The predicted 1890 rate of depreciation was 37.4 percent while the observed rate was 36 percent. For 1892 the predicted rate was −11.9 percent and the observed rate was −12.8 percent.

the "news" effect is persistent, as it was in 1891, there can be large movements in the exchange rate that are not well accounted for by the limited set of fundamentals. Though the exchange rate continued to fall the monetary authorities may still have been doing the right things to stop the flight from the paper peso. After all, by the end of 1891, with the help of new foreign capital flows, specifically the Funding Loan which is discussed in a moment, they had succeeded in lowering the rate of growth of the monetary base from 50 percent to about 6.7 percent. Even so, the public did not yet believe in a regime change.[12]

For some evidence on this matter, the monthly quotations from the foreign exchange market shown in Figure 5.1 are a useful indicator of the public's perceptions of economic policy developments. When the Pellegrini administration took office in August 1890 the gold peso stood at 2.65 paper pesos. By the third quarter of 1891, with gold at 4.21 paper pesos, a return to parity must have looked like a very remote possibility. Negative short-run reaction in the foreign exchange market could have reflected the grave uncertainties at the time reforms were begun. The "news" relevant to the formation of expectations regarding the future policy regime was, for a while, the driving force pushing the market exchange rate well above its fundamental determinants.

12. A simple example illustrates the problem of divergence between economic policy facts and market beliefs, that is to say, a multiple equilibria problem. Assume, for example, a Cagan-type of money demand that is a function of the expected depreciation rate and suppose that purchasing power parity prevails with stable foreign prices in the short run such that, without loss of generality, $p_t^* = \log P_t^* = 0$. Then domestic prices are equal to the exchange rate $p_t = e_t$ and domestic inflation is equal to the rate of depreciation $E_t e_{t+1} - e_t = E_t p_{t+1} - p_t$. Hence, the domestic demand for money can be written as

$$m_t - e_t = -a(E_t e_{t+1} - e_t),$$

where $a > 0$, m_t is the paper money stock at time t, e_t is the exchange rate at time t, and E_t is the expectation operator at time t. Suppose now that the expected evolution of the paper money stock is given by

$$E_t m_{t+1} = E_t m_{t+2} = E_t m_{t+3} = \ldots = (1 - \phi)m_t + \phi(m_t + b).$$

Here, the money stock is expected to be fixed from next period onward and is equal to a linear combination of the current paper money stock and a higher stock $b > 0$ with the weights being their respective expected probabilities. Solving recursively for e_t in terms of m_t yields

$$e_t = m_t + \frac{a}{1+a}\phi b.$$

This expression states that in the short run the exchange rate e_t may differ from its fundamental, the actual money stock m_t, if the probability ϕ assigned to a higher money stock $m_t + b$ in the near future is strongly positive. If the market belief was that, despite all the intended reforms, the inflationary regime would persist for a while, then a higher probability would have been attached to a higher future money stock, and the larger would have been the deviation of the exchange rate from its fundamental. For a discussion of the determination of the exchange rate with an emphasis on the role of "news" see Frenkel (1981) and Dornbusch (1983). The problem of a divergence between economic policy facts and market beliefs concerning the risk of a discrete devaluation is sometimes called *the peso problem*. See also Lizondo (1983).

The External Debt

To take pressure off the foreign exchange market, the government attempted to roll over the service of its external debt. They sought a one-year moratorium in the form of a Funding Loan of four million pounds, but negotiations were interrupted when, in November 1890, Barings bank failed.[13] Finally, though, their efforts paid off when, on January 23, 1891, the Argentine negotiator Victorino de la Plaza finally signed a much larger contract with a syndicate of merchant banks in a deal coordinated by the Bank of England. The agreement granted the government a 6 percent funding loan of fifteen million pounds to cover the full service of external debt over the following three years.

As might be expected, the external loan was conditional on several provisions, the most severe of these placing clear constraints on the conduct of domestic monetary policy. Admittedly, the Conversion Office had adopted currency contraction as a desired aim of policy to be achieved at some point in time. Article 16 of the Funding Loan agreement was much more explicit, and set a precise redemption timetable: the Conversion Office would have to retire each year, for three consecutive years, fifteen million pesos of bank notes from circulation—cumulatively about 20 percent of monetary base.[14]

Thus, with a tighter monetary policy in sight, in April 1891 the government decided to suspend the convertibility of deposits into currency at the official banks. The banks were already suffering a severe drain of deposits, and it was announced that substantial reforms in the banking system would be enacted. To that end, in October 1891, Congress created a new bank out of the ruins of the old Banco Nacional called the Banco de la Nación Argentina (BNA), a "semipublic" institution. It was intended that the Banco de la Nación Argentina be established with an initial private capital base of fifty million pesos and shares were to be offered for public subscription.

This plan was derailed when the share issue failed: investors, if there were any at all, regarded the project with deep apprehension and abstained from buying any shares. Ultimately the government "backed" the capital base with fictitious claims that were created by converting the bank into a state institution. To give a flavor of the market climate and the reaction to the project consider the opinion of the correspondent to *The Economist* newspaper in a column published on November 28:

> The new Bank of the Argentine Nation will open its doors to the public on the 9th [of December]. Its 50 million of inconvertible notes will rapidly get into circulation, as the provision for issuing them in series of ten millions is merely a blind, and the inevitable economic result of a battle between coin and inconvertible and depreciated paper currency must issue. The imported gold will be driven away faster than it came, and our currency will be in a worse plight than ever.

13. Williams (1920, pp. 117–18).
14. Data from *Memorias de Hacienda* (1891, Anexo 15, pp. 43–60).

Cartoon 5.2. *Hacer un mate sin yerba es algo dificil, pero hacerlo chupar: "that is the question."* (To make a *mate* without herbs is something difficult, but to make it drinkable: that is the question.)
Notes: This cartoon is a critique of the plan to rescue the Banco de la Nación Argentina. President Carlos Pellegrini holds a *mate* with the label Banco de la Nación; the lady is public confidence, expressing her lack of faith in the plan. Broken *mates* lie on the floor. The kettle is labeled *la mision* (the mission to London?) and the stove is labeled the Congress. The container for *yerba* and sugar lies empty on the table, an allusion to the parlous state of the bank's balance sheet.
Source: El mosquito, año 29, no. 1491, August 16, 1891.

Why was the market afraid of the Banco de la Nación Argentina initiative? There were reasonable fears that the banking project would degenerate into cronyism and political manipulation, as in previous experiences with state banks. But the architects of the plan were not unaware of such fears and took care to make the institutional design more robust. There were a couple of clauses intended to prevent abuse of the bank by the state.

First, in an effort to separate commercial banking functions from government finances, the project put severe limits on the amount of credit that could be extended to the federal treasury. Specifically, rules stated that the Banco de la

Nación "may not lend money to any public power or municipality other than the national government, whose credit with the Bank must not exceed two million pesos" (Article 12). Furthermore, the bank "would not use deposits as funding for public loans" (Article 14).

Second, minimum reserve requirements were imposed on the bank to prevent the money creation associated with excessive credit expansion. Originally, reserves equal to a minimum of 25 percent of total deposits were to be maintained in the vaults of the bank. In June 1892, a new decree established that additional reserves, a "guaranteed fund," equivalent to 75 percent of private deposits were to be deposited at the Conversion Office.[15]

Decisive Reforms, 1892–99

In short, by mid-1891 a package of measures had implemented deep reforms of fiscal and monetary policy. There had been a large tax reform. There was a draconian adjustment in the banking regime centering on the liquidation of the Banco Nacional and the Banco de la Provincia de Buenos Aires. A new independent body had been established to control the monetary base. And, with these reforms afoot, there had been a successful renegotiation of the repayment schedule for the external government debt. We now discuss the short-run response of the Argentine economy to this stabilization attempt.

The tentative reforms of 1890–91 were incapable of cementing in place expectations of a new stable regime. But the beginning of 1892 marked a turning point in the public's beliefs about the viability of the reform package. The cause of the reversal of expectations was the widespread conviction that Luis Sáenz Peña, an advocate for fiscal retrenchment, would be elected the next president of the Republic for the term from 1892 to 1898:

> When in February 1892, it became known that Dr. Sáenz Peña, a highly esteemed member of the Supreme Court, was to be the next President, the premium declined forty points within a month, and there were those who said that the gold premium depended simply on political conditions.... The paper peso would surely appreciate under wise political treatment; public confidence is a powerful factor in a depreciated paper situation, though scarcely sufficient to make a paper peso worth $0.25 become the equal of $1 gold without other forces cooperating.[16]

Sáenz Peña's appointment as the new constitutional president of Argentina in October 1892 seemed to calm the nervous expectations of Argentina's economic agents and bolster the viability of the economic reform package.

The confirmation as finance minister of Juan José Romero, an outspoken defender of convertibility and the gold standard, then produced a further rapid

15. Charter of the Banco de la Nación, from Tornquist (1919, pp. 311–12). Decree of June 1892, from Banco de la Nación Argentina, *Memorias* (1892, p. 3).

16. Williams (1920, p. 141). Here was a clear example of the "news" effect at work.

appreciation in the value of the paper peso on the foreign exchange market. Judged by market sentiment, policy was finally headed in the right direction. Critically, Romero understood that the monetary policy goal, in this case an eventual return to the gold standard, could not be achieved without ensuring coordination and consistency with fiscal policy and without better management of the external debt.[17]

The External Debt

Romero disliked the terms of the 1891 Funding Loan, the centerpiece of the de la Plaza–Bank of England agreement. Instead he proposed to the Rothschild Committee, another bank syndicate, that Argentina should pay its external obligations based on its own fiscal capacity and not on new loans from outside financed at high interest rates. Romero feared that Argentina would end up in a Ponzi scheme, that is, an unsustainable schedule for debt payments based on perpetual rollovers where the level of debt explodes in the long run:

> If [the government] were to satisfy all the obligations of the internal and external public debt, as well as the sum total of the guarantees, all the revenues of the Nation would scarcely suffice to cover those services alone. . . . We are paying our debts by creating daily a more burdensome debt for the Nation—a disastrous system which should be put to an end.[18]

Thus followed a new round of negotiations, the result of which came to be called the Romero Agreement. Under the new terms, Argentina was granted a more generous rescheduling of its debt service: first, between 1893 and 1898 the government was required to pay half the level of original debt service recognized in the de la Plaza–Bank of England agreement; second, from 1898 it would pay the full level of debt service; and third, from 1901 the government would begin to amortize principal as well. Under this new arrangement the short-run shock to fiscal policy was alleviated and the government would have ample time to anticipate and plan for the increased future payments.

As Romero intended, the plan eliminated the possibility of an explosive debt situation. To show that this was a real possibility, let us consider the government budget constraint and assume that there is an ongoing deficit DEF_t that is entirely bond financed. In this case the change in the stock of debt B_t can be expressed as

$$B_t - B_{t-1} = DEF_t + r_t B_{t-1}, \tag{5.1}$$

17. It is interesting here to note that Romero, an economic conservative, was a member of the Union Cívica party and in December 1889 he had been part of the so-called Revolutionary Junta that plotted the overthrow of President Juárez Celman (Alonso 2000, p. 61).
18. Shepherd (1933, pp. 39–40).

Table 5.2. *The Burdensome Funding Loan Agreement*

	Interest Rate		Output	Coefficient	Debt-Output
Year	Nominal	Real	Growth Rate	(1+r)/(1+g)	Ratio (%)
1891	10.3	6.6	-11.0	1.20	72
1892	9.9	16.2	8.6	1.07	90
1893	8.9	10.8	5.0	1.06	91

Notes and sources: See text. The interest rate of the Funding Loan is calculated as the stated 6 percent interest rate on the bond, divided by the average price quotation of the bond from *The South American Journal.* The real interest rate is calculated as $(1+i)/(1+\pi^*)-1$, where i is the interest rate and π^* is the world inflation rate proxied by the U.K. Board of Trade price index from Mitchell (1971, p. 476). The rate of output growth is the annual rate of change of the real activity index as in Appendix 1. The coefficient $(1+r)/(1+g)$ is as described in the text. The figures for the stock of debt are from Appendix 1.

where

$$B_t = \text{real debt (in constant pesos);}$$
$$DEF_t = \text{real primary deficit (in constant pesos);}$$
$$r_t = \text{real interest rate.}$$

Assume that real output Y_t grows at an exogenous rate g, so that

$$Y_t = (1+g)Y_{t-1}. \tag{5.2}$$

It is then easy to see that the debt-output ratio has dynamics given by

$$\frac{B_t}{Y_t} = \frac{1+r}{1+g}\frac{B_{t-1}}{Y_{t-1}} + \frac{1}{1+g}\frac{DEF_t}{Y_{t-1}}. \tag{5.3}$$

This first-order difference equation implies that the debt-output ratio B/Y will grow indefinitely in Ponzi fashion so long as the real rate of interest exceeds the real growth rate of the economy.[19]

The figures in Table 5.2 indicate that Argentine debt service was rolled over at extremely high real interest rates. The high rates are explained, in part, by the low credit rating of the Argentine government in European capital markets after the crash; and, as a result, the bonds of the Funding Loan could only be floated at heavy discounts in excess of forty percent. In addition, the steady world deflation of the 1891–95 period augmented the real rate of interest still further. With the benefit of hindsight we can now see why Finance Minister Romero felt that the 1891 Funding Loan agreement was a "disastrous system" that needed to be stopped.

Monetary Reforms

When it came to exchange-rate stabilization, Romero favored the idea of letting the market value of the paper peso appreciate, but he opposed any policy of

19. For analysis of debt, deficits and debt restructuring see Blanchard (1983) and Sjaastad (1983).

Table 5.3. *Selected Statistics, 1891–99*

Year	Money Base	Money Supply	Price Level (1886=100)	Paper-Gold Exchange Rate	Real Output Index	Average of Exports & Imports	Money Velocity Variant 1	Money Velocity Variant 2
1891	261	417	253	3.74	6,535	89	3.08	100
1892	282	387	201	3.29	7,113	108	2.88	115
1893	307	415	189	3.24	7,466	113	2.64	110
1894	299	419	185	3.58	8,040	119	2.76	127
1895	297	435	221	3.44	8,093	135	3.19	133
1896	295	437	187	2.96	8,768	144	2.93	122
1897	293	440	194	2.91	8,198	124	2.82	103
1898	292	443	187	2.57	8,888	159	2.93	115
1899	291	463	161	2.25	9,666	184	2.62	112

Notes and sources: Money base and money supply in millions of paper pesos. Real output index in millions of 1950 pesos. Exports and imports in millions of gold pesos. Velocity variant 1 is real output multiplied by the paper-gold exchange rate and divided by the money supply. Velocity variant 2 (an index with 1891=100) is the average of exports and imports multiplied by the paper-gold exchange rate and divided by the money supply. All series from Appendix 1.

withdrawing paper pesos from circulation in order to accelerate deflation and push the paper peso toward par. In a November 1892 report prepared for President Sáenz Peña, he declared that

> In spite of the quantity of money in circulation, an appreciation in its value is occurring with an unusual speed, and this, without doubt, is an encouraging sign for the country's economic future. But we should not forget that the higher the value of the paper currency in circulation, the greater the amount of gold that will be needed for its eventual convertibility. It seems to me that it is appropriate to mention that the administration of Dr. Pellegrini put forward the idea of restoring convertibility at [a devalued gold premium of] 250 percent. The rate that was suggested by the Pellegrini administration for a future conversion is, I believe, a fair rate and a convenient one for the country, and it seems to me that prudence recommends urgent and serious consideration on this important matter.[20]

Unfortunately, even with Romero's willingness to consider convertibility at a weaker parity, the plan was not workable because the Conversion Office had no specie reserves and the government was not in a position to negotiate a gold-based loan that could serve as initial backing for the paper peso.

The figures in the first column of Table 5.3 indicate that the monetary base increased by 7.7 percent in 1892 and by 8.9 percent in 1893, but then fell steadily from 1893 to 1899 by an average compounded rate of 0.9 percent per year. The initial increase in the monetary base did not augment liquidity in the money market because the Banco de la Nación's legal reserve requirements, and the private banks' desires to build up reserves after the crash, had an offsetting effect through the money multiplier.

20. Shepherd (1933, pp. 38–39).

Table 5.4. *Monetary Ratios, 1891–99*

			Reserve Ratio		
Year	Currency Ratio	Reserve Ratio	Banco de la Nación	Other Banks	Money Multiplier
1891	0.50	0.26	0.03	0.36	1.59
1892	0.49	0.47	0.58	0.45	1.37
1893	0.45	0.53	0.89	0.42	1.35
1894	0.41	0.51	0.84	0.41	1.40
1895	0.38	0.48	0.79	0.40	1.47
1896	0.38	0.48	0.66	0.43	1.48
1897	0.38	0.46	0.66	0.41	1.50
1898	0.36	0.47	0.70	0.40	1.52
1899	0.35	0.43	0.62	0.38	1.59

Notes and sources: See Appendix 1.

Further details of the monetary developments of the 1890s are shown in Table 5.4. The broad money supply increased secularly during 1892–99 by an average annual rate of 2.6 percent, a modest increase in a time of rapid economic growth when compared to the 21.1 percent rate experienced during the 1880s boom years. The velocity index (Table 5.3, column 6) displays a somewhat erratic behavior throughout the deflationary period. The evidence suggests that three distinct patterns can be observed. First, there was a period of profound decline in velocity through 1893 and then, after an upward adjustment in 1894 and 1895, a period of almost constant velocity with a slight declining trend toward the end of the period.

Romero's objectives for stable monetary policy were ultimately achieved. The period 1892–99 was characterized by only the slightest rate of monetary expansion, at least if we omit the monetary expansion used to fund the Banco de la Nación Argentina. Essentially, the monetary policy rule used by the Conversion Office amounted to setting a fixed monetary rule á la Friedman.[21]

Fiscal Reforms

On the fiscal side the crucial adjustments were achieved during Romero's tenure, allowing the treasury to post surpluses for four consecutive years from 1892. In reality, given its monetary policy commitment, the government was practically forced to equilibrate the budget after the debacle of 1891–92 and in the face of tightening credit conditions in both the domestic and international markets. With no ability to issue debt issue, and the inflation tax off limits, the deficits had to be eliminated.

The figures in Table 5.1 show that the state of public finances improved markedly from 1892 to 1894. The government moved toward a balanced budget

21. Friedman (1959).

and into surplus. Increased taxation and a sharp improvement in the gold value of fiscal revenues were the important sources of fiscal adjustment, rather than cuts in the level of fiscal expenditures. The healthy state of public finances was weakened in 1895–98 by the impending threat of a border war with Chile. This territorial dispute in southern Patagonia caused a spectacular surge in military expenditures, but by then confidence in capital markets had been restored and, remarkably, the 1895–98 deficits were entirely financed with internal debt and short-term foreign loans, and there was no recourse to the printing press.[22]

Recovery with Deflation

Although the postcrash era was a contractionary time for fiscal and monetary policy, the country's economic agents had anticipated both developments, and, far from retarding the economy, the stabilization was accompanied by a remarkably rapid economic recovery. An average annual real rate of growth of nearly 5 percent was achieved in this decade in the years after the crash. This was a very high growth rate for the late nineteenth century by international standards, and it put Argentina on a course to restore its very high rates of long-run growth.[23]

In 1892, with expectations stabilized and business activity on the rise, there was an increase in the quantity of money demanded that could only be accommodated by a 21 percent decline in domestic prices and a large appreciation.[24] After this big adjustment in 1892, the paper-gold exchange rate fluctuated between 3.2 and 3.6 from 1892 to 1894. From then on it declined at a very rapid pace, a cumulative decline of 37.1 percent in five years from 1894 to 1899. The exchange rate fell from 3.75 paper pesos per gold peso in 1891 to 2.27 in 1899 under a pure float (Figure 5.1).

With a tight monetary base and accelerating economic growth, the income velocity of money could only remain constant or even decline with a protracted deflation in the paper-gold exchange rate and in domestic prices. The real economy recovered and grew even when there was a deflation and an appreciation of the currency. This period of monetary stability was also a time of recovery for the banking sector. The broad money supply expanded by 18 percent due to an increase in the money multiplier, a marked turn around in the process of

22. Defense expenditures rose from 27.8 million paper pesos to 53.8 million in 1895, 63.5 million in 1896, 38.8 million in 1897, and 85.5 million in 1898. See Appendix 1. Short-term foreign loans were advanced by Deutsche Bank of Berlin, Disconto Gescheshaft, and Baring Brothers during 1895–97 in the sum of 24 million gold pesos. See Martínez (1898, pp. 303–11).
23. The 5 percent growth rate compares with a (probably unsustainable) 8.5 percent rate that prevailed in the precrash boom years of the 1880s, and it is only slightly inferior to the rates of growth characteristic of the gold standard years 1900–1913.
24. Friedman and Schwartz (1963) report that European grain crops failed in the summer of 1891 producing a sizeable increase in international crop demand. For Argentina, this represented a chance to increase world market share in crops by a switch in export mix. In 1888, the value share of wheat, corn, and linseed in total exports, was 15 percent; by 1892–93 it was already 31 percent. See Cortés Conde (1979, pp. 90–91).

financial deepening for the official banks after the Baring Crisis had seen a fall of 34 percent in the money multiplier in 1889–91 (Table 5.4).

It is also important to note that the Argentine recovery occurred in the middle of an international recession. In 1892–94 international prices were at their lowest level in the years of the so-called "Great Depression" that characterized large parts of the world economy from 1870 to 1895.[25] This global deflation was quickly transmitted to the very open Argentine economy through the market for goods: between 1891 and 1894, for example, while the nominal rate of foreign exchange appreciated 3.1 percent annually, domestic prices fell by a faster annual rate of 9.3 percent.

The international macroeconomic scene changed radically in 1895. An increase in global monetary liquidity resulted from an increase in the world stock of gold. This increase was due to a various factors, among them new discoveries of gold deposits and a series of technological advances in the refining of the precious metal. After 1894, the international inflation had an effect on Argentina: in the subperiod 1894–99 domestic prices declined by only 12.8 percent despite an even greater appreciation of the paper peso by 37.1 percent.

The Political Economy of Deflation

Argentina's monetary authorities had been successful in fixing the quantity of money and in allowing the value of money to be freely determined by the exchange markets. As a result of this extraordinarily restrictive monetary policy a debate began around 1897 as to whether a return to a convertible monetary regime would be advisable or not. Once again, the conflict over economic policy centered on whether the paper peso should be convertible at its traditional par or at an exchange rate set by the markets. Urban sectors and commercial interests favored a convertibility plan with the old par, while exporters and industrial sectors called for a devalued par.[26]

What was the distributional impact of the deflation on different interest groups? We constructed various measures shown in Table 5.5. An Argentine export profitability index is measured by the paper-gold exchange rate, multiplied by the ratio of the external price of exports to the rural money wages. Rural money wages are used as a proxy for the export sector's variable production costs. The figures suggest that the 1892–94 world depression was the main cause of the decline in the profitability index. In the last half of the decade,

25. Although Britain, for example, escaped most of this deflation, peripheral and settler economies suffered greatly. The economic suffering led to political pressure at times for a change in monetary regime. In 1893 a major financial crisis occurred in the United States when expectations arose that the gold standard would be abandoned due to political pressure from silver standard advocates (Friedman and Schwartz 1963, pp. 89–134; Eichengreen 1996; Frieden 1988; 1997).

26. Ford (1962). Such intersectoral conflicts were seen elsewhere. See Eichengreen (1992a; 1992b) and Frieden (1988; 1997).

Table 5.5. *Urban-Rural Welfare Measures and Interest Rates, 1891–99*

Year	Export Profitability Index (1891=100)	Percent Change in Terms of Trade	Percent Change in U.K. Prices	Index of Food Prices	Urban Wages Deflated by Wholesale Prices	Yield on Internal Bond	Domestic Rate of Inflation
1891	100	19.7	3.5	100	100	10.3	56
1892	84	-8.6	-5.4	117	129	9.2	-21
1893	—	-7.0	-1.7	115	121	8.7	-6
1894	77	-11.1	-5.9	108	139	8.9	-2
1895	147	52.2	-3.0	98	120	8.3	20
1896	73	-3.3	-2.8	105	164	7.7	-15
1897	76	10.0	2.2	147	196	7.8	4
1898	89	12.3	3.5	201	230	7.9	-4
1899	68	-9.0	-1.1	239	263	7.9	-14

Notes and sources: All series from Appendix 1 unless otherwise stated. The export profitability index is the implicit international price of exports multiplied by the paper-gold exchange rate divided by the nominal rural wage (the latter from Cortés Conde 1979, p. 228). U.K. Board of Trade price index from Mitchell (1971, p. 476). Nominal urban wages and prices of food from Cortés Conde (1979, pp. 230 and 226). Domestic rate of inflation is the rate of change of the wholesale price index.

the trend of the profitability index is less clear: monetary forces made the peso appreciate, but this was offset by a rise in world agricultural prices.

For the urban sector we show a real wage index consisting of urban wages deflated by a wholesale price index. It is apparent that urban real wages steadily rose after 1895, but real forces that improved labor's marginal productivity may have played an important role in addition to the monetary deflationary forces. A rise in the relative price of labor and a fall in export profitability may just reflect a "normal" pattern of changing economic conditions in this newly settled country. We doubt that a mere change in the nominal exchange-rate regime would have a persistent effect on the equilibrium values of these real variables.

Aside from distributional conflict, the most notable argument against deflation focused on the economy-wide distortions arising in the credit market due to the zero nominal interest rate floor. The argument originates in the work of the little-known Argentine political economist Silvio Gesell (1862–1930). In his two most famous articles entitled "Monetary Anemia" (1898) and "Monetary Plethora" (1909), Gesell identified the problem of the debt-deflation trap, anticipating Irving Fisher's famous work by almost thirty years:

> If money gets more expensive, debts increase in exact proportion to the rise in the cost of money. Nominally nothing changes, but materially the debt load increases. With the prospect of having to pay triple what one received, who will dare go into debt to start a new industry in the country?.... The increase in the value of money is the common cause for all the country's economic troubles...[27]

27. See Gesell (1898; 1909). Note the discussion on pp. 20–23. See also Fisher (1933a).

Gesell had the brilliant insight that in a monetary economy there is an essential asymmetry between inflationary and deflationary regimes. In an inflationary economy, nominal interest rates usually incorporate an expected-inflation component. Thus, they can freely adjust upward to reflect expected future changes in the purchasing power of the currency. Conversely, in an economy in which prices are falling the nominal interest rate cannot fully adjust to absorb such expectations since it cannot become negative.

What empirical evidence is available to investigate the Gesell hypothesis? Curiously enough, the behavior of interest rates in this period has received no attention in the previous literature. The nominal interest rate, proxied by the yield of long-term internal bonds, showed a marked downward trend over the period; yet, meanwhile, domestic prices were falling rapidly, resulting in very high real interest rates that were rising in the 1890s (Table 5.5).

In this environment a shift toward more expansionary monetary policies—in the form of resumption at the prevailing market exchange rate—appeared to be a wise course of action. It could have saved the economy from a protracted period of high real interest rates that worked to the detriment of finance, investment, and economic growth. If such was the case, why did the government not embrace such a devaluation to a new parity sooner, rather than waiting until the late 1890s to adopt a definitive convertibility plan at a new parity?

At least two counterfactual policy options could be considered. As we have noted, a first option would have been to adopt convertibility in 1893, accommodating the devaluation with a high exchange rate for the paper peso as Pellegrini and Romero had suggested. However, to have implemented convertibility then, in a scenario of unfavorable expectations and great uncertainty, the government would have needed a very credible commitment. Lacking reserves, they would have required a large foreign loan in specie to provide the necessary backing for the monetary base. It is very hard to imagine that in 1893 the government had the solvency and bargaining capacity to get such a loan in the international market. We have seen that the Funding Loan of 1891 afforded only relatively small sums at high real interest rates. Hence, our pessimistic view of this option seems reasonable once we recognize that a very large loan, at least 20 million pounds sterling, would have been needed to achieve total backing for the country's monetary base, and we recall that the Funding Loan of 1891 had been granted to save Argentina from a default situation and *not* as a line of credit to increase the treasury's specie reserves.

A second option would have been the adoption of a higher rate of monetary expansion in order to accommodate the monetary needs of a growing economy, thus avoiding any further deflationary pressure. In principle, this policy could have been followed under a convertibility system or one of a flexible exchange rate, although only under the latter with any effectiveness in the long run. In accordance with modern monetary theory, this course of action would have represented an optimum monetary policy in the Gesell-Friedman sense if the authorities set a target of stable prices. However, it would have depended on a series of unlikely assumptions. First, the government had to have had the relevant information and the technical and legal flexibility to know at what speed it should inject money into the economy; and second, economic agents, just beginning to recover from the catastrophic crisis of 1891, would have to have perceived correctly the government's intentions to neutralize deflationary pressures and not instead see a monetary expansion as yet another return to an inflationary scenario. A floating exchange-rate regime of this kind was probably unthinkable in a period dominated by a rigid policymaking *mentalité* that prized above all adherence to the gold standard, a fixed exchange rate system.

In the early 1890s, then, the prevailing economic doctrines mandated a return to convertibility at par and not to a nominal exchange rate at a level higher than par. At first, Argentina was to make its best effort to play by these rules even if, at the end of the day, an accommodation to a new parity was unavoidable. Thus, after struggling with deflation for almost a decade, the policy goal was finally changed in 1899. The arguments of Gesell, and the export lobby, held sway and a new parity was adopted that matched the prevailing market exchange rate of 2.27 paper pesos per gold peso. The need for further deflation was over and, with macroeconomic stability restored, the long-awaited opening of the Conversion Office for normal exchange operations could go ahead. The stage was set for Argentina's resumption of gold standard convertibility.

6

Calm Before a Storm: The Gold Standard During the Belle Époque, 1899–1914

After the Baring Crisis Argentina endured nine years of adjustments in the financial and real sectors and a pronounced deflation. These dislocations were painful but appeared necessary to get Argentina back in a position to restore external convertibility. Ultimately, convertibility was restored in 1899, and the whole experience has long been considered by scholars an archetypal success story of a peripheral country finding a way to adopt the reforms necessary to establish a credible convertibility commitment for its money.

This chapter examines the fruits of these efforts and studies Argentina's experience under convertibility from 1899 until the international gold standard was suspended by war in 1914. This Belle Époque was an era of rapid economic growth for the country, with large inflows of capital and labor from overseas, an expansion of the agricultural frontier, and a surge in trade that built on a comparative advantage in primary products. Under such auspicious circumstances, any study of the macroeconomic performance of the money and banking system is inevitably rather uneventful, even boring. There were no major crises, and the currency board arrangement functioned well in these undoubtedly good times. As we shall see, the adjustment mechanisms worked smoothly.

Unfortunately, the good times were not to last, and the first signs of a major downturn emerged in 1913, when adverse economic conditions in the London capital market spilled over to Argentina. The advent of war in 1914 severely constrained external markets for capital and goods, plunging Argentina into the biggest recession it had ever experienced. It was in these harder times that the rigidity of the currency-board system was to be seen as a distinct drawback, even though the system emerged from that recession without having been compromised. Argentina's reputation for having a firm gold standard commitment was further augmented, even at great cost to the domestic economy. Looking ahead, it would be the memories of this political-economy tradeoff in the 1910s, and of the older 1890s debate over the deflationary dangers of the gold standard regime, that would set the stage for the ultimate test of the monetary system in the early 1930s.

Year	Interest Rate Nominal	Interest Rate Real	Output Growth Rate	Coefficient (1+r)/(1+g)	Debt-Output Ratio (%)
1891	10.3	6.6	-11.0	1.20	72
1892	9.9	16.2	8.6	1.07	90
1893	8.9	10.8	5.0	1.06	91

The Adoption of Convertibility

As we have noted, a heated debate had raged in the late 1890s over what kind of monetary system would be best in light of the then-current international financial situation. All points of view could be heard. During the deflation, many had voiced their ardent disapproval of the negative effects of the paper peso's appreciation since 1895. Others, conversely, had been horrified at the prior depreciation and the continued deviation from the old parity. Gesell had argued against the damaging effects of deflation on investment and real activity. Pellegrini and his followers thought a convertibility plan necessary to eliminate "that element of anarchy and destruction—inconvertible fiduciary money."[1]

A large sector of the intelligentsia in money and banking circles, including highly respected ex-ministers of finance, held a relatively skeptical position as to the possibility of imposing convertibility and fixed exchange rates with adequate backing in specie. While it eventually became clear that convertibility would be the policy objective, this did not settle all of the questions. Doctrinal discussion centered on two principal issues.

First, there was no agreement regarding the legally fixed exchange rate parity that should be chosen in order to make convertibility operable. Various ideas surfaced, including the possibility of initially converting the paper peso at the market parity, and then converging to the old parity over an extended period of time during which a "sliding scale" of adjustments in the value of the gold premium would be applied.[2] In the end, the Pellegrini recommendation was accepted, with the country adopting convertibility at the prevailing market exchange rate of 2.27 paper pesos per gold peso.[3]

Second, reasonable doubts existed over the adequacy of fiscal reforms that would assure the credibility of the Conversion Office in its task of exchanging paper for specie. The level of specie reserves was likely to be very low, and it was feared that the mechanism, therefore, could not be maintained in the event of a speculative attack on the paper peso. Despite these concerns, at the inauguration of Congress in 1899, President Julio A. Roca (1898–1904) declared his intention to see convertibility restored as quickly as possible, announcing that

> To achieve that result, we recommend the formation of a significant specie reserve. One of the causes that has most influenced the variation in the value of paper money is the lack of confidence in the direction the government is taking. Convertibility obliges us to reorganize and 'moralize' the mechanisms of the administration, to introduce all

1. Moyano Llerena (1935, pp. 48–49).
2. A minority on the Finance Committee in the lower chamber of Congress had proposed a scale of gradual reductions in the gold premium at a rate of 5 gold cents every six months until the old par was reached. It would have taken five and a half years to reach par under such a mechanism (Moyano Llerena 1935, pp. 62–63).
3. Moyano Llerena (1935) notes the important intellectual and political influence of Senator Carlos Pellegrini, the former President, in the adoption of convertibility in 1899. On the economic thought of Pellegrini, see Gallo (1997).

the economies possible in the budget, avoiding exaggerated expenditures, reducing or eliminating certain taxes, and re-establishing equilibrium in the public finances. Also the provincial governments have to play their part in this project. It is a fact that the number of administrative personnel in every province is more than superior to the needs. The bulk of those employees who delay the progress of the public administration only represent useless and harmful expenses and a burden that must be subtracted from the productive work force.[4]

The Law of Conversion (Law 3871) was passed on October 31, 1899, by Congress, establishing convertibility promised in 1891. The Finance Minister at the time was José Maria Rosa. From that moment, and for fifteen uninterrupted years, Argentina was to maintain gold standard convertibility at an exchange rate of 2.27 paper pesos per gold peso.[5]

The first article of the law established a clear and simple monetary regime. The Conversion Office would have the singular responsibility of exchanging paper for specie (and vice versa) at a rate of exchange fixed by law at 44 gold cents for each paper peso. Thus, any expansion or contraction in the amount of cash in circulation would exactly match the variations in the level of specie reserves on hand at the Conversion Office. With such a system of 100 percent marginal gold backing for the currency, there was a strict and inelastic relationship between variations in the stock of metallic reserves and variations in the monetary base. Consequently, all key autonomous monetary policy functions were proscribed, such as operating on the open market to buy or sell public bonds in order to influence the level of interest rates, or the use of rediscounts to provide liquidity. In addition, there could not be any other types of guarantees offered by the Conversion Office, such as the provision of Lender-of-Last-Resort assistance to the financial system. The money supply had been rendered completely endogenous by this choice of regime.

Another interesting aspect of the Law of 1899 was the degree of independence from political interference granted to the Conversion Office. The monetary authority was to be administered by a board of five directors chosen by the executive branch, each subject to approval by the Senate, and all appointed to a term in office of five years.[6] This was a clear and transparent attempt to enhance the credibility of the institution by keeping it at arm's length from the various branches of the government that might interfere with or apply pressure to the monetary authority as a way to seek fiscal or monetary policy relief in hard times. The plan was successful in this respect, and under these arrangements the Conversion Office maintained strict independence from the Executive, the

4. Quoted in Fernández López (1993).
5. For details of how Finance Minister Rosa coped with the consequences of the law see Rosa (1909), and on Rosa's participation in these debates see Gallo (1977).
6. According to Moyano Llerena (1935, p. 87) "the principal guarantee of the Caja is its separation from the Government and, in addition, that its administrators are personally responsible for any illegal application of the Caja's funds."

treasury, and the Banco de la Nación Argentina until the outbreak of the First World War in August 1914, when external convertibility was suspended.

Obviously, as the skeptics had noted, the most pressing problem facing the government was the creation of an initial reserve in specie that could guarantee, to some extent at least, the paper in circulation. This was vital in order to sustain a belief that parity could be defended in the event that the general public decided to test the convertibility of its paper pesos into gold. To say that the government's initial position was not very promising would be an understatement. The level of specie reserves at the Conversion Office throughout the period 1891–99 was zero. Originally it had been thought that the Conversion Office should have a reserve of approximately 30 million gold pesos, sufficient to back almost 25 percent of the monetary base. Article 4 of the Law of Conversion sought to generate fiscal revenue for this purpose, but this proved to be impossible in the time available, and it was not until 1910 that this goal was achieved.[7] In the end, under the constraints of no fiscal resources, no foreign gold loans, and no specie reserve whatsoever—and in a leap of great faith—the law went into effect anyway. This meant that in order to maintain convertibility in the early years of the law, it was going to be necessary to generate positive net inflows of specie. Otherwise the plan would surely fail.

The Gold Standard Adjustment Mechanism

For the student of Argentine monetary history, the 1900–1913 gold standard period is relatively uneventful in that volatility arising from autonomous fluctuations in the stock of money and the paper-gold exchange rate were removed as independent sources of economic disturbances. The gold standard years were noteworthy for a sharp growth in the Argentine real output and the mild inflation of domestic prices, the latter a reflection of the swift increase in the world money supply during the so-called Golden Age of 1902–12. Key macroeconomic statistics for this period are shown in Table 6.1.

The monetary regime proved durable and credible in these years. From November 1899 and until the outbreak of the First World War, the Conversion Office stood ready to automatically exchange paper pesos for gold, and vice versa, on demand and at a fixed exchange rate of 2.27 paper pesos for each gold peso. The figures in Table 6.1 show that this rule was strictly obeyed by the monetary authorities. In all years, the increase in the monetary base was fully 100 percent backed by the inflow of gold reserves at the Conversion Office. By adopting and adhering to a very strict gold exchange rule, the Conversion Office surrendered its control over the quantity of money, which became endogenously determined in the money market.

7. Moyano Llerena (1935, pp. 85 and 88–90).

Table 6.1. *Monetary and Fiscal Indicators, 1900–1913*

	Conversion Office			Money	Domestic	Real		Fiscal Deficit as a	
	Monetary		Money	Multi-	Price	Output	Money	Percentage of	
Year	Base	Gold	Supply	plier	Level	Index	Velocity	Receipts	GDP
1900	295	0	482	1.63	182	9,430	2.78	5.1	0.6
1901	296	0	472	1.60	159	10,220	2.68	5.6	0.7
1902	296	0	498	1.68	175	10,020	2.74	27.7	3.2
1903	380	87	640	1.69	165	11,450	2.30	3.8	0.4
1904	407	114	761	1.87	169	12,670	2.19	3.5	0.4
1905	498	205	944	1.89	184	14,350	2.18	0.0	0.0
1906	526	233	972	1.85	195	15,070	2.36	2.0	0.2
1907	531	239	981	1.85	201	15,390	2.46	1.0	0.1
1908	581	288	1,121	1.93	193	16,900	2.27	-0.8	-0.1
1909	685	392	1,390	2.03	210	17,730	2.09	26.5	2.5
1910	715	422	1,580	2.21	227	19,020	2.13	33.9	3.0
1911	722	429	1,635	2.26	226	19,370	2.09	33.9	3.1
1912	799	506	1,775	2.22	231	20,950	2.13	17.6	1.6
1913	823	529	1,673	2.03	232	21,160	2.29	16.2	1.5

Notes and sources: Monetary base, gold, and money supply in millions of paper pesos. Real output index in millions of 1950 pesos. Fiscal deficit as a percentage of GDP is estimated as the fiscal deficit deflated by wholesale price index divided by the real output index. See Appendix 1.

How did the market adjust? Starting from a situation of equilibrium in the money market the adjustment mechanism operated as follows. An increase in domestic real income led to an increased demand for money. This was satisfied by an inflow of specie and an increase in foreign reserves at the Conversion Office. This in turn led to an expansion of the monetary base and—via the money multiplier—a corresponding increase in the broad money supply. Thus, in this type of regime, the variable that quickly adjusts to restore equilibrium is the domestic money stock. In short, this theory states that gold flows restore equilibrium in the money market via an adjustment in the money supply, and they have no independent influence on other macroeconomic variables.

The key assumptions here are that prices and interest rates are internationally determined on world markets via purchasing power parity (PPP) and interest parity. Are such assumptions justified? We have already noted that PPP appeared to hold for Argentina in this period (see Appendix 4). This result is none too surprising given the very high share of foreign trade in output. What about international interest arbitrage? Recall that Argentina became a substantial long-term international borrower in the second half of the nineteenth century. Figure 6.1, which plots the Argentine-European external bond yield differential on an annual basis, shows that the required yield to hold an external Argentine bond was always higher than the yield of a comparable long-term European bond, the Rendita Italiana. For the entire 1884–13 period, the Ar-

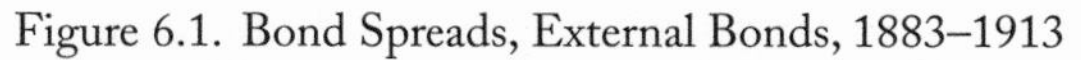

Figure 6.1. Bond Spreads, External Bonds, 1883–1913

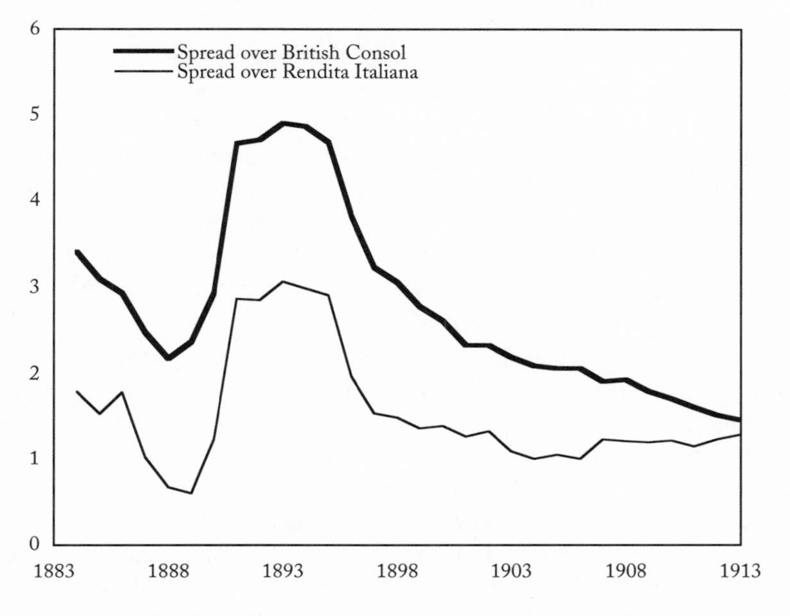

Notes and sources: See Appendix 1.

Figure 6.2. Bond Yields, External and Internal Bonds, 1883–1913

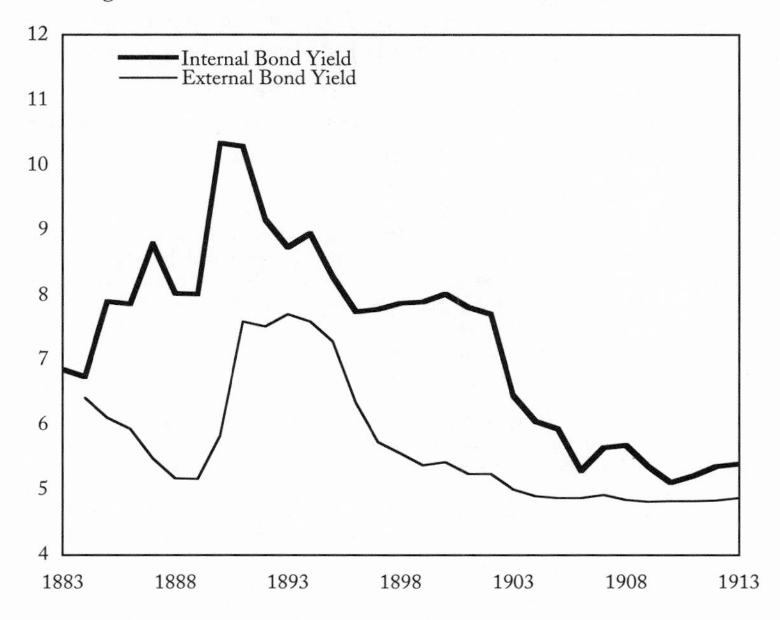

Notes and sources: See Appendix 1.

gentine long rate was, on average, 2.8 percentage points higher than that of the United Kingdom and 1.5 percentage points higher than that of Italy.

However, the chart also shows remarkable changes in the magnitude and evolution of the spread for the various subperiods of analysis. For example, whenever financial markets perceived that the Argentine government was not following prudent fiscal and monetary measures, Argentine debt instruments were rated as poor risks, and traded at a big discount, despite the explicit government guarantee. From 1889 to 1894, the abrupt rise in the risk spread was driven by the Baring Crisis, and the yield "surcharge" on Argentine external bonds (at least for those that were not in default) amounted to 4 or 5 percentage points in the London market.

After 1895, the fears that Argentina would repudiate its external debt started to subside. The external bond spread abruptly declined until 1900, reaching a steady low plateau during the gold standard years and continuing with a modest declining trend relative to the British consol. Figure 6.2 confirms the fact that the abrupt fall in the spread that occurred from 1895 to 1899 was entirely dominated by movements in the yields of the Argentine external bonds. After 1902 there is a clear convergence of the domestic bond yield to the external yield. When the exchange rate and default risk were minimized, capital markets were again closely linked, and the Argentine long-term interest rate was almost equal to the long-term rate of the international capital markets.

If we accept the preliminary evidence in favor of goods and capital market arbitrage, a simple test can be conducted to analyze the operation of the gold standard in Argentina for the years 1904–13. The test consists of comparing the actual contribution of the inflow of gold to changes in the domestic money stock with the residuals of the change in the demand for the money minus the changes produced by domestic sources (that is, changes in the money multiplier). Table 6.2 exhibits the results of the test.[8]

8. The methodology is as follows. The postulated money demand takes a standard form (see Appendix 4) where real money balances depend on real income Y and the interest rate i, with $\ln(M_t/P_t) = a + b\ln Y_t + c\ln(1 + i_t) + u_t$. The actual rate of change of money supply due to foreign sources equals to the rate of change of gold reserves times the backing ratio

$$\frac{G_{t-1}}{MB_{t-1}}\frac{\Delta G_t}{G_{t-1}},$$

where G is gold reserves at the Conversion Office, MB is monetary base, and we assume for this purpose a fixed money multiplier M/MB. The predicted rate of change of the money supply due to foreign sources is the rate of change in predicted nominal demand for money from the money demand equation minus the rate of change of money supply due to domestic sources. The latter term is calculated as the actual total rate of change of money supply minus the actual rate of change of money supply due to foreign sources, namely,

$$\frac{\Delta M_t}{M_{t-1}} - \frac{G_{t-1}}{MB_{t-1}}\frac{\Delta G_t}{G_{t-1}},$$

where M is the stock of money. See McCloskey and Zecher (1976, pp. 357–85).

Table 6.2. *Effects of Gold Reserves on Money Supply, 1904–13*

Year	Predicted Effect, Using Specification A	Predicted Effect, Using Specification B	Actual Change
1904	5.9	10.9	7.3
1905	22.6	23.9	22.3
1906	18.9	8.1	5.7
1907	0.3	1.0	1.0
1908	2.4	3.0	9.1
1909	12.8	13.7	17.8
1910	1.3	8.4	4.6
1911	-2.8	-3.4	0.8
1912	11.1	11.9	10.7
1913	8.6	9.3	3.0

Notes and sources: Annual rates of change. Column A uses long-term interest rates in the money demand equation; column B uses short-term rates. See text.

The correlation between predicted and actual reserve flows lends support to the monetary theory of the balance of payments as applied to Argentina for this period. That is, the demand for money in excess of supply provided by domestic sources is mainly satisfied by adjustments in gold reserves, a reflection of the balance of payments adjustment.

Money, Prices, and Real Activity under the Gold Standard

We have seen how the Argentine economy achieved convertibility, and we also examined how the new regime operated. Yet this tells us little about the more important end result of any policy reform package: what it meant for broad long-term economic achievement. How well did the Argentine economy perform under the new gold standard regime? To answer that question, we now briefly review some of the key events of the 1900–1913 period.

International and Domestic Overview

In the period 1899–1914 the international economy was characterized by extreme financial and monetary liquidity in international markets due to a sustained increase in the world stock of gold. This expansion reached 3.5 percent annually between 1890 and 1914, well above the 1.5 percent annual average growth between 1866 and 1890.[9] Under the international gold standard system these growth rates produced a generalized increase in the means of payment in the central countries and brought about an extraordinary increase in the level of activity and in prices. In Great Britain in the period 1899–13, the real economy grew at an accumulated rate of 16.8 percent, while the price index grew at 12.3

9. Data from Friedman and Schwartz (1963, p. 137).

percent. In the United States, the accumulated growth rates of the economy and of prices were 51.9 percent and 28.4 percent, respectively.

Argentina also underwent an important period of expansion in the real sector of the economy with the level of real output growing in 1899–1914 at an accumulated rate of 78.5 percent, equal to an average annual rate of 5.8 percent. In another reflection of the increase in the international stock of money, Argentina imported external inflationary pressures. The price level rose at an accumulated rate of 36.3 percent during this period, an average of 2.6 percent annually. Following a severe depression in prices at the beginning of the century (1899–1901), which brought a fall of 15 percent in price levels, the subsequent tendency for prices to rise reflected extraordinary improvements in the terms of trade for all countries that exported agricultural goods. The increase in exports plus the continued inflow of capital into Argentina had a strong correlation with the country's real, financial, and monetary performance.

From the point of view of monetary policy, the Conversion Office respected the rules of the game. The monetary authorities lost control of the quantity of the monetary base, which was left to be determined endogenously by the domestic money market. According to the monetary approach to the balance of payments, movements of specie became the vehicle by which equilibrium was restored to the market through adjustments in the specie stock, and from Table 2.4 we saw that the entire increase of the monetary base from 1900 to 1913 was exactly equal to the rise in the level of specie at the Conversion Office.

Bank Money and Financial Deepening

The growth of the monetary base was surpassed by that of bank money, which grew at an accumulated rate of 161.5 percent, or an annual rate of 12.2 percent. Bank money, and the money multiplier, clearly showed procyclical tendencies. After an accentuated fall after the Baring Crisis, the multiplier rose from a low of 1.2 in 1893 to a high of 2.2 in 1912. Judged by this statistic alone, this recovery could not match the financial deepening achieved in the 1880s during the period of the Law of National Guaranteed Banks.

Nevertheless, we feel certain that the deepening of financial intermediation which occurred in the later period was more genuine than in the previous expansive experience since, in the later case, the country's economic agents made real use of bank deposits as an alternative monetary asset. In the boom of 1889, for each "guaranteed" peso held by the public, little more than two pesos of commercial deposits existed. By 1912, for each peso in the hands of the public, there were more than three pesos in private commercial deposits. For some comparative perspective here, in the United States the ratio of deposits to cash was 3.4 in 1890 and 6.8 in 1910. This process of expansion of money or bank credit can be explained by the behavior of the level of reserves in the financial system and the ratio of cash to deposits held by the public.

Bank Reserves and the Risk of Runs

While the reserve ratio, the ratio of bank reserves to deposits, remained quite high in Argentina, it fell from an average of 50 percent for the decade of the 1890s to about 30 percent in 1910. This fall in aggregate reserves explained 8 percent of the change in the broad money supply during this period of considerable economic and monetary expansion. It is interesting to note that even when the Banco de la Nación Argentina began to play an important role in financial markets, the bank remained very conservative in terms of loans, maintaining reserve ratios as high as 62 percent in 1903 and no lower than the 31 percent level seen in 1912. The private banks in Argentina had lower reserve levels with a maximum of 31 percent in 1901 and a minimum of 24 percent in 1911.

Given the monetary regime, such a cautious attitude toward bank reserves is, as we have suggested, not surprising, and we will explore this question more deeply in the next chapter. For now, we again stress that the system of fractional-reserve banks functioned in the absence of a Lender of Last Resort, since neither the Conversion Office nor the Banco de la Nación Argentina had the authority to advance rediscounted funds in the event of a massive run on the deposits of private banks.[10] This seeming structural weakness was offset by a high level of reserves relative to countries whose central banks had discretionary rediscount policies. In fact, the reserve ratios in the Argentine financial system under the gold standard were *three times higher* than those in the United States—even though the United States, prior to the creation of the Federal Reserve Bank in 1913, was, like Argentina, without a formal Lender of Last Resort.

However, Argentina had virtually no mechanisms, public or private, to prevent liquidity crises, even absent a Lender of Last Resort. In contrast, the United States had the clearing houses and other institutions formed to forestall financial panic, a system that was buttressed by the Aldrich-Vreeland Act of 1908 under which a group of highly capitalized banks formed the National Currency Association.[11] No such institutions existed in the Argentine financial system, a structural weakness that would become evident in the crisis of 1914.

10. See our subsequent chapter on internal and external convertibility. In fact, the Banco de la Nación Argentina did make some small rediscounts after a change to its rules circa 1904. But major rediscounting powers were not available until 1914, when a new emergency law was passed. We discuss this legal change at the end of this chapter.

11. These banks were authorized to rediscount the portfolio of banks suffering a run on deposits by the public. Within limits, banks with problems could convert their assets into cash to halt any generalized run by depositors and forestall a credit crunch. Several authors maintain that the Aldrich-Vreeland Act provided the mechanism by which the United States avoided a serious financial crisis in August 1914. See Friedman and Schwartz (1963, pp. 170–71) and Timberlake (1978).

Cash, Deposits, and Public Behavior

How did the general public behave in the new regime? Confidence in the banking system clearly recovered from the pessimistic scenario of the 1890s following the Baring Crisis. This is well illustrated by the evolution of cash and money. We noted earlier that financial deepening, measured by the increase in private deposits, can serve as a force to expand the monetary holdings of the public. The ratio of cash to money was 36 percent when the Conversion Law was approved in 1899. In 1901 the ratio peaked at 38 percent, and then fell monotonically, reaching a plateau at about 24 percent in 1911. This secular trend fed into the expansion of money until 1912, the first year in which the economy began to feel symptoms of financial fragility. If we recall that the stock of money can be split into base money and banking money, the growth of the latter explains the 55 percent of the growth in the stock of broad money in the economy during this period.

Prices and the Real Exchange Rate

Strengthened by credibility, the real exchange rate appreciated relative to the pound sterling by 15 percent in the period 1899 to 1914. The dynamics of the real exchange rate in this case resemble the recent experiences with stabilization in developing countries based on a fixed exchange rate as a nominal anchor. Put another way, the inflow of capital to the Argentine economy implied an increase in the quantity of base money and, as a result, in the quantity of broad money—where the increase in the level of bank money was 60 percent over and above the change in the monetary base. This monetary expansion produced an increase in aggregate demand and domestic prices started to rise more rapidly than the level of international inflation.

The sustained price boom was reflected in many indicators. One example is a crude index of real estate prices based on the price per square meter of residential properties in the city of Buenos Aires.[12] The index shows a clear cyclical evolution: first, a real estate boom in 1887–90 with an increase of 210 percent in prices; a major depression in 1890–94 with a fall of 50 percent; a stagnation in 1895–1903; and finally a large increase of more than 350 percent under the gold standard from 1904 to 1913. The sensitivity of these asset prices to international movements of capital can be seen clearly during the financial crisis of 1914, with a fall of 33 percent in a single year.[13]

12. While clearly imperfect, the index is a useful proxy for the evolution of nontradable goods prices. Given the significant international mobility of labor during this period, an index of real estate prices is perhaps a better proxy for aggregate demand than, say, nominal salaries.

13. On this unpublished price index, see della Paolera (1999b). The primary source was the *Anuario Estadístico de la Ciudad de Buenos Aires* (Annual Report of Statistics for the City of Buenos Aires), which provides detailed information in 14 parishes on the number, size, and prices of properties sold. The index weights each parish according to sales.

Summary: The Pros and Cons of the Gold Standard

On the eve of the First World War, few observers would have grumbled at the economic performance achieved by Argentina over the preceding decade. By 1912 most macroeconomic indicators were at their best-ever levels. Monetary circulation had backing in specie of 63 percent. Country risk measured by the bond spread between domestic and international fixed income assets was as low as 1.5 percent. A steady increase in the real quantity of money continued at a rate of 7 percent per annum. The federal budget deficit was no higher than 20 percent of fiscal revenues. The ratio of public debt to national output was as low as 35 percent, having been more than 100 percent in 1891.

Argentina' s potential for such a dynamic upswing was recognized by Alec Ford. He emphasized the importance of the international economic cycle on the economy of a peripheral country that had credibly adopted the gold standard. In his view, the gold standard maximized an economy's ability to attract international investors in periods of international bonanza. However, by symmetry, simultaneously Argentina had to face the key weakness of this kind of regime. For Great Britain, perhaps, the adoption of the gold standard mitigated the consequences of unfavorable external shocks; but for emerging market countries like Argentina, the convertibility system left the economy very sensitive to sudden shocks in the country's terms of trade or in international interest rates. Ford's vision was thus of a gold standard that amplified economic cycles:

> It is easy to understand the dislike of some Argentines for a system which dictated that a slump must be aggravated by monetary reactions, although, doubtless, they had forgotten that the same system served to enhance booms.[14]

In truth, many Argentines were aware of both the upside and the downside. In 1909, not long after the United States recovered from a menacing financial crisis in 1907, Silvio Gesell again put his finger on a key issue. In his work *La plétora monetaria de 1909 y la anemia monetaria de 1898* (Monetary Plethora in 1909 and Monetary Anemia in 1898) he sounded a note of caution that might have seemed out of place as capital inflows surged during Argentina's great boom:

> Our money is so intimately and solidly linked to gold, as the pound sterling is and even more so than the franc and the mark.... If, in some faroff country with a gold standard, a crisis develops, this crisis will have immediate repercussions for the Argentine paper currency.... And it should be that way, as that is what the Law of Conversion is all about. He that enjoys the advantages of an international money must also accept its inconveniences, the pros and the cons of monetary solidarity.[15]

Still, one might imagine that few were listening to Gesell's warning at a time of unprecedented growth and prosperity. In the Argentine economy, exuberance,

14. Ford (1962, p. 188).
15. Gesell (1909, p. 56).

rational and otherwise, was at all time high. Taking all these factors into consideration, it is likely that the inhabitants of Argentina were not at all prepared for the severe foreign-exchange and financial crisis—a "twin crisis"—that was about to hit the country in 1914.

The Foreign Exchange and Financial Crisis of 1914

The First World War was a tremendous negative external shock to an economy as open as Argentina's. It maintained fluid international economic relationships with both sides of the conflict, but it was financially tied to the pound sterling. Eventually the conflict would end, but by then it would have destroyed the harmony of the international monetary system based on the gold standard, the very regime that Argentina had fought so hard to credibly join. With the exception of the United States, core countries had decided by mid-1914 to let the value of their monies depreciate relative to gold, and Argentina had little choice but to join them by abandoning convertibility in August 1914.[16]

Warning Signs

Even as early as the beginning of 1913, contractionary financial and monetary policies adopted in London started to have a strong effect on the Argentine domestic economy. The Bank of England raised its discount rate from 3.4 percent in 1912 to 5 percent by late 1913.

By dint of the close arbitrage linkages of purchasing power parity and interest parity, such shocks were rapidly transmitted to domestic markets, and the figures in Table 6.3 allow us to see some of the impacts. The seemingly unstoppable increase in the domestic monetary base that had been witnessed for over a decade was swiftly halted. Then, for the first time since the implementation of the convertibility law, a reverse in specie flows caused a reduction in the money supply of 4.8 percent. A 6.4 percent decline in bank deposits at the same moment reflected the spillover of these effects into the broad money market.

These were early, yet clear indications that Argentina was about to import deflationary pressures from Europe. In 1913, the annual rate of price inflation slowed from 2.6 percent to 0.2 percent, and the growth rate of the economy slowed to a discouraging 1.0 percent. Bankruptcies increased by 20 percent relative to 1912, and, as we have already mentioned, there was a 33 percent drop in residential real estate values in the city of Buenos Aires in one year.

The sudden cyclical deterioration in a very broad group of economic and financial indicators—including the values of real estate and farm land, the scale

16. The United States imposed restrictions on the export of specie during 1917–19, but maintained the convertibility of dollars to gold within its borders. In June 1919, the free movement of capital was reestablished (Bordo and Kydland 1992, pp. 22–24).

Table 6.3. *Financial Crisis Indicators, 1913–14*

Year	1912	1913	1914	1915
Monetary Base, Percentage Change	10.7	2.9	-2.4	23.0
Gold Backing of Monetary Base, Percent	71.8	72.6	66.3	72.5
Money Supply, Percentage Change	9.3	-5.3	-9.5	16.0
Banking Money, Percentage Change	8.2	-11.7	-16.3	8.0
Bank Reserves, All Banks, Percent	28.6	32.4	33.8	42.2
Bank Reserves, Bank of London, Percent	30.6	34.0	Feb. 46.0	Jan. 68.5
			Apr. 53.0	
Bank Deposits, Percentage Change	8.1	-6.9	-14.2	23.4
Wholesale Prices, Percentage Change	2.0	0.2	1.2	6.0
Commercial Bankruptices, Percentage Change	—	20	Annual 175	—
			Jul.–Dec. 232	
Real Output, Percentage Change	8.0	1.0	-11.0	1.0
Exchange Rate, Paper Pesos per Gold Peso	2.27	2.27	2.27	2.31

Notes and sources: See Appendix 1.

of bankruptcies, and the volume of deposits—gave only a hint of the difficulties that the financial system was to face as the deflation threat developed. In a deflationary scenario, leveraged financial entities are in grave danger. There is a marked change in the relative values of banks' assets and liabilities. In a deflation, economic agents look for liquidity. This entails an increase in the use of cash versus deposits (bank liabilities) and a decrease in the propensity to hold illiquid assets (assets that normally form a part of banks' portfolios). This portfolio shift implied a general deterioration in the indicators of liquidity and solvency of the financial system.

Another microeconomic ratio we must keep in mind when considering a deleterious external shock to an open economy is the relationship between the monetary liabilities and the reserves in specie, that is, the ratio between inside money and outside money. At the start of 1912 the ratio of specie reserves to broad money was 29 percent; that is, the quantity of domestic money was roughly three times the specie at the Conversion Office. This ratio is, of course, a function of two other ratios in the monetary system: the ratio of monetary base to reserves in specie, an indicator of the solvency of the Conversion Office in terms of being able to maintain the external convertibility of the peso; and the ratio of broad money supply to the monetary base, the money multiplier, which reflects the existence of a financial system with fractional reserves.

The banks create secondary money, or bank money, by means of the deposits they hold. The inherent instability of fractional reserves arises because the general public may believe that a peso in the pocket is better than one on deposit. A contraction in the money multiplier follows, which reduces the quantity of money in the economy. The economy moves from deflation to financial crisis when the public begins to panic, or run, by trying to convert all its deposits into

Cartoon 6.1. *En Europa, la tierra de Perogrullo, a la mano cerrada se llama* puño, *y en la Argentina, a lo mano cerrada se llama* ruina. (In Europe, the land of platitudes, the closed hand is called *fist,* and in Argentina the closed hand is called *ruin.*)

Notes: This cartoon conveys a flavor of the international transmission of the 1913 economic crisis. In emerging markets it is the financial market that delivers the blow, then as now. The fist carries the label *crédito* (credit). Abandoned factories rot in the background as unpaid bills lie on the ground.

Source: PBT, no. 455, August 16, 1913.

pesos. With bank reserves only a fraction of total deposits, the intervention of a monetary authority is needed to provide the liquidity necessary to preserve the stability of the financial system.

Unfortunately, given the institutional context, Lender-of-Last-Resort actions were explicitly *not* a responsibility of the Conversion Office, or anybody else. Thus, in the 1913 scenario it is easy for us to see, once again, the trade-off between internal convertibility (stabilizing the domestic financial system) and external convertibility (maintaining the monetary standard which guarantees the value of the money).

The Banking Crisis

Argentina's battle with these tensions reached a critical point in August 1914. We can take an insider's look at the anatomy of this financial crisis by looking at the minutes of the Bank of London and the River Plate, at that time perhaps the most important private commercial bank in the financial system.[17] We should note that this bank always maintained a more conservative policy than others. Toward the end of 1913, its level of aggregate reserves was 32 percent as shown in Table 6.3.

In April 1914, the Bank of London and the River Plate increased the level of its reserves considerably to 53 percent, a response to an increase in the rediscount rate from 3 percent to 4 percent by the Bank of England. The bank also continually monitored an index of commercial bankruptcies in Buenos Aires. In 1913, the annual bankruptcy rate exceeded that of 1912 by more than 20 percent; by the third quarter of 1914 bankruptcies were increasing at an annual rate of 175 percent, and by 232 percent in the final quarter, as shown in Table 6.3. A severe downturn in real activity was underway.

Such statistics were "leading indicators" of real activity, and clear signals of the financial situation of firms seeking credit. This information was public, since it was regularly published by the Buenos Aires Stock Exchange (Bolsa de Comercio). So it was possible, therefore, for economic agents to infer the change in the quality of the portfolio of the consolidated banking system. In a deflation, the fall in the quality of bank assets could trigger a run by creating negative expectations as to the future solidity of the financial system.

From Table 6.3 we see that in 1914 Argentina's financial system had a level of fractional reserves equivalent to 34 percent. For comparison, the United States had a reserve ratio of 12 percent, and none of the European countries had a ratio in excess of 5 percent. Argentina also had a more accentuated preference for liquidity. The ratio of cash to money in the public's hands was almost 23 percent. By contrast, in the United States the proportion was 13 percent.

17. The primary source is the BOLSA (Bank of London and South America) archive, University College Library, London. See especially folios 192–95, 199–205, and 286 from 1914.

On the face of it, the Argentine financial system seemed, according to these indicators, to be better prepared to face a situation of illiquidity. In the early days of August 1914, however, a run on deposits of unexpected dimensions occurred.

Policy Response

The major institutions in the banking system, under the leadership of the President of the Banco de la Nación Argentina, pressured the government to call a bank and foreign exchange holiday for one week. The banks hoped that a cooling-off period would put a stop to the panic and avoid a suspension of payments by several commercial banks.[18] The government acceded to the request, and, during the week of August 3, a variety of proposals were presented for resolving the crisis.

The presidents of the most important banks met daily, and on August 4 they presented a proposal which suggested that the government make a transitory emergency issue of currency to enable the Banco de la Nación Argentina to rediscount or make guaranteed advances to the banks. This proposal was put into effect. So too was a proposal to suspend withdrawals of specie from the Conversion Office and the banks.

Still, political agreement on these plans was not complete. In the minutes the Bank of London and the River Plate commented that the Executive opposed the idea of an emergency issue, and instead favored using the Conversion Fund *(fondo de conversión)* of 30 million gold pesos as a way to rediscount the commercial paper of banks with problems. At first, Congress approved a Presidential decree declaring a moratorium of 30 days on all financial obligations falling due during that period and established that banks must respond with up to 20 percent of the deposits that were to fall due. The Banco de la Nación was authorized to convert the Conversion Fund to paper and to use these funds to rediscount commercial obligations.

In the end, the use of emergency issues of currency was approved, despite the opposition of the Executive Branch. However, as a safeguard it was required that money in circulation could never have a backing in specie of less than 40 percent (at the moment the law passed, 72 percent of the money base was backed in specie). The new laws therefore offered the possibility of an expansion of the money supply that was more elastic in response to external shocks.[19]

18. The run on the banks also put pressure on the Bank of London and the River Plate, which had one of the highest reserve levels in the entire system. They reported that "in the face of such unusual circumstances we could not insist that our financial position was such as to withstand all the demands that could be made upon us and we accordingly joined our colleagues in the suggestion above [the request for a bank holiday]" (BOLSA, folio 193).
19. The emergency issue was also to be used for rediscounting commercial paper, but only with the consent of the Executive Branch.

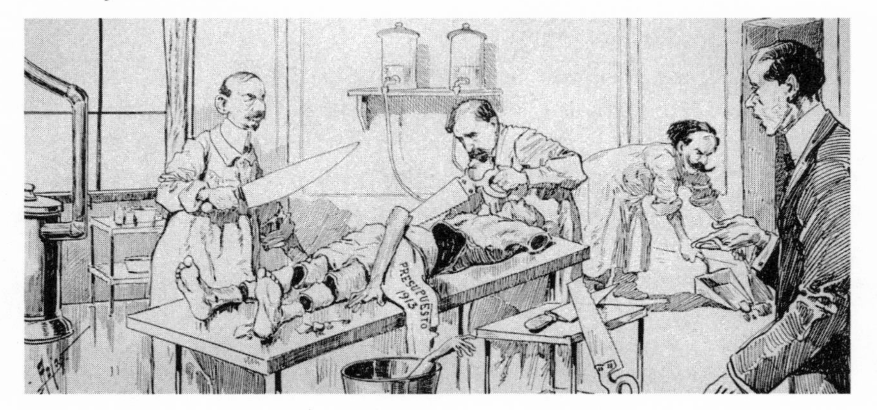

Cartoon 6.2. *Los cirujanos socialistas. — ¿Qué están ustedes haciendo? — La disección. — Pues cualquiera diria que estaban picando carne para hacer embutidos.* (The socialist surgeons. [Person] — What are you doing? [The socialists] — The dissection. [Person] — Because anyone would say that you are grinding meat to make cold cuts.)
Notes: The 1913 economic crisis has hit. The socialist leaders attempting to impose fiscal conservatism on the national budget are (left to right) Nicolás Repetto, Juan B. Justo, and Alfredo Palacios. These were the first three members of the socialist party to become *diputados* (deputies, members of the lower house in Congress). The cartoon shows that in their desire to cut the budget they are dismantling it to see what is inside.
Source: PBT, año 10, no. 444, May 31, 1913.

The emergency laws gave Argentina powerful Lender-of-Last-Resort capabilities, but to a large extent they went unused. The tools were there, but, at least at the Conversion Office, the authorities were reluctant to use them. The currency board felt it would risk its credibility if it broke the gold standard "rules of the game" and issued unbacked money. This was true even as many central banks in the core countries were breaking the same "rules" left and right. If the Conversion Office was unwilling to use its emergency powers to make transitory issues—and if, as seems to have been the case, it had sufficient independence to refrain from doing so given the political pressures—then everything depended on the actions of the largest of the banks, the Banco de la Nación Argentina.

It is interesting to note that the government confronted the financial crisis by authorizing the Banco de la Nación Argentina to use two thirds of the 30 million gold pesos in the Conversion Fund to resolve transitory illiquidity at banks. In this way, the Banco de la Nación Argentina acted in a limited way as a Lender of Last Resort. In 1914 the money supply declined 9.5 percent, deposits 14.2 percent, and bank money 16.3 percent. Yet, despite substantial exchange controls prohibiting the exportation of specie, the exchange rate depreciated less than 2 percent in 1915. This minor adjustment suggests that the country's economic agents felt that any suspension in convertibility was clearly contingent on international events. After this crisis, the recuperation of the financial system was a rapid one, though real output did not recover until 1916.

The End of the Golden Age

For almost fifteen years, the convertibility law of 1899 had provided a sound basis for the macroeconomic policies of the Argentine Republic in the first era of economic globalization. Policymakers realized that, while they were constrained by open economy forces, they could still benefit from "network externalities" in a world enamored of gold standard rules and could use a credible commitment mechanism to overcome a doubtful reputation for fiscal and monetary responsibility.

Unfortunately for the country, most of the features that made the currency board regime so suitable for the Golden Age from 1900 until 1914, also made the system very risky for use in the turbulent interwar period that followed. This was not, of course, Argentina's fault; the outbreak of war was surely exogenous to the country. But the change of scene amply illustrated that large external shocks can quite radically alter the calculation as to what constitutes an optimal monetary, banking, and exchange-rate regime.

The immediate shock of the 1914 crisis was undoubtedly large, and a deep recession followed that cost Argentina a massive cumulative loss of output. However, even after a recovery from this downturn, the problems of macroeconomic and financial instability in the economy were far from solved. The next part of the book traces the subsequent gradual breakdown of the gold standard in Argentina in the interwar period. We argue that one must view this unfolding drama at several levels to fully understand the tensions unleashed by the radical external regime change in 1914.

At a microeconomic level, the banking system had to cope with new shocks, a lack of insurance, and no real Lender-of-Last-Resort capabilities. Yet, at the same time, it faced a marked increase in the demand for capital and intermediation after the retreat of foreign banks and investors. At a regulatory level, the Banco de la Nación asserted itself more forcefully as a "quasi" Lender of Last Resort, and, by venturing beyond what its own rules permitted, it helped keep a troubled banking system alive. At a macroeconomic level, larger external shocks rattled the economy, and the Conversion Office could do little but follow its prescribed mechanical functions, since it chose to play by its own rules. Finally, the inconsistencies in the whole framework were exposed by the world depression of the 1930s, and the threat of failure in both internal and external convertibility would eventually destroy the entire system.

Part Four

The Travails of the Interwar Years

7

Distress Signals: Financial Fragility in the Interwar Period

The 1914–39 period defined a critical transition in Argentine economic history, yet the signs of future retardation and recurring crises were not so obvious. Even scholars with the most cursory acquaintance with the historical record can point to this key period as a regime shift, when the move from convergence and relative prosperity to divergence and relative backwardness begun. All histories single out the interwar period, perhaps even the very year 1929, as the decisive break point.[1]

One may wonder if this emphasis justified. In its economic performance Argentina fared no worse than other settler economies in the transition to the interwar period. That is, despite important and violent shifts in the terms of trade and the virtual state of autarky in international capital markets, the Argentine economy managed to overcome both the depths of the 1914–18 and 1929–31 crises. How was this possible, in an economy that at the turn of the century was still a primary production economy? How should it affect our view of the origins of Argentine relative retardation?

As the first part of this book has made clear, Argentina staged a remarkable comeback from the Baring Crisis of the 1890s, and the inconsistent policy choices of the 1880s and earlier that had precipitated that famous fiasco. The recovery was centered on an extreme version of macroeconomic orthodoxy that coupled fiscal discipline with a seemingly iron-clad guarantee of monetary convertibility. The latter gold-standard commitment was considered an essential vehicle for building a new level of credibility in world capital markets starting from almost nothing.

Despite how unlikely the success of such an announced strategy might have seemed in 1891, by 1914 Argentina had emerged as the favorite of emerging market investors during the height of the classical gold standard. The new institutions appeared to be holding. Monetary stability was firm, and in a climate of surging economic growth, investment was high, capital inflows abundant,

1. Di Tella and Zymelman (1967); Díaz Alejandro (1970; 1984); Cortés Conde (1979); Taylor (1994); della Paolera and Ortiz (1995).

and the financial sector was in a phase of healthy expansion after the wounds of the 1890s crisis had started to heal.

This rosy scenario was rudely disturbed by a set of totally exogenous economic shocks associated with the First World War, shocks in the global economy that were to test the economic policy regime that Argentina had set in place. The regime was, of course, predicated on certain assumptions: that the gold standard would endure, that global capital markets would remain stable and liquid, and that trade in goods would remain open and facilitate Argentina's specialized strategy of exchanging primary product exports for manufactured imports.

The final part of our book examines the implications of this change in the external regime as it affected Argentine economic performance during the interwar period in general, and during the 1930s Great Depression in particular. To do so, we will need to set the stage by considering the state of the Argentine economy at the end of the Belle Époque. Our work is certainly a money and banking study, but we know that the Argentine monetary regime exhibited some remarkable continuity from 1890 until 1935, as the Conversion Office remained in control of the money supply and followed its strict rules of the game.

Yet while the monetary side remained fairly stable, an important part of the changing context in our study is the financial landscape of Argentina. After being virtually eradicated in the 1890s, domestic banks regrouped and expanded until 1914, and were joined in their work by an expanding group of foreign banks. A small but growing stock market also made itself felt, although equity markets were small next to debt markets and banking finance. After 1914, all these markets faced new constraints as external adjustments forced the Argentine economy down unexpected paths.

Our aim in this chapter is to address two sets of major questions about events in financial markets. First, exactly how remarkable was interwar financial development relative to previous and subsequent trends in Argentina and relative to other countries' long-run experience? What were the financial magnitudes involved? How much capital was mobilized and allocated? And what can we infer about the capacity of financial development to significantly improve Argentina's long-run rates of saving, investment and economic growth?

Second, what independent sources of macroeconomic instability were originated by financial shocks in this evolving domestic financial system? It requires us to assess the inherent fragility of the domestic financial system: could it produce financial shocks that could influence business cycles?[2] In addition, the economy soon faced one of the worst international depressions that saw world-

2. In particular, banking intermediaries have an inherent instability under the so-called Diamond-Dybvig (1983) framework. Since banks insure the nominal value in deposit contracts and they create high-powered deposits they are subject to runs from investors. In a scenario of generalized runs, the expectation of the bankruptcy of an otherwise safe institution is self-fulfilling.

wide financial panics and collapses. How did the institutional features of the emerging financial markets propagate, or dampen, shocks that originated in the real sector economy? Before we engage discussion of these topics, we first review the major elements of the theory of finance and development.

Finance and Development in Theory

The influence of the development of financial and capital markets on economic growth and the emergence of market economies has been debated by economists and economic historians since Adam Smith. Theoretical and empirical studies have focused on the role of financial deepening on the process of economic growth.

As early as 1912, the Austrian Joseph Schumpeter in his *Theory of Economic Development* argued that finance scarcity was a serious obstacle to development. Economic historians such as Davis, Cameron, Gerschenkron, and Goldsmith made pioneering empirical contributions showing that financial markets were "necessary" institutions in the early stages of industrialization of today's developed countries. By following a comparative approach, these studies claim that a lack of well-functioning capital markets institutions is central in explaining the relative backwardness of some continental European countries.[3]

Two contributions that can help us organize an analytical framework for studying the finance-growth nexus and assessing the quantitative importance of the financial system for economic development are the works of Townsend and Levine. They note that with perfect information and no transaction costs, there will be basically no need for financial intermediaries. Otherwise, intermediation provides a potentially valuable service.[4] The value-added characteristics of financial institutions, some of which were listed by Levine, are key functions that could increase the prospects for economic development:

1. To deepen the use of money and near-monies for transaction purposes to move beyond the technology of a barter-exchange system (i.e., the development of stable and credible monetary and financial institutions);
2. To ease the trading, hedging, and pooling of risk by reducing the uncertainty about the timing and settlement of intertemporal economic transactions (i.e., innovation in the creation of liquid financial instruments);

3. See Schumpeter (1936); Gerschenkron (1962); Davis (1963); Cameron et al. (1967); Goldsmith (1969). More recently authors such as Gurley and Shaw (1955), McKinnon (1973), Shaw (1973), and Fry (1995) have studied the recent experience of a large sample of developed and developing countries. They examine the channels of transmission from financial intermediation to growth by inspecting institutional and economic forces such as legal regulation, and the influence of interest rates on savings and investments.
4. Townsend (1983); Levine (1996). A straightforward question about the functional role and usefulness of capital markets, and especially banks, was posed by De Long (1991) in his paper "Did J. P. Morgan's Men Add Value? An Economist's Perspective on Financial Capitalism." The same question might be asked of any intermediary, in any country, at any time.

3. To ease the linkages between savers and investors by reducing the need for information so that available *short-run* funding from surplus economic units will flow to those short-of-funds investors who can promise a higher expected rate of return for their *long-run* projects (i.e., improved efficiency in allocating resources by transforming the maturity of assets);[5]
4. To mobilize savings by the pooling of capital from disparate savers for investment to obtain efficient scales of operation in firms (i.e., a mobilization of savings can produce a fall in the cost of external finance for firms and entrepreneurs allowing them to choose their first-best techniques);
5. To lower the cost of finance and interest rates, and thus enhance the resiliency of financial institutions to systemic fragility and provide for the flourishing of new entrepreneurs and new firms that otherwise could not have existed.

When the factors mentioned above are in operation, financial intermediation will enhance capital accumulation and, most importantly, technological adaptation and innovation. All these have the potential, in turn, to speed economic growth.

Stylized Facts

Let us now turn to a first preliminary inspection of the available macrodata for Argentina to establish some links between measures of financial deepening and economic performance. Few scholars have tackled this subject and very little has been written on the interaction in Argentina between financial development and aggregate economic activity for the 1913–39 period.[6]

A vague consensus suggests that some financial development took place, though it was not all that might have been hoped for:

> While the financial history of Latin America remains to be written, it appears that by the 1920s most countries had succeeded in establishing commercial banks of the (then) traditional sort.... Although there was no "financial repression," critics pointed to a lack of medium and long-term credit, particularly to finance industry and non-export agriculture...[7]

5. Levine (1996) notes that "the link between liquidity and economic development arises because some high-return projects require a long-term commitment of capital, but savers do not like to relinquish control of their savings for long periods. Thus, if the financial system does not augment the liquidity of long-term investments, less investment is likely to occur in the high (risk-adjusted) return projects...." This is a crucial function because when performed in an efficient manner it enables entrepreneurs to overcome the problem of borrowing or credit rationing. Following Calomiris (1993), if financial intermediation did not develop beyond short-term credit and lending practices, the allocation of resources and the nature and speed of economic growth will be affected because the choice of inputs in production will be biased toward variable-cost inputs and against investment in fixed capital.
6. See, however, della Paolera and Ortiz (1995).
7. Díaz Alejandro (1985a, p. 2).

In his landmark history, Díaz Alejandro offers further evidence for significant financial deepening in the interwar period.[8] The domestic debt market featured an expanding array of debt instruments in fixed money terms, and mortgage activity grew. There was an increase in bank channels of mobilizing finance, notably via rapidly expanding savings accounts which expanded from 8 percent of output in 1913–14 to 22 percent in 1928–29. Monetization also expanded, and a traditional indicator, the ratio of monetary assets to output, rose from 46 percent in 1913–14 to 55 percent in 1928–29.

Not all signs were good, however. The equity market remained thin, and "companies relied primarily on bank credit for short-term financing and on retained earnings and ad hoc arrangements for long-term financing." Trading on the Bolsa was dominated by mortgage paper and government bonds, and only around 10 percent of trades were in corporate stocks. In banking one institution obviously loomed large, the Banco de la Nación Argentina, which accounted for more than two-fifths of the assets of the entire banking system, and which, in the absence of a central bank, had a quasi-public function. Despite these caveats, the evidence seemed favorable: "the domestic contribution to financing pre-1930 capital accumulation was large and tended to grow" and suggested that by 1930 Argentina had become a "highly monetized" economy with an "expanding [domestic] capital market."[9]

More than thirty years after Díaz Alejandro's essay, a pioneering work built on scarce data, we think it time to re-examine these issues and explore the relationship between the development of domestic financial markets and economic growth for the 1913–39 period. But we have so far lacked a detailed analysis of the linkages between financial development, inside-money deepening, credit creation, the efficiency and level of investment, and economic growth. For the case of Argentina, an emerging economy, the role of financial development is an essential element in understanding what happened after 1914.

The Argentine economy suffered an immediate shock at the onset of the First World War. The British supply of financial services proved to be unreliable when international capital markets dried up. Thus, there was a need to substitute for foreign mobilization and accumulation of resources by domestic sources which would have to rely on a domestic financial technology.[10] As Levine noted:

> England's financial system did a better job at identifying and funding profitable ventures than most countries in the mid-1800s.... Indeed, England's advanced financial system also did a good job at identifying profitable ventures in other countries, such as Canada, the United States, and Australia during the 19th Century. England was able to "export" financial services (as well as financial capital) to many economies with underdeveloped financial systems.[11]

8. Díaz Alejandro (1970, pp. 28–35).
9. Díaz Alejandro (1970, pp. 33–34).
10. Taylor (1992).
11. Levine (1996, p. 14).

The very same process was at work in parts of Latin America, notably in Argentina—perhaps to an even greater extent given its extreme degree of dependence on foreign capital. In this way an Anglo-Argentine elite came to dominate the financial landscape of turn-of-the-century Buenos Aires. About one half of Argentine capital was foreign owned, either directly or indirectly in 1913, a far higher percentage than in any other major lending nation at the time, and the bulk of that foreign capital was British in origin.

Why was Argentina so dependent on foreign capital in this period? This is a challenging question, and to discuss it fully would venture beyond the bounds of the present book, but it is a question worth dwelling on for a few moments to appreciate the dimensions of Argentina's external economic shock in 1914. Before this date, and ever since the devastation of the banking system in the Baring Crisis, a very large share of asset accumulation had been financed by capital inflows. The foreign capital stock in total size amounted to perhaps one half of the total domestic capital stock of the nation—a spectacular figure probably never equaled before or since as a measure of foreign capital penetration.

Notwithstanding the willingness of foreign savings supply to finance investment in Argentina, the observation also prompts the question as to why domestic savings were so scanty in the first place. A number of hypotheses suggest themselves. One is that the arrested development of the domestic financial system prevented the effective mobilization of domestic savings supply. But this assumes that such savings were there to be mobilized. An alternative, or at least complementary, explanation suggests that the low level of savings in Argentina had other causes, notably the unusually high demographic burden in the country. With a rapidly growing population, and a large share of dependent children in the age distribution, Argentine households would be expected to be in a phase of high consumption before 1914.[12]

Considering both of these mechanisms indicates why investment and economic growth could be sharply curtailed by a closure of external capital markets. Neither mechanism is susceptible to very rapid adjustment. Financial development is usually a slow process that takes decades to reach fruition, as many studies have shown. Similarly, the demographic structure is a very slowly evolving feature of the economy, for two reasons.

First, large demographic burdens can take a generation to be transmitted from the child-dependent component of the age distribution into the productive labor force component. Second, fertility rates are themselves slowly evolving variables and so present another reason to expect great persistence in the demographic structure. For example, the persistent demographic burden in Argentina in the interwar period could explain the much lower rates of saving, and hence investment, there as compared to the rest of the world, and most if not all of

12. This paragraph and the one that follows draw on Taylor (1992).

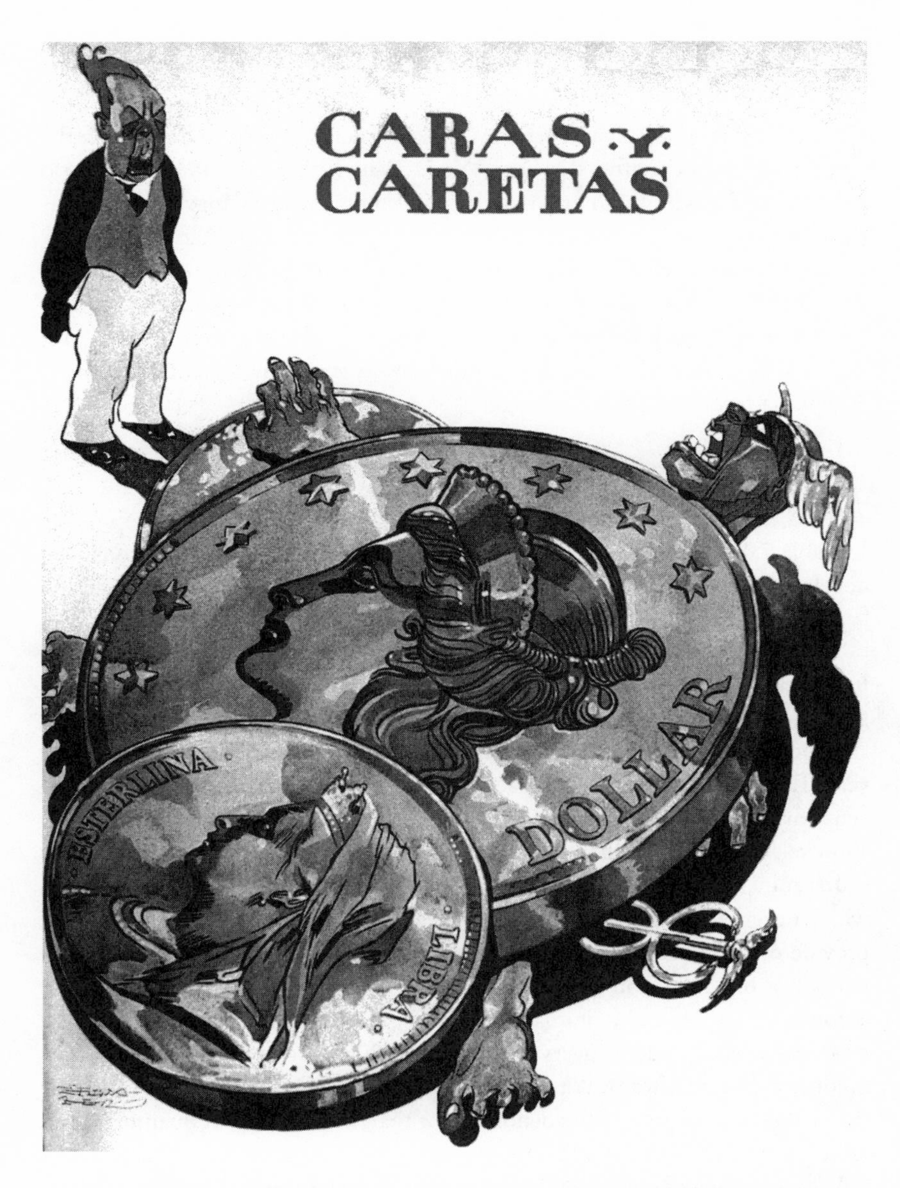

Cartoon 7.1. *Con las manos en los bolsillos. Comercio — ¡Socorro! ¡Socorro! Irigoyen — Espera que venga mi término; despues hablaremos.* (With their hands in their pockets. Business — Help! Help! Irigoyen — Wait until my term comes; then we'll talk.)
Notes: A comment on interwar economic retardation. Ex-President Irigoyen, the man with his hands in his pockets, could not be re-elected so Alvear became the new president, putting Irigoyen on the sidelines. Business is shown being crushed by the dollar and the pound. It is interesting that the dollar is shown as being bigger than the pound.
Source: Caras y caretas, año 23, no. 1181, May 21, 1921.

the emerging relative retardation of the national level of income per capita by global standards.

International political and economic engagements started to dissolve in the autarkic atmosphere after the First World War, with ramifications for world markets, and especially international capital mobility.[13] Savings-scarce countries, like Argentina, whose prior development had been built around a heavy dependence on foreign lending were bound to feel a tightening of capital constraints, unless they could mobilize and allocate domestic supplies of capital to substitute effectively for the rapidly receding supplies of foreign capital. Yet such a realignment of the development process was no simple matter. How did Argentina respond to this challenge?

The Argentine Context

In Table 7.1 we offer some preliminary macroeconomic indicators of financial development and economic growth from 1900 to 1939. Let us examine the broad development indicators in the upper part of the table.

The figures show that the Argentine economy suffered a significant slowdown in economic growth after the First World War. From an average per capita real growth rate of about 3.5 percent per year for the first decade of the century, Argentina only rebounded in the twenties to a growth rate of 1.7 percent per year. The 1915–19 period is characterized by a dismal performance of the real economy, even by international standards, but the depression years 1930–35 show relatively little decline by the same yardstick.[14]

Instrumental in both recessions were dramatic declines in investment activity, which never recovered its level of 1905–1914. Several open economy indicators provide evidence of the increased autarky of the Argentine economy in this period: a big reduction in capital inflows measured by the ratio of current account to output, and a dramatic worsening in the terms of trade. Despite a modest terms of trade recovery in the mid-1920s, exports as a share of output gradually decline after peaking during the later years of the First World War (more due to a collapse in the denominator than a rise in export quantum), and fall even further in the 1930s.

We would like to examine the association, if any, between economic development and measures of financial development. There are two typical proxies for the degree of financial intermediation. First, one can use a ratio of monetary aggregates to output, typically the broad money stock M3 defined as the sum of currency in hands of the public plus demand deposits and interest bearing deposits and liabilities of banks and nonbank intermediaries (denoted DEPTH).

13. Obstfeld and Taylor (1998).
14. Taylor (1992).

Table 7.1. *Finance and Development, 1900–1939*

Period	1900 –04	1905 –09	1910 –14	1915 –19	1920 –24	1925 –29	1930 –34	1935 –39
A. Broad Development Indicators								
Per Capita GDP (1913=100)	76	93	98	83	98	109	99	106
Saving/GDP (%)	7	10	4	10	4	11	6	11
Investment/GDP (%)	9	16	15	7	10	13	9	11
Current Account/GDP (%)	-1	-6	-11	3	-6	-2	-3	0
Terms of Trade (1913=100)	88	103	104	88	64	83	73	95
Exports/GDP (%)	27	27	24	30	24	24	16	17
B. Financial Development Indicators								
DEPTH=M3/GDP (%)	35	38	40	43	49	47	50	41
CREDIT=Loans/GDP (%)	—	27	34	29	37	36	43	29
NETCREDIT=Private Loans/GDP (%)	—	19	24	18	22	21	23	16
Savings Accounts/GDP (%)	—	5	7	10	15	18	21	17
Stock Market Turnover/GDP (%)	26	19	10	6	11	7	7	10
Bank Stocks Price Index (Dec. 1913=100)	70	104	62	73	65	74	46	—
Stock Market Price Index (Dec. 1913=100)	57	77	94	140	107	142	—	—
Relative Price of Bank Stocks	122	135	66	52	61	52	—	—

Notes: GDP is gross domestic product. The terms of trade is the ratio of export to import prices.
Sources: From Appendix 1 except population and stock market turnover from Comité Nacional de Geografía (1941); saving, investment, and current account ratios from Taylor (1998); terms of trade from Di Tella and Zymelman (1967), and post-1914 from IEERAL (1986); export ratio from Balboa (1972); savings accounts from *Revista de Economía Argentina* (February 1938); stock market price index from Nakamura and Zarazaga (1999).

Second, one can use the level of credit activity provided by the banking system as a ratio of output (denoted CREDIT).[15]

The usual caveats concerning the variable DEPTH and the use of M3 as an indicator of financial and capital market depth arise. Any definition of monetary aggregates or banking credit might be a weak indicator of capital markets development if it is the case that a significant percentage of industrial finance occurs outside the financial system.

For alternative domestic channels of investment such as the Buenos Aires Stock Exchange Market we only have fragmentary evidence on its quantitative importance, which we will discuss shortly.[16] Notwithstanding conceptual difficulties, the ratio of M3 to output is the traditional indicator of financial or monetary sophistication of an economy in most of the relevant historical

15. The DEPTH measure follows King and Levine (1993); CREDIT follows De Gregorio and Guidotti (1995). We have constructed, on the basis of a consolidated monetary database, annual and monthly data for a monetary aggregate that resembles M3. We have also collected monthly data on the loan activities of the Argentine banking system for the second definition, relying on the pioneering work of Baiocco (1937).

16. See the work in progress by Nakamura and Zarazaga (1999). However, in their paper they attempt to construct a preliminary index of the prices of stocks in the Buenos Aires Stock Exchange, which we include in the above table, not the size of the market capitalization. This issue, as to exactly how much finance was raised via equity instruments, is a subject for future research.

studies. In different studies, it has been shown that higher per capita incomes in developing economies are associated with higher degrees of monetization and secular declines in money velocity.[17]

The variable CREDIT is perhaps a more accurate indicator of financial development, as it measures the amount of credit effectively intermediated by banks. As banks develop their capacity to create banking money should increase. Related to this indicator, we want to analyze the credit to the private sector net of the loans of the most important official or quasi-public bank, the Banco de la Nación Argentina (BNA). We then use the ratio of non-BNA credit to output as an indicator. Thus, we abstract from a bank that was the financial agent of the government, and this indicator should be effectively related to the level and efficiency of *privately financed* investment (NETCREDIT).

We also include in the lower part of Table 7.1 some other financial variables covering various aspects of bank and nonbank financial activity. We have a measure of the growth of savings accounts relative to output. From the Buenos Aires Bolsa we show an indicator of stock-market turnover volume relative to output, an index of banks' stock prices, and an index of all stock prices. These indices allow us to get a sense of how banking performed relative to the rest of the equity market in price terms, and how the two finance channels, debt and equity, performed in terms of activity.

From our monetary and financial data we can infer that all was not well in the Argentine financial system. The DEPTH measure is certainly misleading. The ratio of M3 to output increased in a sustained fashion from 35 percent at the beginning of the century to reach a high of 50 percent at the onset of the Great Depression. But the optimistic picture changes when we observe the behavior of more detailed statistics of banking credit. Even the DEPTH measure drops back to 41 percent by 1935. However, when financial development is proxied by credit to the economy—and especially by net credit as a proxy of privately created loans for investment—the vitality of the emerging financial system is more questionable.

Total credit did rise appreciably prior to the slump, from a low of 27 percent in 1905 to a high of 43 percent in 1930. But net credit as a fraction of output fell during the First World War, recovered a little in the middle of the 1920s, only to plunge, together with output, during the years of the Great Depression. Thus the widely used M3-to-output ratio depicts a monetizing economy, but one which nonetheless did not deliver financial development in the form of a bank credit expansion to the same degree. By either measure, trough-to-peak gains never amounted to more than increases from 27 to 37 percent (DEPTH) and 18 to 24 percent (NETCREDIT), but even these modest gains were reversed.

17. For the monetary history of the United States and United Kingdom see Friedman and Schwartz (1982); for the monetary history of different European countries see Bordo and Jonung (1987); and for recent experiences see Fry (1985), and King and Levine (1992).

It is not just the credit data that suggest the banking sector had its problems. If banks were the best available technology to channel savings to investments, then their situation as perceived by the market participants did not flourish during the interwar period. From 1913 to 1935, the market value of the industry declined by more than 50 percent as shown by the quotation of an index of bank stock prices. The relative value of banking as an industry had declined dramatically even by 1930, the first year in which the deflationary effects of the Depression were felt domestically. Relative to other stocks, bank stocks had fallen in price by about 60 percent relative to their pre-1914 peak. This decline in market value of banks calls into question whether banks were an effective technology to channel savings to investments in interwar Argentina, an issue that will receive further scrutiny.

As for alternative sources of finance, there was little relief from the equity market either, and stock market turnover suggests a stock market of dwindling importance: turnover relative to output fell by more than half from 1900 to the 1930s. Turnover is not the same as new capitalization, but even so, the data are suggestive of a weak stock market unable to deliver a dynamic and growing source of industrial and commercial finance when such funding was exactly the type needed by the Argentine interwar economy. Further research is surely warranted on the evolution of the *Bolsa* to uncover its workings in this period.[18]

However, to be fair, not all signs were disappointing, and certainly the expansion of savings accounts, in particular, from 5 to 21 percent in 1905–1930, has attracted attention. It was this trend, and the increase in monetization (DEPTH), led Díaz Alejandro to see an "expanding capital market." But more concrete measures of financial development results (in terms of credit delivered and the health of bank stocks) do not seem to justify this rosy view. And most tellingly of all, more savings accounts and more monetization, at the end of the day, could not by themselves deliver large and sustained increases in loan activity, and thus deliver an impact on the private finance of investment via the credit channel, the ultimate benchmark for financial development.

Hence, the standard measures of "financial development"—DEPTH and CREDIT—need to be interpreted with caution in this and other historical contexts. On the face of it increases in these measures of about 15 percentage points (as seen in interwar Argentina) should deliver impressive gains in growth performance. According to cross-section studies of the impact of financial development on growth using contemporary data, such changes would be worth about 0.5 percent per annum in growth performance, via improved mobilization and allocation of capital.[19]

That kind of boost to growth failed to materialize in Argentina. The figures in the upper part of Table 7.1 on saving and investment show the disappointing

18. See Nakamura and Zarazaga (1999).
19. King and Levine (1993); De Gregorio and Guidotti (1995).

bottom line. In the absence of foreign savings during the interwar years, the dwindling current account deficits meant that Argentine had to finance most of domestic investment out of domestic saving. Yet the home financial system could not respond to the challenge.

After 1914 savings rates climbed only modestly, averaging just 8 percent of output; investment rates declined to average about 10 percent of output, much less than the investment rates of 15 to 16 percent seen in 1905–14 and so heavily financed by foreign capital inflows. After 1914 foreign capital only contributed an inflow of about 2 percent of output on average.

Economic retardation was the result of this new capital constraint.[20] The financial system failed in its two core *microeconomic* tasks: it could neither successfully mobilize more capital (quantities did not increase appreciably); nor did the allocation of capital improve in efficiency (indeed bank stock price declines suggest a shift to poorer quality assets over time). The *macroeconomic* results were predictable, but to understand why the domestic system failed we need to understand its own institutional shortcomings, and so why it faced a much harder task than the foreign financial intermediaries it was seeking to replace.

International Perspectives on Financial Development

A key set of motivating questions for this chapter asked how remarkable was interwar financial development in Argentina. Those questions are, at least in part, comparative questions: if we assess Argentine growth relative to that of other countries, so we must also seek international benchmarks for financial development. This is very much the spirit of the modern studies using large cross-sectional databases covering scores of countries. We cannot hope to match this sample size given the availability of historical data before 1945, but, just as we did in the Introduction for income per capita comparisons, we can now compare Argentine experience to a sample of a few well-chosen developed and developing countries in Figure 7.1.[21]

The sample includes Argentina, plus three benchmark rich "core" countries (Britain, the United States, and Germany) and three developing "peripheral" countries (Italy, Portugal, and Spain). As noted earlier, in 1913 Argentina was one of the five or so richest countries in the world and would have been

20. Taylor (1992).
21. The figure shows two measures of financial development, both using M3, the only monetary aggregate available for this purpose. The first measure is the DEPTH measure, the ratio of M3 to output for seven countries from 1913 to 1939. The second measure is *real* M3 per capita, measured in 1928 prices, and converted to U.S. dollars at 1928 parities. Unfortunately, we were unable to obtain currency in the hands of the public for such a broad sample (so as to examine shifts in the use of deposits versus currency). Nor were we able to get measures corresponding to our preferred CREDIT variable, a measure of bank financing in the economy.

Figure 7.1. International Comparisons of Financial Deepening, 1913–39

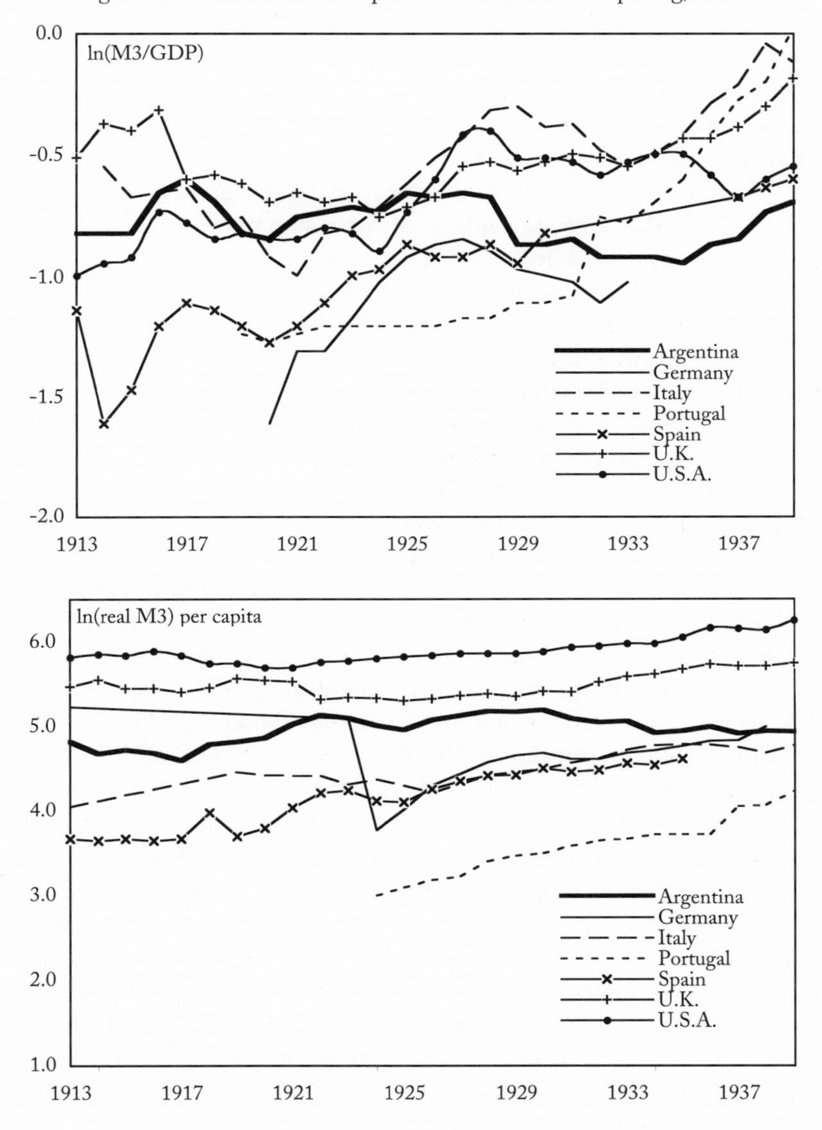

Notes and sources: For Argentina, see Appendix 1. Other countries from Mitchell (1992, 1993) and Bordo (unpublished data).

considered a good candidate for comparison with the first reference group. But by the postwar decades Argentina's position had certainly sunk into the developing-country sample and had fallen well behind the three European peripheral countries included in the second reference group. Can we find evidence of such a reversal of fortunes in this financial data?

The first chart shows that in 1913, Argentina's DEPTH measure was only just behind that of the three core countries, and after the shocks associated with the First World War, Argentina briefly surpassed all countries in the sample on this measures of financial deepening. This success proved short-lived. A brief financial crisis in Argentina in the mid-1920s brought the DEPTH measure down to its initial level. The only core country by then below Argentina was Germany, whose own financial system had been wrecked by chaos and financial repression during the hyperinflation. There was then some stability up to 1929, but other periphery countries saw very rapid increases in DEPTH over the same years, which Argentina could not match. In the 1930s, Argentina faced further financial crises, reducing the DEPTH measure below that of *all* other countries in the sample by the late 1930s, excepting Germany. But Germany was by then an economy with serious problems financial and otherwise—heavily controlled currencies, an increasingly command-type economy, and crowding-out via militarization—all serving to strain the private financial system.

A similar story is told by the evolution of real M3 per capita in the second chart. Again, Argentina started near the top of the financial league table in 1913, and its relative position improved a little by the early 1920s. But after 1920 almost nothing happened to change the Argentine level of real M3 per capita, whereas in *all* other countries, this measure of real financial activity per person was continually increasing, even in the 1930s. The core countries all surpassed Argentina in the level of this variable by the 1930s, and only Portugal and Italy (barely) had a lower level, although they were converging rapidly.

Both of these measures indicate that in terms of financial development Argentina began in 1913 in a very strong position, consistent with its claim to be one of the richest economies in the world. However, this position was continuously eroded in relative terms in the interwar period, such that by the late 1930s, Argentina had experienced virtually no net increase in financial depth. Despite wars and the Great Depression, most other countries posted gains in the same period. It is very telling that Argentine financial development looks good only in comparison with a financial disaster case like Germany.

This sequence of events suggests that we examine the Argentine interwar financial system and economic growth in more detail. Figure 7.2 provides a starting point, and the figures depict time series of output per capita, and two measures of financial development: currency in the hands of the public as a share of output, and banking money as a share of output. According to the established theories of finance and development, the ratio of currency to output

Figure 7.2. Financial Deepening and Economic Performance, 1900–1940

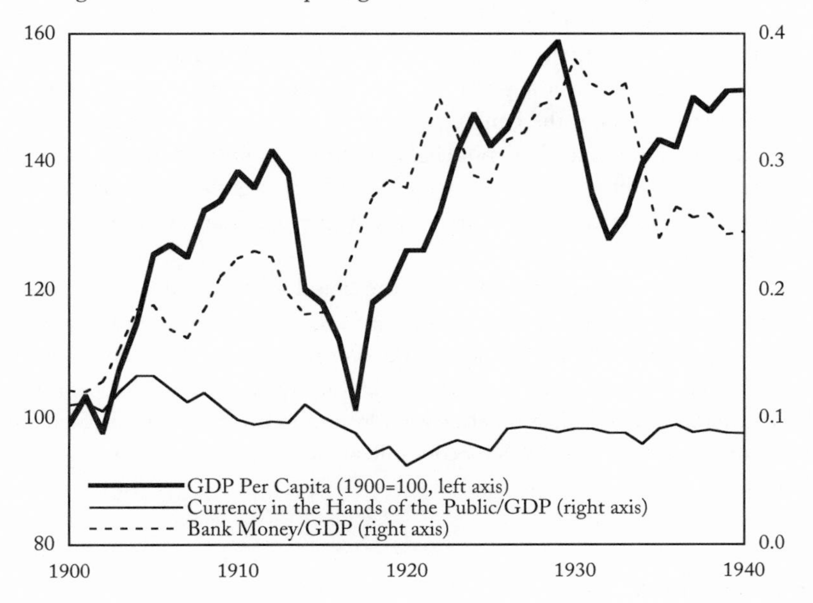

Notes and sources: See Appendix 1.

should remain constant or even fall, and the ratio of banking money to output should rise as development proceeds. Such changes would reflect an increase in sophistication with the public's substitution of assets in the financial system (banking money) for simple cash in hand.[22]

The time path of output per capita shows the two major crises: the First World War and the Great Depression, with the latter *less* severe then the former. There are also minor recessions in 1906–07 (as in the United States) and in 1924–25. These cyclical events, both big and small, can be seen to have parallels in financial activity in the second and third figures. The currency ratio is seen to be declining dramatically from a high of 15 percent to about 6 percent in 1920, albeit with some reversal at the beginning in the 1914 crisis. But thereafter the currency-to-output ratio holds steady and even increases slightly, reaching a level of 9 to 10 percent in the 1930s.

Thus, the substitution of banking system assets for cash seems to grind to a halt in Argentina soon after the First World War. This trend break is also evident in the path of the bank money ratio, which shows volatility around an upward trend before 1920 (almost doubling from 15 to 30 percent). There is then no trend at all from 1920 to 1929 (with a minicollapse in the mid-

22. Townsend (1983).

1920s), and a marked decline in the 1930s (almost falling back to 20 percent, comparable to pre-1914 levels).[23]

In fact, one can argue that there is even evidence of financial retardation or involution after 1920, as the public substitutes back toward currency, and away from financial assets in the banking system. The interwar trends are certainly disturbing, and they may shed more light on the beginnings of Argentina's long-run retardation. However, the macroeconomic data gathered so far can only provide weak evidence of the failure of the Argentine financial system between the wars.

We are still poorly equipped to trace the causal relationship between, on the one hand, the institutional structure of the Argentine economy and its position in a changing international economy, and, on the other hand, internal developments in the financial system and their relationship to economic development. To understand these linkages better we now aim to provide an integrated view of the macroeconomic and microeconomic workings of the interwar Argentine financial system.

Institutional and Economic Fragilities

Without further digression, we must therefore ask what were the institutional and economic impediments to the establishment of a fully fledged and resilient financial system during the interwar period? To understand why Argentina suffered recurrent financial distress it is important to introduce here the concept of intertwined macroeconomic monetary and financial risk for a small, open economy under a fixed exchange-rate regime like the gold standard.

Crucial here is the institutional and historical fact that, until 1935, the Argentine monetary and financial regime operated without a central bank. Until that time, a potential cause of a suboptimal financial structure came from the existence of a different kind of monetary authority, the Conversion Office. The Conversion Office could not act as a Lender of Last Resort of the financial system without threatening its macroeconomic responsibility of defending the external value of the domestic currency.

Macroeconomic Twin-Risk: Exchange-Rate Regime and Financial Structure

The almost simultaneous problems of exchange-rate crises and financial crises were a recurrent problem for Argentina, and this type of "twin crisis" economic

23. We also examined correlations of real output per person and the two financial variables. The correlations are striking: before 1920, the economy appears to be developing as per the standard economic model: real economic growth moves in parallel with the relative expansion of the financial system, and the substitution away from cash. After 1920, these correlations completely break down.

phenomenon is now better understood.[24] The complicated dynamics of a regime that combined a high ratio of inside to outside money (a fractional-reserve financial system) and a fixed exchange-rate regime (the Gold Standard) had become all too apparent by 1914. The "central banker to the world"—the Bank of England—had decided on a course of successive and dramatic increases in its discount rate. The years 1913–14 were thus characterized by a devastating foreign shock to the Argentine economy in general, and to the monetary and financial regime in particular.

In Table 7.2 we show the anatomy of several financial crises to highlight the main channels of transmission to the real economy. We include three important financial crises from our period of study: first, looking back, the 1890–91 Baring Crisis; next, the financial crash of 1913–14; and, last, the 1930–31 downturn. A common characteristic of real financial crises is the fall in bank money, or in the ratio of inside to outside money. This is due to a persistent run on bank deposits, and it is usually associated with a severe loss in output. In 1913–14 we see that, although a major devaluation of the currency was avoided—to avoid a repeat of one major cost of the Baring Crisis—another price was paid instead. The banking industry was devastated. Bank stock prices fell by 38 percent in one year. There was an intense process of capital crunch—the use of capital to pay out depositors when assets fail. Paid-in capital fell by more than one tenth in less than twelve months.

We note also that the destruction in the banking industry in 1913–14, measured by the price of bank stocks, was far worse than the collapse of overall stocks, which declined by a "mere" 6 percent. Suppose that the quotation of bank stocks reflected the expected net present value of the future stream of income of the industry. Then, judging by what happened ex post, one is tempted to say that investors and economic agents had a very accurate perception that the First World War had had a devastating effect on the health of financial and capital markets institutions.

By 1930–31, prices of bank stocks were again at the same level as they had been in 1914, but general stocks were up by 47 percent, and the nominal paid-in-capital stood below the 1913 level. In other words, it seems that financial markets were losing strength at each successive stage of financial distress. Even when a recovery was in place after a shock hit the system, investment in the industry never recovered its previous level.

To show the links between the expected solvency of the banks as determined, simultaneously, by monetary and real factors, we construct a simple econometric model. We perform a time-series regression of bank stock prices on two variables: the level of bankruptcies (a proxy for the distress of borrowers or the state of affairs in the real sector); and current and lagged values of the gold

24. Kaminsky and Reinhart (1999).

Table 7.2. *Anatomy of Three Financial Crises*

	Baring Crisis		World War One		Great Depression	
	1890	1891	1913	1914	1930	1931
A. Real Activity						
Real Output (% Change)		-10.9		-11.0		-3.9
B. Monetary Variables						
Money Supply (% Change, M0)		-25.9		-10.7		-8.3
Money Base (% Change, M3)		6.7		-3.6		1.3
Bank Money (% Change, M3-M0)		—		-17.5		-11.3
International Reserves Backing (%)	21.0	4.0	72.6	66.3	82.1	47.6
Exchange Rate (% Change, Paper-Gold)		45.0		1.7		25.0
Inflation (% Change, WPI)		56.0		1.2		-3.3
C. Banking Variables						
Deposits (% Change)		-47.2		-15.4		-8.6
Banking Fractional Reserves (%)	20.0	27.0	32.4	33.8	11.6	14.9
Money Multiplier (M3/M0)	2.3	1.6	2.1	1.9	3.7	3.3
D. Financial Market Variables						
Ex Post Real Interest Rate (%, Internal)		—		6.5		10.8
Nominal Interest Rates (%)						
High Month	—	10.3	8.1	8.8	7.7	7.9
Low Month	—	—	7.5	7.5	6.4	6.7
Bank Stock Prices (Dec. 1913 = 100)	—	—	100	62	69	64
Stock Price Index (Dec. 1913 = 100)	—	—	100	94	147	—
Paid-In Capital (millions $mn)	—	—	513	449	498	485

Sources: From Appendix 1 except stock price index from Nakamura and Zarazaga (1999).

stock (a control for the domestic money-market situation and also possibly to be interpreted as a proxy for country macrorisk). All variables are in log levels. The results are reported in the upper part of Table 7.3.

The principal inferences to be drawn from the model are twofold. First, an increase in bankruptcies lowers the market value of banks. The long-run elasticity is -0.2, so an increase of 10 percent in bankruptcies lowers the price of bank stocks by 2 percent in the long run. Second, a gold inflow (an improvement in the balance of payments) eases the monetary liquidity of the economy and has a positive impact on the financial intermediation industry. A rise of 10 percent in the stock of gold increases the monthly price of bank stocks by 3.6 percent in the long run.

In this model we see that the solvency of banks is crucially linked to a principal macroeconomic variable: the level of gold stock, mostly consisting of international reserves at the Conversion Office. From the point of view of individual bankers and investors, who set the "price" of banks, this variable, like the bankruptcy level, would be seen as exogenous—hence our choice of specification. The gold stock, in turn, is related to the choice and stability of the level of the exchange rate.

Table 7.3. *Model of Banks with "Twin Risk"*

A. Bank Stock Prices, Bankruptcies, and Macroeconomic Risk	
Dependent Variable	ln Bank Stock Price
Constant	-0.02
	(0.23)
Trend	0.00
	(0.07)
ln Bankruptcies	-0.01
	(2.28)
ln Gold Stock	-0.30
	(2.18)
ln Gold Stock (*t* -1)	0.52
	(2.12)
ln Gold Stock (*t* -2)	-0.20
	(1.42)
ln Bank Stock Price (*t* -1)	0.96
	(47.80)
Long-run elasticities	
ln Bankruptcies	-0.20
ln Gold Stock	0.36
R-squared	0.96
Number of observations	222
SEE	0.03

B. Lending by Type of Bank as a Reaction to Gold Flows and Bank Stock Prices		
Type of Bank	Domestic	Foreign
Dependent Variable	ln Loans	ln Loans
Constant	0.06	-0.08
	(1.31)	(1.34)
Trend	0.00	0.00
	(0.77)	(0.30)
ln Gold Stock	0.03	0.05
	(2.72)	(3.26)
ln Bank Stock Price	0.02	0.03
	(1.93)	(1.60)
ln Loans (*t* -1)	1.05	0.69
	(17.20)	(13.10)
ln Loans (*t* -2)	-0.08	0.27
	(1.41)	(5.28)
Long-run elasticities		
ln Gold Stock	0.70	1.22
ln Bank Stock Price	0.66	0.70
R-squared	1.00	0.99
Number of observations	343	343
SEE	0.02	0.04

Notes and sources: See text and Appendix 1.

The above transmission mechanism distinctly parallels the seminal ideas of Bernanke, who argued that the financial system constituted an additional channel through which monetary crises could cause havoc in the real economy. The above model is fairly simple and describes the first-order effect by which the terms of Argentina's deviation from gold standard rules can have a definite impact on the "pricing" of banks by exacerbating gold outflows. As it stands, we can trace out important independent effects of the real and monetary sectors on the perceived solvency of banks.[25]

Finally, note that we have developed a satisfactory microeconomic model of these channels as they affect bank "pricing." In the next chapter we will return to consider the problems of internal drain and external drain in a more formal macroeconomic model.

Microeconomics of Banking

We might now ask what was the effective cost, in terms of lending, of having a fragile financial regime subject to the risk of twin crises. This is a difficult question to tackle without examining the microeconomic behavior of banks. Thanks to the construction of a new data set based on the monumental work of Baiocco, we can now assess the microeconomic behavior of banks and see how such behavior affected the availability of credit in the economy.[26]

In Figure 7.3 we display the share in the loans in the financial system. We show three types of bank: the Banco de la Nación, the most important official bank; the other domestic banks, such as the Banco Frances del Rio de la Plata, Nuevo Banco Italiano, Banco Español; and the foreign banks. One striking feature of the data is that from 1910 until 1930, domestic banks' share in total loans declined from almost 50 percent to less than 35 percent. Foreign banks could hardly maintain a share of 20 percent in the same period. The Banco de la Nación's share jumped from 28 to 45 percent. In short, it appeared that the private sector was losing ground in the capital market to the state bank.

In Figure 7.4, the evolution of paid-in capital of banks is reported. It is interesting to note the dramatic "capital crunches" suffered by domestic banks during financial crises or distress. In the 1914 crisis, the domestic banks lost almost half their capital; in the short-lived drain of 1922–23 they lost 25 percent; and in 1934, as we said previously, their capital was almost the same as in 1913. How did these shocks to bank capital affect intermediation? In a virtually unregulated banking environment, the bankers could optimize their

25. See Bernanke (1983). A second-order effect of an expected depreciation of the currency via the behavior of depositors (investors) in a fractional reserve banking system also deserves comment here. But our data preclude a detailed econometric analysis of this effect, usually referred to as twin exchange-rate and financial crises. In the case of a discrete devaluation this is the well-known *peso problem*.

26. Baiocco (1937).

Figure 7.3. Loans by Bank Type, 1910–35

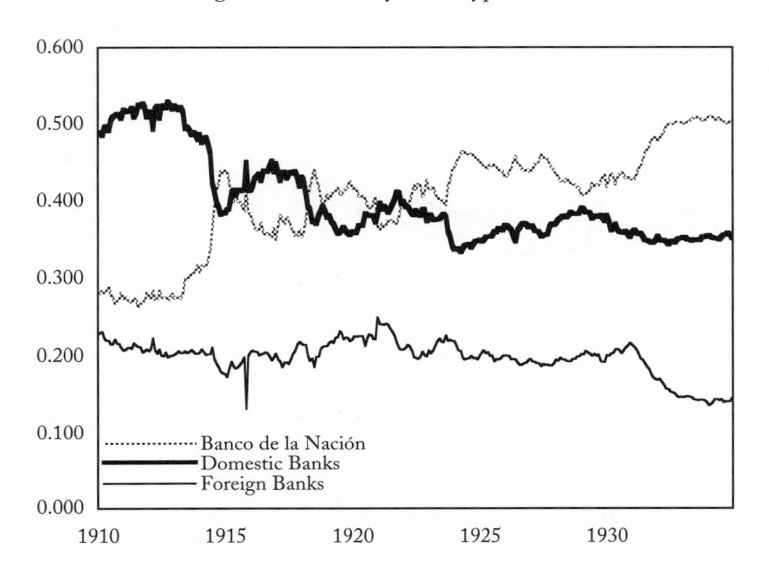

Notes and sources: Units are shares of total loans. See Appendix 1.

asset holdings and portfolios, so we think of leverage, the ratio of risky loans to paid-in-capital, as being the most important choice variable in the industry.

In Figure 7.5, we observe that, excluding the Banco de la Nación, domestic banks had a leverage ratio much lower than the leverage of foreign-owned banks. We believe that differences in capital constraints and in attitudes toward the tolerated riskiness of assets might explain the micro differences in lending. Foreign-owned banks could choose a higher loan-to-capital ratio for two reasons. First, foreign banks could rely more on their international headquarters to avert and overcome financial crises, unlike domestic banks that had no Lender of Last Resort until the central bank appeared in 1935. Second, foreign banks were lending to "safer" assets, giving them a mix of risk and returns that allowed them to carry a higher leverage, since they specialized in trade financing where exchange-rate risk, self-liquidating characteristics, and collateral risk are all well-hedged.

Our interpretation of the differences in observed leverages across banks of different type follows that of the official line as presented in the official banking census of 1925.[27] In the census, the disparity between the loan-capital ratios is *not* attributed to systematic differences in fractional banking reserves. For example, in December 1925, foreign banks maintained a loan-capital ratio of

27. República Argentina (1926).

Figure 7.4. Capital by Bank Type, 1910–35

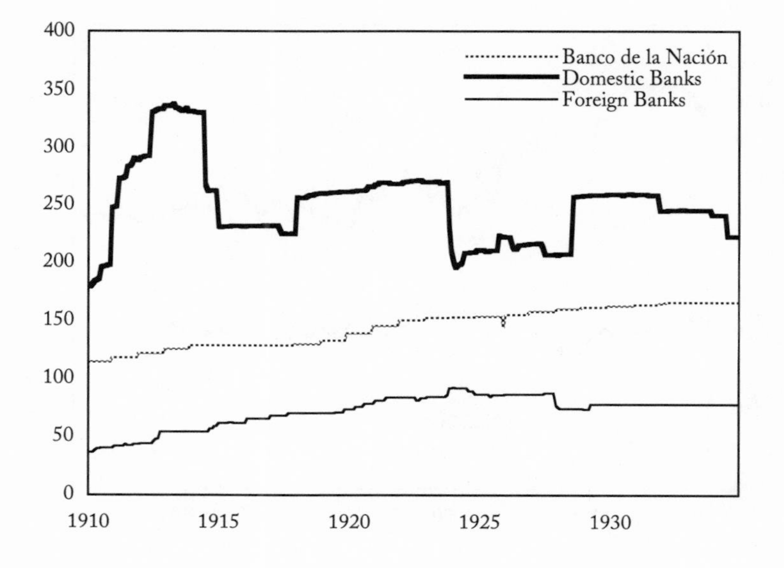

Notes and sources: Units are millions of paper pesos. See Appendix 1.

6.3 while having a reserve-deposit ratio of 29 percent; domestic banks had a loan-capital ratio of 5.3 and a reserve-deposit ratio of 21 percent.

All the same, this observation is still fully consistent with domestic banks having greater portfolio risk than foreign banks.[28] Domestic banks had to hold more capital because they were longer in riskier and more illiquid assets; foreign banks had high liquidity but more lending intermediation too. How can this be reconciled? First, not surprisingly a large share of funding comes through deposits, and deposit-capital ratios, as a first approximation, explain the observed differences in loan-capital ratios. However, on top of this, domestic banks relied exclusively on capital, reserves, and deposits to effect lending; foreign banks could rely on profits generated internationally and, especially, on easy access to open letters of credit from international correspondent banks. In other words, foreign banks could leverage more easily by using international credit and diversification.

The evidence suggests that only foreign-banks could have a net-indebtedness position vis-á-vis correspondents in the rest of the world. That is they could channel resources from abroad but only for investing in very safe and short-term assets. For example, long-term loans and mortgage loans represented 16 percent of assets in domestic banks, but only 4 percent in foreign banks. Conversely,

28. See the model of Calomiris (1993).

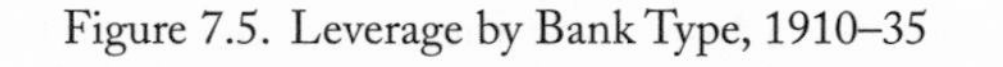

Figure 7.5. Leverage by Bank Type, 1910–35

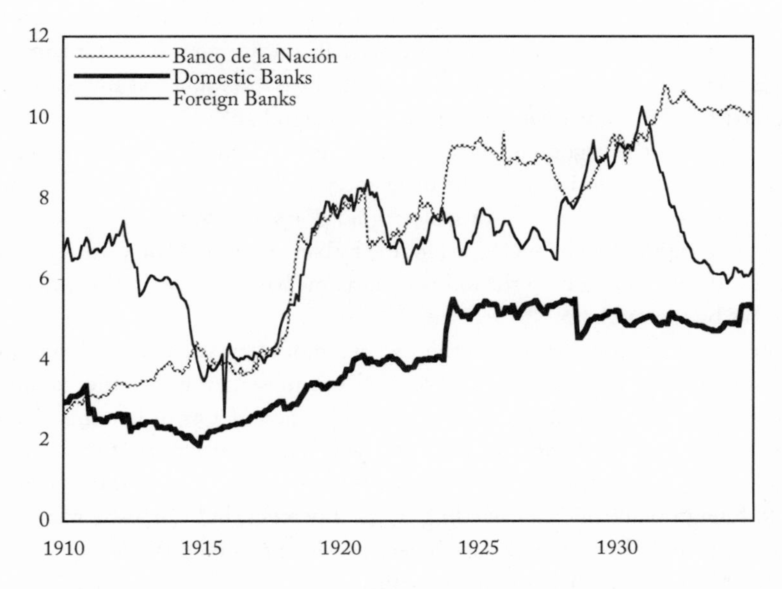

Notes and sources: Leverage shown is loan-to-capital ratio. See Appendix 1.

short-term loans accounted for 22 percent in domestic banks versus 45 percent in foreign banks.[29]

The second important behavioral consideration is that changes in leverage are more important as a response to changing business cycle conditions in the case of foreign banks. This is apparent from the data presented in figures 7.4 and 7.5, where we can see that when financial crises or exchange rate crises arise, severe capital crunches occur in domestic banks but no severe curtailment of paid-in capital occurs in the other banks. Therefore, it was principally the domestic banks, who were more prone to long-term lending, that were exposed to capital crunches.

We argue that this was because they could not rely on international diversification to smooth out financial runs or crises. Under stressful conditions, domestic banks might have been forced to call back loans, but a total transformation of assets to pay back short-term debt was, in general, neither sufficient nor feasible: therefore, capital was squeezed out. In contrast, foreign banks

29. República Argentina (1926, p. 39). In the census it is shown that foreign-owned banks typically had a net debtor position, that is they were recipients of financial capital from correspondent banks abroad which was applied to trade lines. Domestic banks and the Banco de la Nación had a net creditor position vis-à-vis such *corresponsales en el exterior*. For 1925, the net debtor position for foreign banks was equivalent to 60 percent of total paid-in-capital of those banks (República Argentina 1926, pp. 26–27 and 44).

could immediately call up loans, and they could decide not to open up new letters of credit. In the former case, idiosyncratic risks could not be by-passed by domestic banks and the adjustment mechanism during a downturn in the business cycle was a capital crunch. In the latter case, lending was immediately curtailed to effect adjustment in the case of foreign banks.

To reinforce the argument, in the lower part of Table 7.3 we use another econometric model to illustrate the differences in lending behavior. Loans are taken to be a function of two variables: gold flows, to show how inflows and outflows of capital are channeled to lending by bank type; and bank stock prices, to assess the performance of the industry and how bankers react to the "pricing" of banks by the market.

The results are consistent with theory: in a monetary, small, open economy, gold inflows and increases in the expected net present value of the banking industry should be conducive to an increase in the amount of lending. Note also the long-run elasticities of lending by type of bank with respect to the level of gold stock of the economy: if there is an increase of 10 percent in the gold stock, foreign banks increase lending by 12.2 percent, but domestic banks by only 7 percent. Foreign banks seem very sensitive to liquidity considerations and to changes in the balance of payments.[30]

To display these effects more clearly, Figure 7.6 displays impulse-response functions for the two types of banks based on the dynamic equations estimated in Table 7.3. It is apparent that full adjustment by the banks takes a number of years. Even after 36 months, a 10 percent decline in gold stocks translates into only a 5.4 percent (8.2 percent) fall in loans for domestic (respectively, foreign) banks, whereas the long-run adjustment would be 10 percent (12.2 percent). Evidently, banks could not adjust their loan portfolios overnight, so external shocks had long-lasting effects, as banks continued to adjust their lending activity over several years.

We have thus found structural differences in lending behavior as a response to macroeconomic and microeconomic events in different types of banks, domestic and foreign. This is an extremely important result, one that has not been identified in previous studies of banking in emerging markets in a historical perspective, nor in contemporary studies.

The Interwar Financial System: Success or Failure?

Much of the existing literature on Argentine financial development offers a somewhat optimistic view of the interwar period. We disagree with this interpretation. Marshaling new evidence both for Argentina in time series, and relative to other countries in cross section, we see weakness in the financial

30. There are no significant differences in relation to the elasticity of loans to changes in the bank stock prices but it is worth noting that the elasticity is again very high.

Figure 7.6. Response of Bank Loans to a Shock to Gold Stock

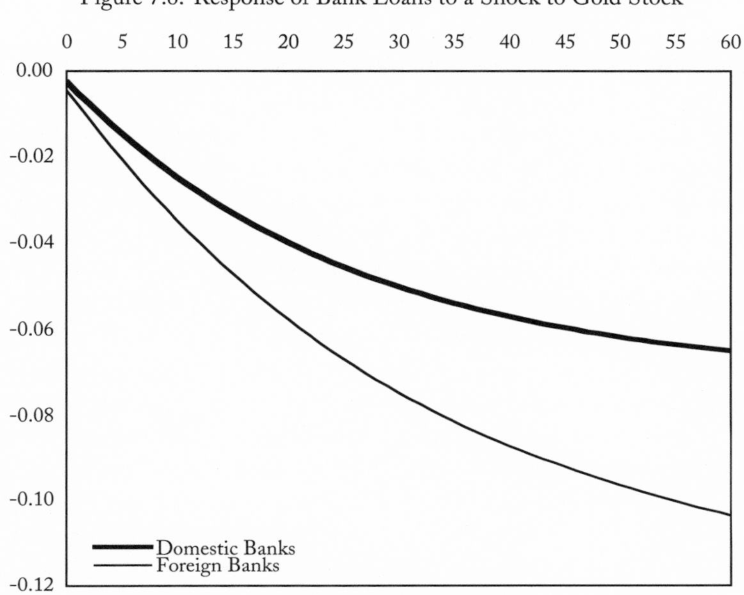

Notes and sources: See text. Horizontal axis shows time in months; vertical axis ln(loans).

system between the wars. According to this new view, we have reason to suspect the financial system as one cause of Argentina's relative retardation after 1914. Moreover, our work pinpoints two important institutional features of the interwar financial system.

First, we highlighted the macroeconomic "twin risk": under a fixed exchange-rate regime, without a Lender of Last Resort, the fractional-reserve financial system was prone to systemic risks triggered by external shocks via gold flows. Second, we examined the micro behavior of banks in that setting, and we found significant differences between domestic and foreign banks. Adverse external shocks damaged the value of all banks, but elicited a larger and swifter adjustment of lending by foreign banks. However, in terms of capital adjustment, only the domestic banks suffered "capital crunches."

The two types of banks differed in asset risks, type of lending, and they served different niches after 1914. Foreign banks narrowed their lending activities to specialize in liquid short-term commercial loans, leaving domestic banks to supply longer-term loans up in firms and real estate. They also crucially differed in terms of exposure to risk. *Ceteris paribus,* a foreign bank was less likely to fail. First, it could pool risk via international diversification: in a time of crisis foreign banks could call on overseas partners for liquidity; for example, a bank's London headquarters. Second, it could avoid systemic risk by its link to a monetary authority that acted as a lender of last resort. If the crisis was very severe then central banks would intervene—for example, the London headquarters of the bank would enlist the support of the Bank of England, as indeed happened during the 1890 Baring Crisis.

Given these considerations, Argentine domestic banks were forced to choose a lower leverage: they had to maintain a higher capital cushion. Hence a barrier to economic growth would emerge as a result of the arrested development of the financial system. Or, put another way, Argentina paid a price for the disintegration of world capital markets that went beyond just the loss of foreign capital inflows. The domestic financial also faced a loss of intermediation services when it became more risky as a result of isolation from global diversification and risk pooling. Domestic banks could not fill the void left by the retreat of foreign capital after 1914; lower leverage meant that they could not mobilize finance to the same extent and thus could not facilitate so easily the accumulation and allocation of capital in this emerging economy.

8

Bailing Out: Internal versus External Convertibility

In the previous chapter we discussed the evolution of the Argentine financial system before and after the First World War. The various diagnostic tests that we performed suggested the system was in relatively poor shape throughout the interwar period, but it is the aim of this chapter to point out the critical juncture at which the collapse of the system seemed perilously close. To understand this turn of events, we rely on the often overlooked distinction between external and internal convertibility.

From 1914 until 1927, Argentina's currency was inconvertible; the window of the Conversion Office was, so to speak, closed. Thus, the national gold stock was safe, and no external drain (a conversion of notes to specie) could take place. Ipso facto, there could therefore be no conversion of deposits to specie either, so that an internal drain was temporarily ruled out by the inconvertible currency.

A key question for Argentine policymakers as they contemplated rejoining the gold standard in the late 1920s—although it is anyone's guess as to whether they considered this possibility—was whether this stable state of affairs would still prevail if convertibility were resumed. That is, if some adverse shocks hit the macroeconomy or the banking sector, or both, could the system be subject to a "meltdown" scenario, with a run on both the banks and the currency board itself? To address this question, we must examine whether the banking system maintained the same sound inside-money practices that enabled the prewar convertibility regime to function so well.

With the wisdom of hindsight, we employ a simple model and econometric test to show that unsound practices led to an unstable outcome in 1927–29. Our finding helps account for the fleeting two-year convertibility period 1927–29 and the sudden demise of the interwar gold standard in Argentina. Since this kind of experience was not unique to Argentina, the approach also has wider ramifications for other currency and banking crises under fixed exchange rates, both in the Great Depression and in recent years.

Crises—Internal and External

In the wake of recent developing-country macroeconomic-financial crises, one of the more pressing questions confronting researchers and policymakers has been to discover what kind of money and banking regime might be optimal for a small open economy.[1] The problem is of course acute in the context of a fixed exchange-rate regime, a system usually motivated by a desire to dampen external price volatility or discipline domestic monetary and fiscal policy in the wake of hyperinflationary experience. Such regimes can take a variety of forms, such as a discretionary central bank adhering to a peg or a more rigid institution such as a currency board with hard rules designed to "tie the hands." Whatever the form, the key dilemma of the money-banking nexus is never far away: how can goals of external convertibility (a fixed exchange rate) and internal convertibility (a working fractional-reserve banking system) be simultaneously met?

As is well known, problems in both macroeconomic and financial areas can strike together, the so-called "twin crises," and the exact causal relationship between the two remains an area for research.[2] Recent events powerfully demonstrated this type of dynamic in an era of globalization, and the combination of pegged rates and weak banking systems is now seen as a major cause of the Asian crises of 1997–98. However, noting the contrast to the fragile exchange-rate regimes that just collapsed, some observers now advocate one type of institutional innovation that seemed to weather all of the recent storms. The Hong Kong Currency Board and the Argentine Convertibility Plan apparently coped well with a dismal international financial situation and are under study as possible models for more robust designs in other countries. Can these schemes be a basis for a monetary and financial design that will function well in this kind of global economic environment? We think a combination of theory and history can provide some answers.

From a historical perspective we note that the late-nineteenth and early-twentieth century experience of the periphery has much in common with the current situation. Emerging markets on the periphery were joining the ever-expanding markets of the core, there was widespread use of a fixed exchange-rate system, and fledgling banking systems were learning how to function in this new environment. In our study of Argentine history we find that the present types of problems have earlier ancestors in the turbulent interwar economy.

1. In the Asian crises of 1997–98 considerable difficulty was caused by a weak financial sector in general, and, specifically, the large number of insolvent banks that had been propped up for many years in an environment of lax regulation and supervision. At the time of crisis, the size of bad assets in the financial sector threatened either to destroy the entire superstructure for intermediation, or else require substantial subsidies to cover the large gaps between true assets and liabilities. In countries like Korea and Indonesia, a very large clean up of the banking sector was precipitated, requiring considerable real resources. For a discussion of the recent crises and the relationship between banking sector weaknesses and macroeconomic crisis, see Eichengreen (1999), Roubini (n.d.b), and World Bank (1999).
2. Kaminsky and Reinhart (1999).

More important, we find that the Argentine institutional structure in money and banking changed considerably in the first decades of the twentieth century, as did its vulnerability.

If we are to analyze this historical episode from a theoretical perspective, we need to turn to a set of models that integrate banking and financial crises into models of currency crisis. However, the so-called first- and second-generation models of currency crisis finessed the distinction between inside and outside money and the banking sector was excluded from the analysis.[3] More recently, and motivated in part by the contours of recent crises, scholars have turned their attention to the problem of twin crises—that is, the internal and external convertibility problem. This embryonic literature draws on ideas found in some vintage papers in the literature, notably the work of Díaz Alejandro, but the theoretical base is still being developed with close attention to how we can best match the empirical regularities.[4] In that spirit, we draw on an older and somewhat neglected model of the money-banking nexus by Dornbusch and Frenkel, an approach they applied to an even more distant historical situation.[5]

The Dornbusch-Frenkel theory was developed to illustrate the short-run dynamics of the gold standard regime and the operations of the Bank of England in the crisis of 1847. This elegant model addressed the actions of two quasi-independent parts of the Bank: the Issue Department and the Banking Department. The former was concerned with outside money, the paper note issue and its gold backing; the latter dealt with inside money, and engaged in normal commercial banking operations, yet it also had a special role as the banker to the state, being responsible for handling government debt. The model traces the dynamics of gold backing for the currency (subject to *external drain*) and the backing of banking deposits by reserves (subject to *internal drain*).

This approach is notable for its multiple equilibrium possibilities. There can be a stable "good equilibrium" with high reserve ratios and a high gold stock in a strong banking environment where neither internal nor external drain threaten the system. There can also be an unstable "bad equilibrium" with low reserve ratios and a tendency to banking collapse with full internal—and possibly some external—drain. In the former equilibrium, confidence in the bank runs high, and an interest-rate defense is feasible, but in the latter case confidence is so low that an interest-rate defense is self-defeating and the drain only increases.

3. In early currency-crisis models a fixed exchange rate collapsed when money printing was used to finance a fiscal gap (Krugman 1979). In later models, self-fulfilling crises were also shown to be possible, where external markets punish a good borrower and the withdrawal of capital leads to collapse (Obstfeld 1994; 1996).
4. Díaz Alejandro (1985b). For a survey of the issues see Eichengreen (1998). Theoretical work includes papers by Velasco (1987) and Calvo (1996; 1998). A key empirical contribution is the paper by Kaminsky and Reinhart (1999).
5. Dornbusch and Frenkel (1984). In a recent important contribution, Miller (1996) refines and expands the Dornbusch-Frenkel model, incorporating a Krugman-style approach to a speculative attack and incorporating forward-looking expectations.

We think the applicability of this model to the Argentine situation in the years 1900–1935 is clear: the currency board, the Conversion Office, was the analog of the Issue Department, and the quasi-state bank, the Banco de la Nación Argentina (BNA), functioned just like the Banking Department. The two were linked to the same public-sector balance sheet in the sense that they were both government agencies and, in practice, the Conversion Office was eventually called on to make rediscounts to the state bank to keep it afloat. That is, the state bank (and possibly some of the big private banks) received ex post—and quite possibly expected ex ante—implicit state guarantees via a de facto banking insurance provision.

What are the implications of our analysis? At one level, there are general implications for the study of the interwar period and the demise of the gold standard. We know a great deal about outside money in this era: much has been written about monetary authorities, the impact of the trilemma, and political-economy issues. Yet we know much less about inside money: the role of the financial sector as a possible source of regime inconsistency is less understood. If the lessons of the Argentine experience can be applied to other countries' histories then we might get a better sense of the conflicts between money and banking regimes in the 1920s and 1930s, and a clearer view of the slender tightrope on which policymakers were poised. This could yield a more nuanced explanation of what many see as a still largely unanswered puzzle: why the gold standard, a system that had functioned so well before 1914, was suddenly "unsafe for use" in the 1920s. [6]

At a narrower level, our work has direct implications for the institutional design of money and banking regimes. Suppose a fixed exchange-rate, or *external convertible,* regime is credible. Our paper suggests that commercial banks can be in a permanently sustainable situation *for sure* only if they specialize in administering the means of payment of the economy—that is, if they become *narrow banks.* Such specialization would leave riskier banking activity to other *uninsured* institutions such as investment houses and merchant banks (Fama 1985). This might be the only design in which one can attain the goals of *both* external and internal convertibility *even under a very bad state of nature.*

Simply put, under the traditional design of a gold-exchange standard (or currency board) and a banking regime you can only "price" outside money—but not banking deposits, the main component of inside money. In the event of a crisis of confidence, such as a Diamond-Dybvig run on deposits, the system might end up being governed by the dynamics of a bad (unstable) equilibrium from which there is no escape.[7] Such dynamics would destroy internal and

6. Some references works on the interwar period and its long-run context are Eichengreen and Sachs (1985); Eichengreen (1992a; 1992b; 1996); Temin (1989). The quoted phrase is Temin's.
7. Diamond and Dybvig (1983).

external convertibility alike, taking down the institutions of both—the currency board and the banks—with it.

To sum up, having a strong and credible currency board may be no defense against a crisis if the banking sector is rotten and a nasty shock occurs. This sentiment has been often expressed in policymaking circles in the wake of the recent crises, especially by those who reject the idea of currency boards as a universal panacea.[8] Still researchers seek more empirical support for the argument, and, given that the debate rages on, we think there is value in having explored the problem here with a more formal, theoretical, and empirical treatment.

The Argentine Banking Environment and Its Evolution

As we noted in earlier chapters, after the catastrophic crisis in 1890–91 the government took great care in designing a new regime to replace the fragile decentralized system of the past. It was hoped that a new money and banking regime would usher in an era of stability sufficient to permit Argentina to rejoin the gold standard. Two institutions were central to the plan. The first was the currency board: for the first time the state centralized the power to issue money within the new Conversion Office. The second was the newly reformed state bank: The Banco Nacional was liquidated during the Baring financial crisis in 1891 and was refounded as the Banco de la Nación Argentina in 1891. The two institutions were kept at arm's length so as to effectively isolate two functions. External convertibility was to be the sole task of the conversion office. Internal convertibility was the domain of the Banco de la Nación and the private financial system.

The new state bank had multiple roles as the financial agent of the state, a development bank, and as one of the biggest commercial banks. Could it handle all these tasks safely? A new charter was put in place governing bank reserves at the Banco de la Nación so as to limit its rediscounting capacity. Despite being seemingly "too big to fail," and clearly susceptible to the moral hazard risks that attach to any banking institution with implicit state guarantees, the Banco de la Nación maintained an admirably clean balance sheet in the period of recovery and smooth economic growth from 1892 to 1913 (Table 8.1). As a fraction of overall banking activity, its use of rediscounts was small even after a relaxation of banking laws in 1904; nonperforming loans were few; leverage was not excessive and there appeared to be adequate capital on the balance sheet (Figure 8.1). The reserve-deposit ratios stayed very high, well over 50 percent in most years before the war (Figure 8.2).

8. For a discussion of recent issues in banking structure to prevent crises, see, for example, the "Economics Focus" discussion of narrow banks and subordinated debt ideas ("Better than Basle," *The Economist*, June 19, 1999). On the role of currency boards as incomplete insurance against crisis, see, for example Gavin and Hausmann (1998) and Feldstein (1999). For a more trenchant critique of currency boards see Roubini (n.d.a).

Table 8.1. *Banco de la Nación, Balance Sheet Items, 1892–1934*

	Loans							Liabilities		Ratios		
	Total	Redisc	To	Non-	Banking Reserves			Cap-	Dep-	Redisc.	Non-Perf.	Capital
Year			Govt.	Perf.	Total	Gold	Paper	ital	osits	to Loans	to Loans	to Loans
1892	33	0	—	0	22	1	21	50	37	0.00	0.01	1.52
1893	46	0	—	1	52	5	47	50	57	0.00	0.01	1.09
1894	51	0	—	1	49	1	47	50	57	0.00	0.02	0.98
1895	56	0	—	1	46	2	44	50	58	0.00	0.02	0.89
1896	68	0	—	1	39	2	37	50	58	0.00	0.01	0.74
1897	72	0	—	1	40	3	37	50	59	0.00	0.02	0.69
1898	74	0	—	1	48	3	45	50	67	0.00	0.01	0.68
1899	81	0	—	1	45	3	43	50	72	0.00	0.01	0.62
1900	87	0	—	1	63	18	44	50	77	0.00	0.02	0.57
1901	88	0	—	2	68	25	43	50	78	0.00	0.02	0.57
1902	80	0	—	2	62	19	43	50	80	0.00	0.03	0.63
1903	78	0	—	2	99	34	66	50	111	0.00	0.02	0.64
1904	98	0	—	1	97	49	47	50	124	0.00	0.01	0.51
1905	166	1	—	1	77	26	51	52	152	0.01	0.00	0.31
1906	178	3	—	1	74	21	52	54	144	0.02	0.00	0.30
1907	222	1	—	1	97	42	55	107	173	0.00	0.01	0.48
1908	254	3	—	2	119	52	68	110	246	0.01	0.01	0.43
1909	302	3	—	2	182	79	103	113	347	0.01	0.01	0.38
1910	367	4	—	3	177	83	94	117	391	0.01	0.01	0.32
1911	415	6	—	5	217	77	139	121	413	0.01	0.01	0.29
1912	433	9	—	9	253	86	168	125	478	0.02	0.02	0.29
1913	496	8	—	14	259	73	186	128	541	0.02	0.03	0.26
1914	541	43	—	41	386	65	321	128	605	0.08	0.08	0.24
1915	504	13	—	57	386	23	362	128	692	0.03	0.11	0.25
1916	503	16	—	59	401	34	367	128	756	0.03	0.12	0.25
1917	583	7	72	47	380	84	296	129	871	0.01	0.08	0.22
1918	905	5	411	32	398	82	315	132	1,195	0.01	0.04	0.15
1919	1,064	32	361	24	357	89	268	139	1,250	0.03	0.02	0.13
1920	1,162	29	338	18	462	56	406	145	1,412	0.03	0.02	0.12
1921	1,074	38	148	20	463	53	410	150	1,310	0.04	0.02	0.14
1922	1,225	13	151	35	392	53	340	152	1,396	0.01	0.03	0.12
1923	1,369	107	153	49	326	29	296	152	1,479	0.08	0.04	0.11
1924	1,436	122	154	45	283	19	264	153	1,503	0.08	0.03	0.11
1925	1,386	123	85	36	333	35	298	144	1,499	0.09	0.03	0.10
1926	1,398	147	87	73	355	35	320	157	1,533	0.11	0.05	0.11
1927	1,330	106	76	75	482	161	321	158	1,621	0.08	0.06	0.12
1928	1,336	92	70	99	596	318	278	161	1,749	0.07	0.07	0.12
1929	1,557	156	71	92	262	68	193	162	1,665	0.10	0.06	0.10
1930	1,573	152	67	99	228	3	225	163	1,657	0.10	0.06	0.10
1931	1,724	285	94	117	246	2	243	164	1,457	0.17	0.07	0.10
1932	1,687	316	95	158	261	2	259	165	1,498	0.19	0.09	0.10
1933	1,686	293	336	183	256	2	254	165	1,578	0.17	0.11	0.10
1934	1,669	295	349	182	189	0	189	165	1,565	0.18	0.11	0.10

Notes: Units are millions of paper pesos, except ratios. Data are end-of-year. Gold pesos are converted at market rates before 1899 and at parity of 2.27 after 1899. Before 1905, capital is book value.

Sources: Appendix 1 and balance sheets of Banco de la Nación.

Figure 8.1. Banco de la Nación Balance Sheet, 1892–1934

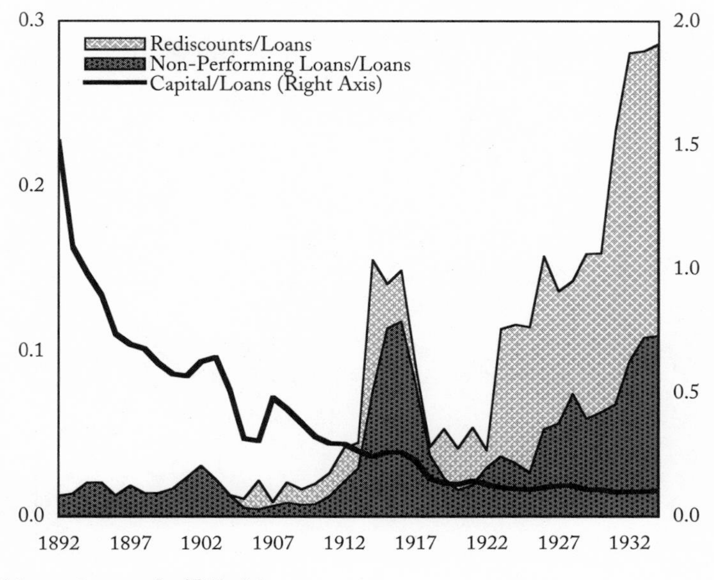

Notes and sources: See Table 8.1.

The system worked well, and a clean separation of the two functions was maintained until the crisis of 1913–14 when an emergency rediscount law was enacted. The dimension of the crisis cannot be overstated: this was by far the biggest recession in Argentine history, and the cumulative loss of output during the trough exceeded such losses in the Baring Crisis and the Great Depression. Real activity slumped and the financial sector consequences were dramatic. Private banks came under pressure as depositors withdrew cash. Curiously, exactly the opposite was happening at the Banco de la Nación, where reserve-deposit ratios climbed (Table 8.2). Clearly, the public perceived the state bank as a "safe haven" for their deposits, perhaps because of its implicit guarantees. With reserve ratios falling to 14 percent in the private banks, the emergency law permitted some relief as the Banco de la Nación began rediscounts to the private banks to supply them with much-needed cash.

The implications of this new economic environment for the state bank's balance sheet after 1914 were dire. Rediscounting surged as a fraction of all banking activity, nonperforming loans started to corrupt the balance sheet in a big way, and the capitalization level of the bank was gradually sinking. We can estimate how much of a difference the rediscount activity made to bank balance sheets by considering a counterfactual experiment. Suppose the Banco de la Nación had not used the emergency powers; then one can recalculate the balance sheets of the Banco de la Nación and the private banks absent the asset

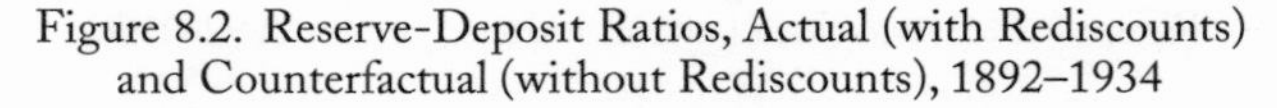
Figure 8.2. Reserve-Deposit Ratios, Actual (with Rediscounts) and Counterfactual (without Rediscounts), 1892–1934

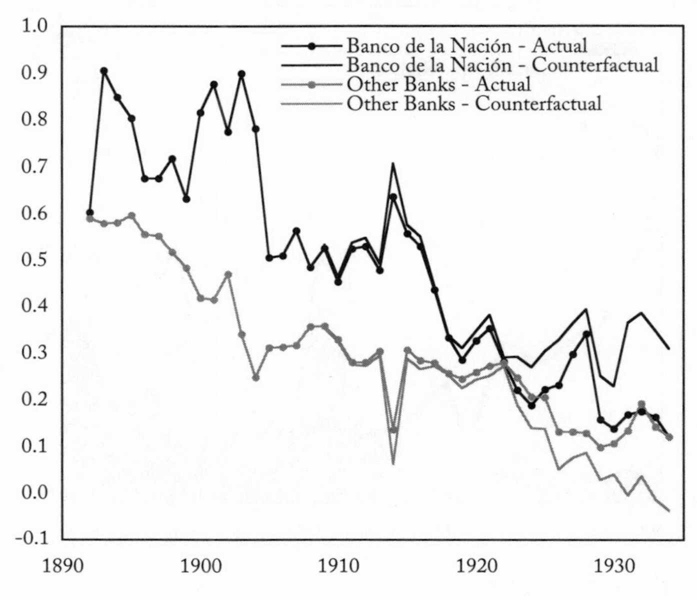

Notes and sources: See Table 8.1.

swap; that is, with cash reserves equal to the rediscounts added to the Banco de la Nación's portfolio, and with the same cash subtracted from the private banks' portfolios.

The impacts are striking when seen in Figure 8.2. For example, in the 1913–14 crisis, absent the rediscount provision, the private banks would have seen their reserve-deposit ratio fall under 10 percent, and dangerously close to total illiquidity at zero. The calamitous situation did abate as the Argentine economy recovered after 1914, but further deterioration in balance sheets came about in the 1920s. Even with rediscounts, private banks saw reserve ratios slide from around 25 percent in 1920 to about 10 percent in 1930. The counterfactual calculation hints at the shocking implication that, without the actions of the Banco de la Nación, the private banks would have failed under a total collapse of liquidity in the early 1930s. Clearly, the rediscount law as it applied to the Banco de la Nación helped a wounded banking system limp along for many years in the interwar period.

Such weaknesses had been exposed during the financial crisis of the late 1880s when a loss of confidence in the banks prompted a massive currency substitution by the public. Still, legislators and policymakers took a seemingly relaxed view even after this chilling experience. Admittedly, note issue had been

Table 8.2. *Selected Banking Ratios, 1892–1934*

	Banking Reserves to Deposits		Banco de la Nación Share of	
	Banco de la Nación	Other Banks	Total Loans	Total Deposits
1892	0.60	0.59	—	0.18
1893	0.91	0.58	—	0.23
1894	0.85	0.58	—	0.22
1895	0.80	0.60	—	0.21
1896	0.68	0.56	—	0.20
1897	0.68	0.55	—	0.20
1898	0.72	0.52	—	0.22
1899	0.63	0.48	—	0.21
1900	0.82	0.42	—	0.20
1901	0.88	0.42	—	0.21
1902	0.78	0.47	—	0.20
1903	0.90	0.34	—	0.23
1904	0.78	0.25	—	0.22
1905	0.51	0.31	—	0.22
1906	0.51	0.31	—	0.20
1907	0.56	0.32	—	0.23
1908	0.49	0.36	0.30	0.28
1909	0.53	0.36	0.29	0.30
1910	0.45	0.33	0.28	0.29
1911	0.52	0.28	0.28	0.30
1912	0.53	0.28	0.28	0.32
1913	0.48	0.30	0.32	0.38
1914	0.64	0.14	0.44	0.51
1915	0.56	0.31	0.39	0.49
1916	0.53	0.28	0.36	0.47
1917	0.44	0.28	0.36	0.46
1918	0.33	0.26	0.40	0.45
1919	0.29	0.25	0.43	0.44
1920	0.33	0.26	0.41	0.43
1921	0.35	0.27	0.40	0.41
1922	0.28	0.28	0.43	0.42
1923	0.22	0.25	0.44	0.45
1924	0.19	0.21	0.46	0.45
1925	0.22	0.20	0.44	0.45
1926	0.23	0.13	0.43	0.45
1927	0.30	0.13	0.42	0.46
1928	0.34	0.13	0.39	0.44
1929	0.16	0.10	0.42	0.43
1930	0.14	0.11	0.40	0.42
1931	0.17	0.13	0.46	0.41
1932	0.17	0.19	0.49	0.42
1933	0.16	0.14	0.49	0.46
1934	0.12	0.12	0.49	0.46

Notes and sources: See Table 8.1. Other banks includes Banco de la Provincia de Buenos Aires, also partly state-owned, and all domestic and foreign private banks.

centralized; but in most other respects an overwhelmingly laissez faire attitude to the banking sector persisted.[9]

In this atmosphere, at least until the beginning of the First World War, the idea of a central bank and more modest plans for regulating and supervising the financial system were foreign to the thinking of the monetary authorities not to mention the banking community itself.[10] Instead, the money and banking system evolved in an ad hoc fashion. Changes were implemented piecemeal through various legislation, notably the emergency law of 1914. The reforms of the 1890s nationalized the currency and instituted a firm nominal anchor, but the question remained then—as it still does today in many developing countries—whether just the act of macroeconomic and monetary stabilization alone can suffice to generate a stable financial environment. Either through choice or neglect, the authorities of the 1892–1914 period appear to have optimistically believed that with the monetary problem solved the banking sector would take care of itself. For several decades, their gamble appeared to pay off.

The 1913–14 crisis was an almost fatal blow for the financial system. Luckily, the Banco de la Nación stood ready to save the day. This is still something of a puzzle. We know the Banco de la Nación did not have an explicit Lender-of-Last-Resort mandate. It was not a true central bank and was given these kinds of powers in an ad hoc fashion. Why was the rediscount law enacted? And why, even then, given its banking objectives, did the Banco de la Nación take on the risks associated with rediscounting to private banks, when the collateral took the form of the low-quality assets then sitting on the private banks' balance sheets? This we consider an important political economy question.[11]

The new rediscounting by the state bank provided a bailout to the private banks once, ex post, they realized that a bad state of the world had hit. In essence, they obtained, if not free, then highly subsidized banking insurance from a government that had made no such commitment ex ante. That such an inconsistent policy choice should have been made says a good deal about the machinations inside the Argentine corridors of power. Rich and powerful interests, including officers and shareholders of the banks, desperately needed cover from the risks they had taken, the loans that had gone bad. Some of

9. There were other institutional gaps. It is frustrating for historians that before 1900 the *Memorias de Hacienda* (Treasury reports) did not systematically include any consolidated monetary and banking statistics.
10. In 1917, President Hipólito Irigoyen (1916–22) made a first attempt, through his Minister of Finance Domingo Salaberry, to establish a central bank and outlined a preliminary project, but the plan did not meet with the approval of Congress.
11. In 1914, the capital and reserves of the Banco de la Nación amounted to 24 percent of loans, while the sum of rediscounts to private banks and nonperforming loans were equivalent to 16 percent of loans—a difficult, but clearly solvent situation. By 1931, the capitalization fell to 10 percent of loans; soft rediscounting and nonperforming loans amounted to 24 percent of loans, and increased to an all-time high of 29 percent by 1934. On top of this potentially insolvent situation, after 1930 the Banco de la Nación had systematically overlent to the government, with treasury-bill rediscounts exceeding the ceiling of 25 percent of capital.

Cartoon 8.1. *El puchero salvador. — Ya está la olla preparada, y pienso salvar la situación, echándole dentro las moratorias, las economias, el empréstito, y los redescuentos. — Pues, va a salir muy flaco el caldo, porque todo eso tiene muy poca substancia.* (The stew of salvation. [Cook] — The pot is prepared, and I think it will save the situation, I am putting in overdue debts, economies, loans, and rediscounts. [Person] — Then the stew will be very thin, because all these have very little substance.)
Notes: This cartoon expresses doubts about the effectiveness of the Emergency Laws of 1914. President Victorino de la Plaza is the cook.
Source: Caras y caretas, año 17, no. 832, September 12, 1914.

those same loans, we also know from confidential records, were loans to the very same officers and shareholders, or to their real or shadow corporations. Such activities certainly give the appearance of corrupt banking operations and probably would not have occurred under a careful system of regulation and supervision.[12]

We do not know what it took for the banks to secure this kind of help, but get it they did—in two forms. The Banco de la Nación from 1914 to 1935 did what it could through rediscounts to keep the banks out of an illiquidity crisis. Ultimately, in 1935, as part of a political economy solution worked out by the government and its new central bank, the banks got the final bailout they sought to head off an insolvency crisis arising from decades of bad loans—a solution with high social costs that we consider below.

In considering the nature of these rescues, we should also mention the information asymmetries that made the ongoing liquidity provision by the state bank in the 1910s and 1920s a bigger bailout than the simple rediscount figures alone suggest. The private banks were trying to offload risks to the state bank. Ideally, the risks they would offload first would be the bad ones. This would likely be private information for them, unknown to the state bank. That is, there was a "market for lemons" problem in the use of loans as collateral whereby private banks have an incentive to use as collateral the worst paper they hold.[13] This problem of adverse selection continually weakened the balance sheet of the Banco de la Nación.

In the end, if the rediscounts themselves went bad—as they were declared to be in the 1935 bailout—the bad collateral would end up on the state balance sheet. In this way, we see that the system was evolving toward a central banking idea in a very incoherent manner. In its rediscounting actions the Banco de la Nación was *not* engaged in pure Lender-of-Last-Resort actions, like a true central bank following Bagehot's principle of lending freely at a penalty rate. Such actions would have left the bad loans with the private banks while extending temporary liquidity. Instead, the state bank was offering a much sweeter, and therefore more risky deal. It allowed the private banks to shed their risks, with ex post (and possibly ex ante) bad paper used as collateral, and lent them cash at only 4.5 percent—far below even the rate the Banco de la Nación offered its customers on time deposits!

Changes in the banking environment in 1913–14, and the interaction between the state and private banks, marked the birth of a severe moral hazard problem for the money and banking regime in Argentina. During the Baring Crisis many banks had been allowed to fail, even very large banks like the Banco

12. The source for this information is the confidential reports of the Instituto Movilizador de Inversiones Bancarias (IMIB), the body appointed in 1935 by the Central Bank to "clean up" the rotten assets of the banking sector. We discuss the activities of the IMIB in a later section.

13. On the "lemons" problem, see Akerlof (1970).

de la Provincia de Buenos Aires. No Lender-of-Last-Resort actions had been taken by the monetary authorities—since no unified monetary authority had then existed. Banking insurance arrived later, in an ad hoc manner, and quite possibly through nefarious means. It was later taken up by the central bank after 1935, generating over the decades since a series of financial sector bailouts, paid for out of seigniorage in times of high inflation, and whose real social costs, like that of the 1935 rescue, have been carefully guarded.

A Model of Fractional Banks in a Gold Standard Regime

As may already be apparent, there were widening tensions during the 1920s between the goals of external and internal convertibility in the Argentine case. During the suspension Argentina had managed the trilemma by allowing a float of the exchange rate, keeping open the option to move capital and have an activist monetary policy.

The activist monetary policy could obviously not emanate from the Conversion Office, which, as we have noted, did not deviate from its mandate to match note issues by gold on the margin. Activism was emerging, however, in the new workings of the Banco de la Nación, which now engaged in large rediscount operations—a policy that amounted to setting a lending rate to the other private banks, a nominal target. Upon resumption of the gold standard, however, the Conversion Office would be aiming to set the exchange rate—potentially a second nominal target, an inconsistency under an open capital market, and a possible source of external drain in a bad state of nature.

The second inconsistency, and the focus of this section, was the internal problem of drain from the banking system. A fractional reserve system allows agents to convert deposits into cash on demand.[14] The problem is that this is not sustainable in the event of one or more sufficiently bad shocks that create a run, or internal drain. Unlike a central bank, the Banco de la Nación could not bail itself out by issuing currency to itself—it could only get itself bailed out by the Conversion Office, which could, by resort to its emergency rediscount provision, issue currency not backed by gold.

This is our view of events in the 1900–1914 and 1927–29 gold standard regimes. Agents perceived an implicit unified balance sheet of the two state institutions, the Conversion Office and the Banco de la Nación. Thus the dynamics of outside and inside money were to be inextricably linked, and the health of each institution depended on the behavior of the other. The way we approach modeling these dynamics is through the dual-equilibrium version of the Dornbusch-Frenkel (1984) model already mentioned.

14. Thus we think it no surprise that Salama (1997) finds a correlation of gold stocks and the Banco de la Nación reserve-deposit ratio. This just describes the process of linked internal and external drains, and in our model we put quite a different interpretation on this phenomenon.

In the model, the Conversion Office has a balance sheet that consists of liabilities in the form of circulating notes MB (high-powered money or monetary base), and assets comprised of gold G and securities S. Here S consists of the balance sheet counterpart fixed fiduciary issue, the virtual assets that offset the unbacked notes in circulation. Here, $MB = G + S$. The Banco de la Nación, the state bank, has a balance sheet with liabilities comprised of banking deposits both private D and public D', and assets in the form of note reserves R (vault cash) and loans L. Here, $R + L = D + D'$. The financial model hinges on an appropriate specification of money demand. Consider the broad money stock M, consisting of currency in the hands of the public plus private deposits at banks. Then, it is easy to verify that,

$$M = \frac{1+c}{c+r\alpha}(G+S) = m(c,r)(G+S), \tag{8.1}$$

where $m(c,r) = (1+c)/(c+r\alpha)$ is the money multiplier, $\alpha = (D+D')/D$ is the ratio of total to private deposits, $r = R/(D+D')$ is the reserve-to-total-deposit ratio of the bank, and $c = (MB - R)/D$ is the currency-to-private-deposit ratio of the (nonbank) public. Clearly, $\partial m/\partial r < 0$ and we can also assume that $\partial m/\partial c < 0$, since $r\alpha = R/D < 1$ in the empirically relevant range.[15]

The currency-to-private-deposit ratio c desired by the public is now assumed to depend on how banks behave, specifically through the reserve-to-total-deposit ratio r chosen by the bank. A higher reserve ratio at the bank inspires confidence and leads to a lower demand for currency, so that $c = c(r)$, where $c' < 0$. We can then write broad money M as

$$M = \tilde{m}(r)(G+S), \tag{8.2}$$

where $\tilde{m}(r) = m(c(r), r)$.

Note that the relationship of the multiplier to the reserve-to-total-deposit ratio r is ambiguous: $\tilde{m}'(r) < 0$ and $\tilde{m}'(r) > 0$ are both possible and we consider this in a moment. Money market equilibrium will generate an equilibrium interest rate such that

$$\tilde{m}(r)(G+S) = L(i,y), \tag{8.3}$$

where $L_i < 0$, $L_y > 0$. Supposing that output y remains exogenous in the short run, we can solve for the interest rate

$$i = i(r, G; \ldots), \tag{8.4}$$

15. See Friedman and Schwartz (1963) for the derivation. Following Dornbusch and Frenkel (1984), we are ignoring here the role of other private banks. That is, we treat the Banco de la Nación, which already accounted for 50 percent of the banking sector by the 1930s, as a proxy for the entire system. However, an alternative view would be to integrate the balance sheets of the Banco de la Nación and the private banks and study the dynamics of the entire system. This is justified, if, as actually happened, the private banks have an implicit insurance guarantee from the state bank. We repeated the exercise with this aggregation of all the banks and the results were unchanged.

where $i_G < 0$.

We introduce dynamics as follows. Bank policy is assumed to be driven by a desired reserve-deposit ratio $\tilde{r}(i)$, where $\tilde{r}$ is a decreasing function of the interest rate i. Here, better lending opportunities lead the bank to reduce the liquidity of its balance sheet in a prudent way so as to seek profits. Still, the bank is cautious, so the actual adjustment of r to its target level $\tilde{r}$ is posited to be a partial adjustment process, as the bank updates its portfolio position in light of new information, such that

$$\dot{r} = \nu(\tilde{r}(i) - r), \tag{8.5}$$

where $\tilde{r}' < 0$ and ν is a positive adjustment-speed parameter. Finally, this being a small open economy with a fixed exchange rate, we assume a rate of gold inflow that is driven by deviations of the local interest rate i from the world rate i^*. Thus,

$$\dot{G} = G(i - i^*; \ldots), \tag{8.6}$$

where $G_i > 0$.

We now have a dynamical system in two variables, r and G. To figure out the nature of the dynamics we consider the multiplier again. The money multiplier m reacts to the reserve-deposit ratio r in two ways. A rise in the ratio means more use of notes by the bank as reserve, directly lowering the multiplier. It also means more confidence in the bank, lowering the currency deposit ratio $c(r)$ and increasing the multiplier via c. If the first effect dominates, then $\tilde{m}'(r) < 0$, and we will show that a stable equilibrium obtains (case one). However, if the second effect dominates an unstable equilibrium obtains, and it is clear why: when $\tilde{m}'(r) > 0$ a bank run would lower r, diminish confidence, raise c (the flight to cash), and further lower m, perpetuating the run (case two).

Next, we can look at the interest rate equation based on money demand. In case one, $i_r > 0$, and an increase in the reserve-deposit ratio by the bank tightens the money market, and lures the public back into holding money balances. In case two, $i_r < 0$, and such actions do not attract the public to money. That is, under case two, the internal convertibility problem overwhelms the system and the interest-rate defense will fail.

The above dynamics lead to a phase diagram in (G, r)-space as shown in Figure 8.3. The direction of trajectories is marked in the various regions delineated by the curves $dr/dt = 0$ and $dG/dt = 0$. The intersections of the curves are the two potential kinds of equilibria, labeled E1 and E2. The point E1 corresponds to case one and is a stable node, a “good” equilibrium. The point E2 corresponds to case two and is an unstable saddle point, a “bad” equilibrium.

A possible stable saddle path for E2 is shown as SS′ and it is important to note that this curve delineates two regions in the plane: above SS′, all paths lead to the stable equilibrium, the sink point at E1. Here, the money and

Figure 8.3. Phase Diagram for the Dynamic Model

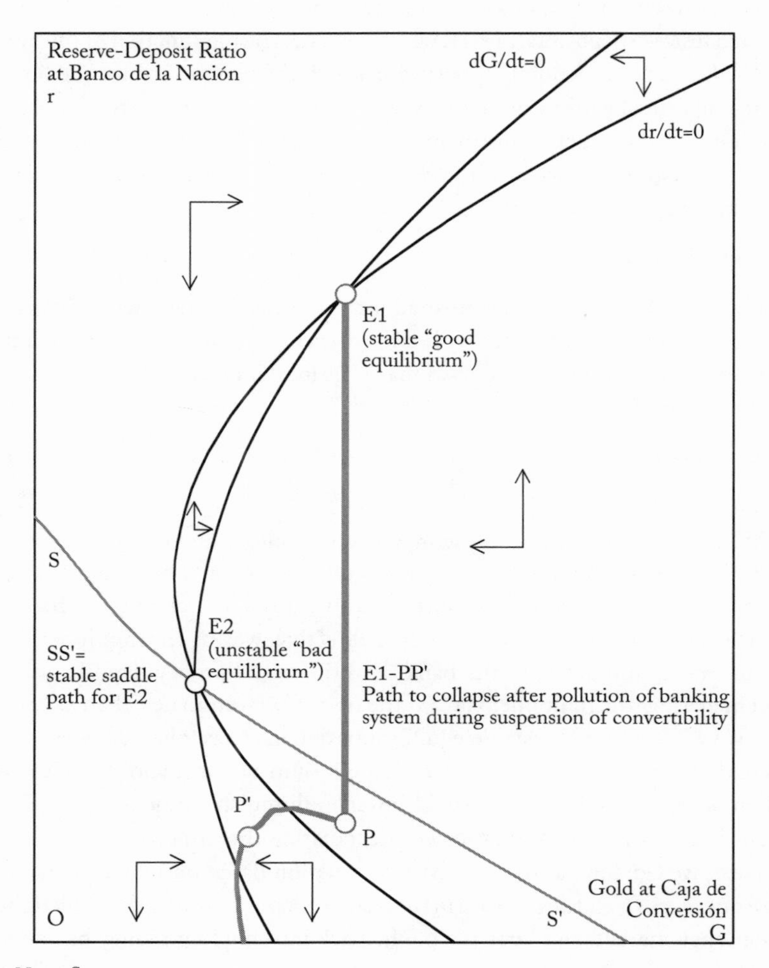

Notes: See text.

banking regime is stable and sustainable in the long run. But below SS′ there is an unstable regime where all paths lead to collapse. Note that this will not generate a crisis in the form of a complete drain of the gold stock—an external convertibility crisis—since the dynamics of G in the unstable region are such as to take paths away from $G = 0$. Rather, it is a region in which the bank collapses—that is, an internal convertibility crisis.[16]

We think this theoretical framework is ideal for the purpose of studying the dynamics of internal and external convertibility in the Argentine case. Moreover, we conceive of the model applying in very different ways in the two periods of convertibility. We have already outlined the major developments in the banking system from 1900 to 1935 in the previous section, and, particularly, the drastic changes at the Banco de la Nación after 1914.

The Banco de la Nación was once a very conservative bank with high reserve ratios and a quasi-narrow objective, but after 1914 it increasingly became a prop to the private baking system and, as a result, its own balance sheet became polluted by the problems of the wider financial system. Reserve ratios fell and the quality of the balance sheet deteriorated. Following resumption of the gold standard in December 1927, the bank experienced a severe drain unlike anything seen before. How could a system that had once worked so well under the old prewar gold standard now fail so miserably?

Our model supplies an answer. The evidence suggests to us that during the Argentine Belle Époque prior to the First World War, the money and banking system was operating in the stable zone of the phase diagram, in the vicinity of the stable equilibrium E1, with high confidence in the regime sustained by high reserve ratios.

Evidence for this type of stable regime is supplied in Table 8.3. We have high-frequency (monthly) data on the gold stocks of the Conversion Office and the reserve and deposit holdings of the bank starting in 1908, and this permits us to estimate a locally linearized version of the model close to E1. To empirically fit the dynamical system we set up a two-equation vector autoregression (VAR) for the reserve ratio and gold stock of the form

$$\begin{pmatrix} \Delta r_t \\ \Delta \log G_t \end{pmatrix} = \alpha_0 + \sum_{s=1}^{p} \alpha_s \begin{pmatrix} r_{t-s} \\ \log G_{t-s} \end{pmatrix} + \sum_{s'=1}^{q} \beta_{s'} \begin{pmatrix} \Delta r_{t-s'} \\ \Delta \log G_{t-s'} \end{pmatrix} + \epsilon_t \quad (8.7)$$

and estimated the model using series from January 1908 to December 1913, the heyday of the classical gold standard.

16. In case one, both curves are upward sloping; the curve $dG/dt = 0$ is steeper, since the interest rate is constant on this curve for external equilibrium; on the $dr/dt = 0$ curve the interest rate is rising to the lower-left to maintain equilibrium at the bank. In case two, both curves are downward sloping; $dG/dt = 0$ is again steeper, with the interest rate constant; on $dr/dt = 0$ the interest rate is rising to the upper-left to maintain equilibrium at the bank. By inspection E1 is seen to be stable (consider, for example, any small rectangle around E1 aligned to the axes: it is a Liapunov stable set). E2 is seen to be a saddle point.

Table 8.3. *Dynamics of Internal and External Convertibility, 1908–13*

A. VAR Estimation		
Dependent Variable	Δr	$\Delta \log G$
r(t -1)	-0.23	0.03
	(0.08)	(0.04)
log G (t -1)	-0.07	-0.10
	(0.07)	(0.03)
Observations	60	60
R-squared	0.14	0.46
Mean of Dependent Variable	0.00	0.00
Standard Error of Estimate	0.05	0.02
Durbin-Watson Statistic	2.20	1.77
B. Covariance Matrix of Residuals		
	0.00207	0.00009
	0.00009	0.00044
C. Stability Test		
Determinant	0.03	
Trace	-0.33	

Notes and sources: See Appendix 1. Lag selection by step-down procedure. Lag of $\Delta \log G$ used in second equation, not shown. Constant terms not shown. log G is subject to preliminary detrending. See text.

After careful model selection we found some simple dynamics consistent with a stable equilibrium of the type E1, and requiring only a simple lag structure, $p = q = 1$.[17] Entries in the matrix α_1 should be negative on the diagonal, and positive off the diagonal and this hypothesis cannot be rejected.[18] Stability would also require that α_1 should have a positive determinant and negative trace, conditions that are met.

Apparently the dynamics were stable in this period, and the same impression obtains from an inspection of the time series of r and log G (the latter detrended) shown in the upper right portion of Figure 8.4. The resemblance to the stable equilibrium E1 depicted in Figure 8.3 is striking. At high levels of reserves and gold, the system was subject to shocks but remained in a neighborhood of its equilibrium. The trajectory fluctuated but it did not explode unidirectionally.[19]

17. Preliminary lag choices were made using the Schwarz criterion on univariate series. Final lag selection was made in the VAR using a step-down procedure to eliminate insignificant lags of each variable. One lag of each level variable was required, plus one lag of ΔG in the G equation. To filter out the long-run expansion of the gold stock, log G was subject to preliminary detrending.
18. One off-diagonal term has the wrong sign but is not significant.
19. Unit root tests suggest that both series are stationary in this sample period. We used the more powerful GLS variant method of the Dickey-Fuller test as introduced by Elliott, Rothenberg, and Stock (1996); the exact test we used is the DF-GLS$_u$ test of Elliott (1999). For the series r (demeaned) and log G (detrended) the test statistics were -2.42 (with a 10 percent critical value of -2.46), and -2.68 (critical value -2.41), respectively.

Figure 8.4. Reserve Ratios and Gold Stocks in Two Convertible Regimes

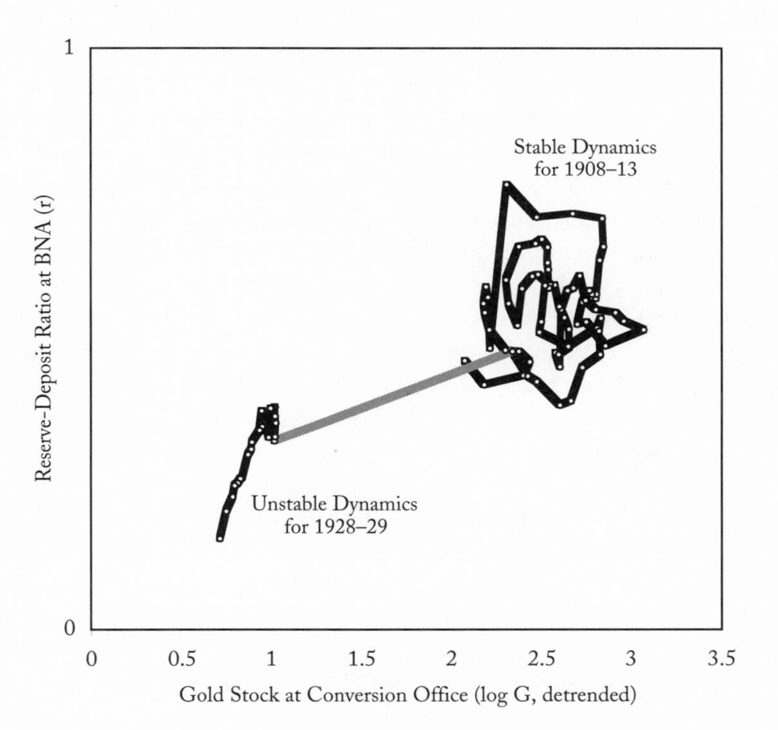

Notes: The series log G is detrended and both series are renormalized for clarity. *Sources:* See Appendix 1.

That is, the gold standard system was a stable one at the beginning of the century because it was combined with prudent inside-money practices.

This regime ended in 1914: external shocks and domestic policy choices made gradual, seemingly innocuous, changes in the institutional framework. The gold standard was suspended, albeit with the intention of resuming. The rediscount provisions of the Banco de la Nación and the Conversion Office introduced some implicit guarantees into the financial system, albeit they were intended as emergency powers. The notion of acting like a central bank became a distinct possibility, at least for the Banco de la Nación, now that some Lender-of-Last-Resort functions were authorized. The creation of these powers did increase the scope for moral hazard. To its credit, the Conversion Office kept its emergency powers largely in reserve. It was not so at the Banco de la Nación, where rediscounting grew steadily after 1914, as a narrow banking orientation gave way to expanding commercial activities.

Had the institutional framework not changed after 1914—had the gold standard rules endured at the Conversion Office and had the bank followed its high-reputation rules—then, of course, the system would have been locked into the stable dynamics for the long run. However, suspension of the prevailing institutions in 1914 caused the system to be buffeted by new political and economic pressures, allowing it to follow a new path without reference to the above dynamical system whose operation had been halted for a time. The system moved ever further from the stable equilibrium E1.

The pollution of the balance sheet of the Banco de la Nación from 1914 to 1927 is represented in Figure 8.3 by the line E1-P. Outside money was in good health, gold stocks in the Conversion Office held firm or even rose, and G did not drop. At the same time, inside money fell into very poor health as the reserve ratio r declined sharply. Thus, we argue, the system arrived at a point like P by the late 1920s. The system could "safely" cross into the unstable region of the phase diagram during the years of suspension, since the dynamics of the model were held in check and the tensions kept at bay.

Yet the institutional pollution of the banking sector, while not a cause for serious concern in the relatively controlled environment of 1914–27, could potentially unleash a dramatic crisis once the full open-economy gold-standard dynamics were set in motion again. Resumption had always been the authorities' intent along the way, despite their tolerance for the dangerous inconsistencies emerging between inside and outside money in the interim. The dynamical system set to work again during the brief 1927–29 resumption, but this time, we conjecture, from new initial conditions at a point like P, with movement along a path like PP′.

How would the system behave in this new region according to theory? Initially, but not for long, the banking system might appear healthy with a slight increase in reserve ratios (r rising), even as gold losses set in (G falling). Yet, eventually, an internal drain would inevitably arise (to the left of the $dr/dt = 0$ curve). The system would head toward collapse on the horizontal axis at P′, unless the dynamics were terminated by some form of institutional change. Either there could be a suspension of internal convertibility such as a bank closure, failure, or "holiday"; or, there could be a suspension of external convertibility, as actually happened when Argentina left the gold standard for good in December 1929.

We have insufficient monthly data to estimate a VAR for this brief period, so we cannot subject the system to the same kinds of tests we did in Table 8.3 for the pre-1914 regime.[20] However, unit root tests confirm an explosive path for r

20. We also note that a VAR might be inappropriate in its linear specification for describing a path like PP′ that lies so far from the equilibrium E2 where a linear approximation might be valid. So it was no surprise that when we did estimate a VAR it did not fit well: we did find unstable saddle characteristics, but with signs that did not conform exactly to the prescriptions of the partial derivatives of the model.

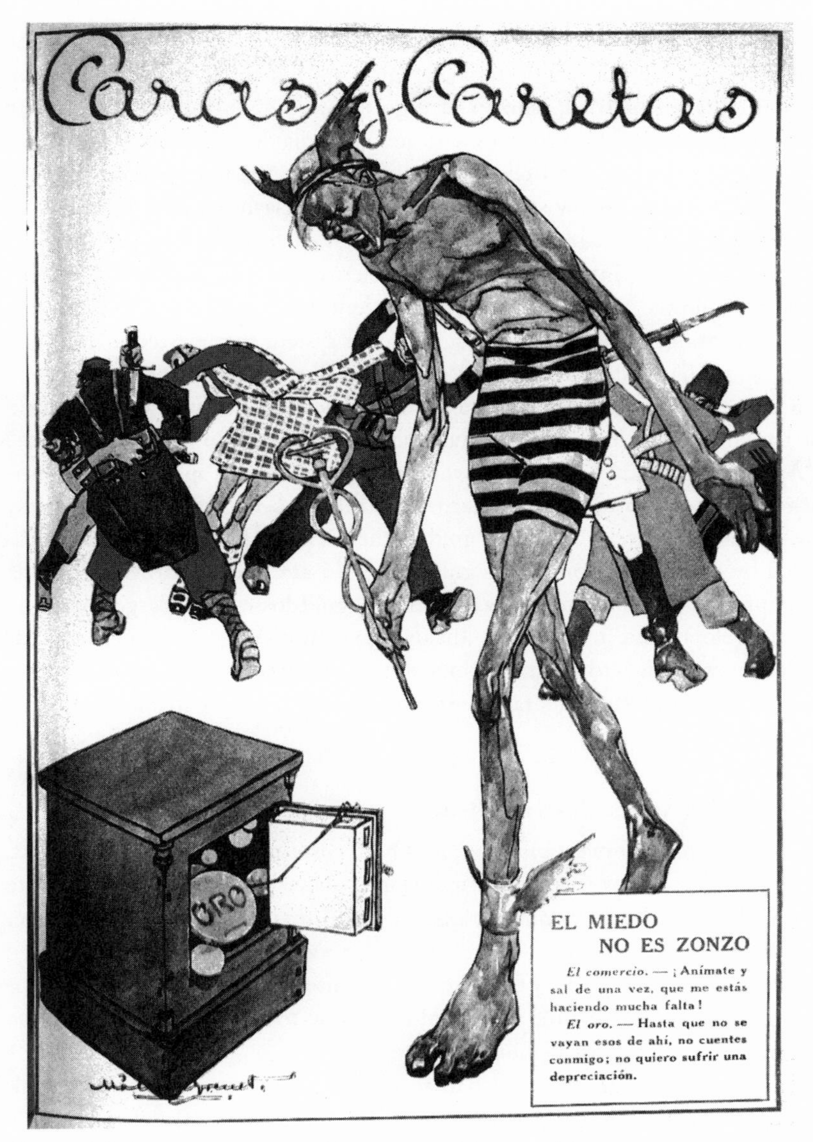

Cartoon 8.2. *El miedo no es zonzo. El comercio — ¡Animate y sal de una vez, que me estás haciendo mucha falta! El oro — Hasta que no se vayan esos de ahi, no cuentes conmigo; no quiero sufrir una depreciación.* (Fear is not stupid. Business — Get moving and get out now, I badly need you! Gold — As long as they [the combatants of the First World War] are still here, don't count on me; I don't want to suffer a depreciation.)

Notes: One month after the outbreak of the First World War, convertibility has been suspended. Business wants liquidity, but under the orthodoxy of the currency board, there is no relief forthcoming: there could be no attempt to expand monetary policy.

Source: Caras y caretas, no. 835, September 26, 1914.

and log G in this period, with both collapsing, and a cursory inspection of the trajectory in the lower left portion of Figure 8.4 illustrates a trajectory much like the putative path PP′ shown in Figure 8.3. Again, the correspondence between the empirical trajectories and the phase diagram is striking.

To sum up, during the Belle Époque era before 1914, a credible currency board and a quasi-narrow state bank avoided any clash between internal and external convertibility, making the provision of each that much more secure. An external shock, internal economic problems, and new political directions after 1914 allowed for some seemingly innocent tinkering with this supposedly solid institutional design. On the surface, the system that existed in 1927–29 did look, to all intents and purposes, very much like the one that had worked so well up to 1913. But certain crucial elements had been allowed to change, and the banking sector, including the state bank, had fallen into very poor shape.

Agents clearly knew this, and when the gold window opened there commenced a massive internal drain (a run on bank deposits) which fed an equally massive external drain (a run on gold at the currency board). The drain was halted by the Conversion Office going off gold after an embarrassingly brief resumption.[21] Outside money was hit hard: gold losses were large, about 40 percent below trend in two years. Inside money was devastated: the Banco de la Nación was now in the same parlous state as the private banks, with a reserve ratio falling about 20 percentage points toward a feeble 10 percent level.[22]

Inconvertible Again: Costs and Benefits

The suspension of convertibility brought both costs and benefits for Argentina. On the upside, a new freedom in monetary policy allowed domestic prices to be delinked from a deflationary global scenario that was to drag many other economies into much deeper depressions. However, as we shall see in the next chapter, this monetary policy freedom was not automatic and faced several institutional hurdles and required some explicit choices to be made about reputation and credibility in the fiscal-monetary nexus.

In a nutshell, Argentina still had to export gold to service debt, but this would mean severe monetary contraction. The choice was either to default on external loans or offset the monetary contraction by printing unbacked notes. Invoking emergency conditions, a sterilization policy was implemented, and a stable price level and money stock were more or less maintained. As we shall

21. Had the conversion office not suspended, the internal drain could have continued to feed the external drain and this could have precipitated a speculative attack and a collapse of the exchange rate regime. See Miller (1996).

22. See Figure 8.2 for these trends. The reserve ratio was disastrously low: for some perspective, we should recall that, as bad as the run on the banks had been in the Baring Crisis, the reserve ratio at the private banks (including the then Banco Nacional) never fell below 22 percent in 1890–91. See Table 3.1.

see in the next chapter, such actions successfully steered Argentina away from a severe recession.

On the downside, the exchange rate was soon floating far from parity after such a change of regime. Put another way, the paper peso price of gold soared. Valued at the market rate, the government's gold reserve was expanding in paper terms. It could have been very tempting to imagine uses for these sudden seigniorage profits, and the policymakers of the time did not lack imagination.

Most worryingly, the costly financial sector debacle was not over. The suspension of 1929 had resolved the tensions in the system by halting the prevailing rules of the game so as to end the unstable dynamics; but it left a much larger problem to be resolved in the longer run. What could be done with a financial system that was on the verge of ruin? Who would bear the costs of fixing the damage? And how big were those costs going to be? We take up this story again when we discuss the formation of the central bank and the extraordinary use of vast seigniorage resources to benefit a privileged few by bailing out the very large fraction of rotten assets that had accumulated on the balance sheets of the nation's private banks.

9

Steering through the Great Depression: Institutions, Expectations, and the Change of Macroeconomic Regime

The experience of Argentina during the Great Depression provides an ideal historical laboratory for the investigation of macroeconomic stability and policy choice in a small open economy under a fixed exchange rate regime.

As in recent developing-country experiences—including examples of contemporary currency boards very similar to Argentina's institutions of the early twentieth century—the essential question is: what happens if you employ a currency board and there is an external crash or deflation threat? This was the nature of the crisis in the 1930s for many countries, and the same potential problem has affected Argentina, Hong Kong, and other countries in the 1990s. What should they do today? To inform that question we ask: What did Argentina do in the past?

The Great Depression began in Argentina in the late 1920s. Like many countries of the periphery, Argentina was exposed to the commodity lottery and the terms of trade worsened in the 1920s.[1] By December 1929, the balance-of-payments crisis was severe and the exchange rate was left to float after a mere two-year resumption of the gold standard.

Recovery began in 1931 as output grew for the first time in several years. By 1934–35 output had regained its 1929 level. Assigning fiscal policy any responsibility for the recovery is implausible: by any measure fiscal policy actually *tightened* during the early 1930s, as in many other Latin American countries and the United States.

However, in monetary policy actions from 1929 to 1935 we see evidence of a change of regime. Many commentators see the creation of the central bank *(Banco Central)* in 1935 as the main monetary policy event of the 1930s in Argentina. We instead emphasize the remarkable decision of the Conversion Office to begin rediscounting in April 1931 and so forge an independent monetary policy. In many ways, we would argue, the Central Bank merely

1. Díaz Alejandro (1983); Kindleberger (1986).

rubber-stamped this new macroeconomic policy regime and continued its operations after 1935.[2]

The Argentine recovery was complete by 1935; and the only pre-1935 change in regime that could be assigned a role in ending the Argentine Great Depression was the action of the Conversion Office. Yet, did it make a difference? We argue that the change of monetary regime was essential to Argentina's recovery in that it helped avert a devastating collapse of prices, and, potentially, of output in 1931–33. Instead of following the United States and other countries into this abyss, Argentina's regime shift destroyed deflationary expectations. Previously extremely high real interest rates were permanently lowered.

In other ways, though, policy was still limited by orthodox thinking. Sterilizations offset gold outflows but never counteracted them. This leads to an important distinction: Temin has argued that recovery from the Depression came through two channels. First, a direct injection of liquidity could lower interest rates and stimulate aggregate demand, something he termed the "Keynes effect." Second, a decisive change in monetary regime could convince agents to discard their pessimistic expectations of deflation, with favorable implications for economic activity via lower ex ante real interest rates, improved balance sheets and asset quality, and so on, termed the "Mundell effect."[3]

Although two escape routes existed, only one was used—but it was enough to avert disaster. Argentina was still a prisoner of its intellectual and economic history, and fear of inflation was still an issue in the midst of slump, as in other countries. The Conversion Office, though willing to follow Prebisch's plan, was not willing to push it as far as it might. There was no "Keynes" effect at work, no large money injection to stimulate aggregate demand as a device to end the Depression more quickly. The channel through which the change in monetary regime had real effects was via the destruction of deflationary expectations, the "Mundell" effect.

Hence we think that the institutional change heralded by the rejection of an old orthodoxy was just as essential to recovery from the Great Depression in the periphery as in the core.[4]

2. In substantive terms, we would argue that the main contribution of the central bank was to put in place a rescue package for the financial sector—by saving the Banco de la Nación—using the proceeds of a large gold revaluation (depreciation). See Salama (1997, p. 21).
3. Temin (1989) noted the impact of these two effects in the 1930s recovery in the core countries, and he too stressed the importance of the Mundell effect and the change of expectations that followed the change of regime. See also Eichengreen (1992a; 1992b). The U.S. experience under Presidents Herbert Hoover and Franklin Delano Roosevelt is a classic example of such a regime shift; see Temin and Wigmore (1990); and Romer (1992).
4. Cross-sectional reduced form analysis of the impact of devaluation on recovery was provided by Campa (1990), following Eichengreen and Sachs (1985). Other studies in this vein include Bernanke and James (1991), and Obstfeld and Taylor (1998). This chapter is perhaps more ambitious in that we focus on a single case-study and examine the structural details of monetary policy and transmission.

Contours of the Argentine Great Depression

The Great Depression marked the end of an epoch where free trade and integration into external capital markets served as the main strategies for economic growth in Latin American countries.[5] For Argentina, although economic problems had retarded economic growth since 1914, there was a pressure to stand by the old liberal orthodoxy. Even during and after the *worst* recession in Argentine history, during the First World War, few policymakers seriously questioned the return to orthodoxy as the goal for the 1920s, to rebuild an economic order predicated on openness in markets and adherence to the gold standard as a monetary rule.[6] This view was only broken as the threat of an even worse international economic collapse loomed in the early 1930s.

Selected data in Table 9.1 show the impact of the Great Depression on the Argentine economy. From 1929 to 1932, Argentina imported severe deflationary pressures from the international economy. If one were to judge by its trade exposure, Argentina was one of the most vulnerable economies in the presence of such sizeable foreign shocks—shocks that, in addition to pure deflation, also included fierce terms of trade declines as countries took their hits in the "commodity lottery."[7] The external terms of trade declined by 24 percent and the foreign (U.S.) price level fell by 26 percent.

In this context it is astonishing that the Argentine Great Depression was so mild and short-lived by international standards. Hence, the notion that an important change in economic policy took place—and saved Argentina from more pronounced suffering—deserves close scrutiny. As can be gleaned from Table 9.1, from peak to trough (1929 to 1932), the domestic real output fell by "only" 14 percent and had even surpassed its 1929 level already by 1935. Deflation, a curse to avoid in the interwar period, was only about 6 percent (in *cumulative* terms) in the same period.

The behavior of output and prices compares favorably, say, to North American gold-standard countries such as the United States and Canada: they had an overall decline from peak to trough of more than 30 percent in real activity, and more than 20 percent in price level.[8] The Argentine performance was also very good by the standards of the periphery in general, and Latin America in particular. In the same 1929–32 period, Mexico's prices and output fell by 19 percent, Chile's real output by 27 percent, and Brazil's by 28 percent.

We note here that currency depreciations were not always directly correlated with the ability to avoid a slump. For example, in Brazil there was a 66 percent

5. Díaz Alejandro (1983; 1984).
6. On the post-1914 slowdown, see Taylor (1992) and Chapter 7.
7. On these deflations, see Kindleberger (1986); Temin (1989); Eichengreen (1992a). On the commodity lottery see Díaz Alejandro (1984). For a discussion of the general experience of the periphery in the 1920s with terms-of-trade shocks see Kindleberger (1986).
8. The data are from Mitchell (1992; 1993).

Table 9.1. *Contours of the Argentine Great Depression*

A. Nominal Variables

Year	Money Base	Gold Stock	Domestic Credit	Money Supply	Exchange Rate	Price Level	Wage Index	Land Prices	Banks' Discount Rate (%)
1913	823	530	293	1,687	2.35	100	100	100	5.4
1928	1,406	1,113	293	4,717	2.32	131	180	296	6.3
1929	1,247	954	293	4,652	2.35	127	178	293	6.9
1930	1,261	968	293	4,660	2.70	122	166	238	6.9
1931	1,245	593	652	4,149	3.40	118	155	260	7.2
1932	1,339	584	755	4,116	3.83	119	146	237	7.1
1933	1,214	561	653	4,061	3.18	114	139	210	6.1
1934	1,172	561	610	4,078	3.89	130	136	196	5.5
1935	1,647	1,354	293	4,180	3.75	128	147	185	5.4
1936	1,685	1,528	157	4,611	3.55	131	153	217	5.6
1937	1,679	1,422	257	4,922	3.28	150	159	252	5.2
1938	1,615	1,296	319	4,811	3.86	140	160	271	5.3
1939	1,796	1,396	400	4,960	4.27	143	166	256	5.8
1940	1,810	1,329	481	5,050	4.30	163	176	248	5.8

B. Real Variables

Year	Terms of Trade	Real Exch. Rate	Components of GDP						Govt. Deficit/ GDP (%)
			Q	C	G	I	X	M	
1913	100	100	4,640	4,322	204	579	1,805	2,270	0.8
1928	99	121	7,780	6,549	406	900	2,901	2,991	1.7
1929	90	126	8,146	6,781	425	1,029	2,847	3,048	2.3
1930	88	144	7,784	6,829	408	871	2,100	2,533	4.3
1931	65	165	7,216	5,248	393	533	2,871	1,651	2.7
1932	68	162	6,966	5,092	393	374	2,636	1,282	1.8
1933	64	139	7,309	5,723	415	418	2,474	1,506	1.7
1934	79	159	7,912	6,085	447	554	2,546	1,584	1.8
1935	79	153	8,275	6,187	538	691	2,754	1,836	1.2
1936	96	148	8,336	6,249	565	824	2,491	1,870	1.7
1937	110	121	8,964	7,145	612	748	2,911	2,381	2.4
1938	101	151	8,979	7,703	634	824	1,963	2,251	2.4
1939	89	162	9,337	7,271	668	691	2,501	1,755	3.6
1940	91	145	9,486	7,588	672	637	2,071	1,461	2.7

Notes: All nominal quantities are millions of paper pesos; real quantities are millions of 1913 pesos; ratios are percent; exchange rate is paper pesos per U.S. dollar; all other series are indices with 1913=100. The components of output are, in order, total output (Q), private consumption (C), government spending (G), private investment (I), exports (X), and imports (M).
Sources: See Appendix 1; Baiocco (1937); IEERAL (1986); della Paolera and Ortiz (1995).

depreciation of its currency, in Mexico 47 percent, while the Argentine paper peso declined by 63 percent with respect to the gold dollar.[9]

We think it is important here to distinguish between a country *choosing* to depreciate as a regime switch versus *being forced* to depreciate in a crisis. There is an enormous difference between: (a) letting the currency depreciate as a mean to restore equilibrium in the money market; and (b) installing a new policy regime à la Sargent that changes expectations and alters the course of economic decisions.[10] If, in the 1930s, Argentina *were* free to choose (or not choose) a full-fledged change in its monetary regime, and if, as we argue, this was as a proactive political-economy decision, then policymakers must have had a lot of room for maneuver.

Indeed they did. From Table 9.1 we note that around 1930, almost 80 percent of the money base was backed with gold—a backing ratio much higher than in any other gold standard country, and a symptom, as we shall see, of Argentina's thirty years of adherence to an especially strict currency-board regime. The massive gold stock was critical, however, even *after* suspension. By using the gold to service external debt obligations the government could maintain a very orthodox fiscal policy. Argentina did not default on foreign debts in the 1930s: a very unusual feat for a peripheral country. In this way a new policy mix was chosen: "sound finance" in the realm of fiscal affairs, and, at the same time, an unorthodox fiduciary monetary regime. The domestic credit component of the money base, frozen for 32 years by the law of 1899, increased to such an extent that it already accounted for 62 percent of the money base by 1932.

Other macroeconomic responses stand out in Table 9.1. Investment fell by about one half in 1929–31 and by another third in 1932. Private consumption fell by about a quarter. Both shifts greatly exceeded the fall in output. This was possible only because an export recovery and massive import compression provided most of the adjustment.[11] As we shall see, agents began to clamor for a change in policies to redress the negative expectations that prevailed. The dramatic declines in output, investment, and consumption ceased, and then reversed, after 1932. It seems the authorities were successful in the regime change, stabilizing the price level and real exchange rate. Export growth and sustained import compression assisted recovery.

9. In larger samples nominal devaluations were correlated with economic recovery in the 1930s. For the core this was shown by Eichengreen and Sachs (1985) and the idea was extended to Latin America by Campa (1990).

10. See Sargent (1983). He applied the idea of regime change to the end of large inflations in history. Temin and Wigmore (1990) applied the idea to the end of deflationary episodes such as the Great Depression.

11. These patterns of adjustment were common in the 1930s depression in Latin America, despite subsequent beliefs in the structuralist and import-substitution schools that the structure of the economy was inflexible and exports could not generate economic expansion. See Twomey (1983) and Bulmer-Thomas (1996).

In short, by 1933 Argentina had circumvented the most devastating effects of the World Depression. Did policy choices make a difference?

The Interwar Gold Standard: Orthodoxy and Heterodoxy

Some authors have characterized the Argentine Great Depression as a definite "blessing"—in the sense of creating an opportunity to adopt new economic policies and institutions in the face of widespread pressure from external governments and economic advisors to stick to orthodox policies. This new institutional regime, by deviating from the prevailing *mentalité* of the orthodox gold standard, is what could have insulated the domestic economy from the dismal global scenario.[12]

Such a regime would have been hard to envisage just a few years earlier given Argentina's position as a periphery economy and its struggle, over more than a century, to securely establish credible monetary, fiscal, and financial institutions. The long effort to adhere to orthodoxy followed from a political consensus in which few doubted the rewards that would (and did) accrue to Argentina in return for embracing globalization in the late nineteenth century and playing by the internationally approved "rules of the game." Free movements of capital, labor, and goods were a key ingredient in Argentina's pre-1914 success. Against this backdrop, we can see what extraordinary intellectual and technocratic obstacles policymakers had to surmount in the 1930s before they could effect a change in the macroeconomic regime, and, in doing so, depart from the prevailing orthodoxy even ahead of most of the developed countries of the core.[13]

Fiscal Policy

We discuss fiscal policy first because of the important constraints it put on monetary policy, even though in itself it was not an area of regime change at all. The historical record shows no shift in Argentina's basic orthodox fiscal stance—of seeking to maintain budget balance—even during the worst years of the Great Depression. This is not a surprising discovery. Even in the economies of the core, the power of fiscal policy was not unleashed to insulate economies from the

12. See, for example, Díaz Alejandro (1983) and Ortiz (1998). Díaz Alejandro states: "Once upon a time foreign money doctors roamed Latin America prescribing fixed exchange rates and passive gold exchange standard monetary rules. Bankers followed in their footsteps, from the halls of Montezuma to the shores of Daiquiri.... This paper will chronicle some of the ways various Latin American economies coped with them. It will be seen that the performance of several economies was remarkably good, under the circumstances."
13. Argentina was one of the first countries to suspended the interwar gold standard in December 1929. At around the same time Australia, New Zealand, and Uruguay suspended. The first suspensions in the core were Britain and Scandinavia in 1931, the same year other Latin American countries suspended. Eichengreen and Sachs (1985); Campa (1990).

Cartoon 9.1. *I-ri-go-yen — Balance Comercial Negativo — Baja del Peso Argentino — Deudas Impagas — Intranquilidad General — Desorientacion. En casa del oculista. Oculista—¿Hasta donde lee? Ministro de Hacienda — No veo más que la primera linea. Oculista — Tiene que usar anteojos, lo mismo que sus colegas.* ([On the optician's chart:] I-ri-go-yen — Negative Trade Balance — Fall of The Argentine Peso — Unpaid Debts — General Unrest — Disorientation. [Dialog:] At the optician's office. Optician — How far can you read? Economy Minister — I can't see more than the first line. Optician — You have to use spectacles, the same as your colleagues.)
Notes: In a cartoon that appeared shortly before the coup by General Uriburu, Irigoyen's government is heavily criticized for doing too little as the international and domestic economic crises worsen.
Source: Caras y caretas, año 32, no. 1625, November 23, 1929.

recession. For example, it is hard to find any evidence of *full employment* deficits in the United States during the 1930s. Indeed, for many years, the net fiscal impact appeared to be contractionary.[14] Moreover, if expansionary deficits were not an option for core countries in the 1930s—with their developed taxation systems and fiscal sophistication—they were, of course, still less of a feasible policy choice for countries at the periphery, given their much less developed government structures for managing, administering, and implementing large spending programs.[15]

The 1930s fiscal experience in Argentina accords with expectations.[16] At the start of the interwar period customs taxes constituted a large share of revenues, as is typical in all developing countries.[17] Consequently, tax revenues were cyclically correlated with trade conditions: during recessions, import contraction was a standard response. Since government spending followed an upward trend, endogenous (although not, by definition *full-employment*) deficits appeared in some of these recessions; and, indeed, temporary deficits were run up in the First World War and in 1921–22.

The fiscal response in the 1930s was not so forgiving. High expenditures were run up in 1928–30 and drastically cut back during 1931–33, generating a big contractionary effect just as the economy fell into the Great Depression. Although customs taxes were falling in line with the trade crisis, *total* taxes were increasing. President José F. Uriburu (1930–32), like Hoover in the United States, was a fiscal conservative and sought orthodox budget balance.[18] One important part of the package was a dramatic increase in direct taxes, in the form of income and wealth taxes, which rose from 25 million pesos (less than 5 percent of all revenues) in the 1920s, to 92 million (almost 15 percent) in 1933. With a broad array of aggressive tax programs, the government raised taxes consistently every year after 1930 and closed the deficit from 240 million pesos in 1929, to just 126 million in 1933 (Figure 9.1). Thus, far from pursuing expansionary fiscal policy via increased *full-employment* deficits, the Argentine fiscal response during the Great Depression was such as to generate not even increases in *actual* deficits, but rather a move toward surplus.[19] So our search for

14. Thus, for example, the classic Keynesian tool of macroeconomic management did not fail, but rather was never really used, as was famously pointed out by Brown (1956). This finding was further reinforced by the work of Peppers (1973); and Romer (1992).
15. This was true of Latin America, where few countries in the 1930s were capable of developing new fiscal programs in response to the Great Depression. Twomey (1983).
16. Díaz Alejandro (1983, p. 21).
17. Such taxes accounted for 199 million out of 370 million pesos of tax revenues in 1913, or about 54 percent.
18. General Uriburu deposed President Irigoyen in September 1930 in the first coup d' état against the constitutional order in the twentieth century.
19. We concur with Díaz Alejandro that "in short, there is no evidence that during the early 1930s the Argentine government sought to increase the full employment budget deficit as a means to compensate for the fall in aggregate demand" (Díaz Alejandro 1983, p. 22).

Figure 9.1. Fiscal Structure, 1910–40

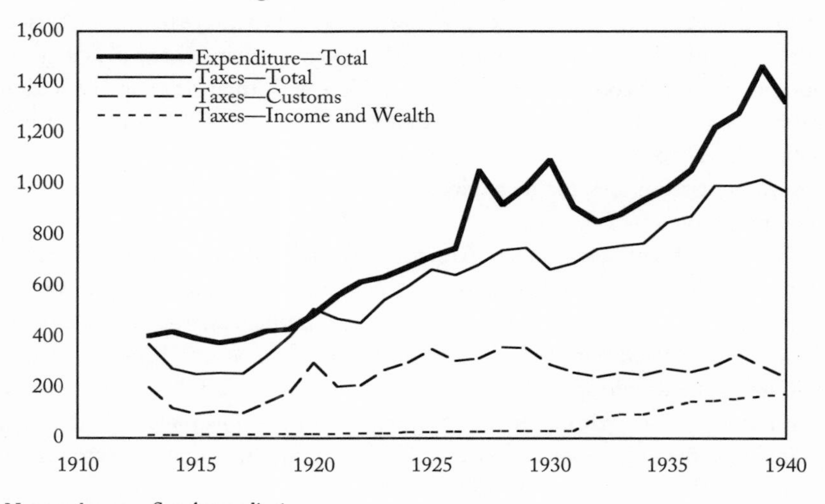

Notes and sources: See Appendix 1.

a source of Argentine economic recovery must focus elsewhere, and we focus on the change in monetary regime.

Curiously, fiscal orthodoxy and monetary tensions were two sides of the same coin, and the link is critical to our understanding of Argentine policy choice. Intense fiscal pressure was felt in many Latin American countries in 1929–30. Tax revenues fell and foreign lenders refused to roll over debts in the worsening international climate. Deflations and depreciations raised the burden of foreign-denominated debt service. The Argentine deficit for 1930 stood at 4.3 percent of output, a marked increase from previous years; debt service had risen from 18 percent of the budget in 1930 to 29 percent in 1932.[20]

Many countries chose to default in this situation, but Argentina never wavered from its external sovereign debt obligations.[21] With external default an anathema—and attempts to raise new borrowings, depress imports, and boost tax revenues proving insufficient in the short run—the only remaining option for servicing the debt was to draw on the last fiscal resource left to the government: the large gold stock sitting idle in the vaults of the Conversion Office. This course was taken, but the price for subscribing to this fiscally orthodox

20. See Table 9.1 and Díaz Alejandro (1983, pp. 20–21).

21. Why? A conventional interpretation is that Argentina maintained debt service so as not to derail the Roca-Runciman trading pact with Britain, understanding that British creditors could not be let down or else severe trade penalties might result from a diplomatic crisis. We offer another, perhaps more compelling, explanation: Argentina sought to maintain its reputation with foreign creditors to maintain access to capital markets, and was indeed successful in this respect during the 1930s.We discuss this issue in a later part of the paper where we focus on contemporary evidence. See also Lindert and Morton (1989) and Tomz (1998).

Table 9.2. *Changes in Gold Stocks and the Money Base, 1900–1935*

		All months			Months with ΔG>0			Months with ΔG <0			Means	
Regime	Dates	*b*	s.e.	*N*	*b*	s.e.	*N*	*b*	s.e.	*N*	ΔG	ΔM
Gold	1900:2–14:7	1.00	.01	174	0.99	.02	87	0.99	.02	52	2.56	2.57
Float	1914:8–19:12	1.00	.01	65	1.00	.01	37	-0.58	.83	5	6.74	6.74
Float	1920:1–27:11	1.00	.06	95	1.00	.04	15	1.30	.39	8	1.90	1.90
Gold	1927:12–29:12	1.00	.01	25	1.03	.03	9	1.00	.01	16	-4.43	-4.43
Float	1930:1–31:3	1.00	.00	15	1.00	.00	2	1.00	.00	12	-4.42	-4.42
Float	1931:4–35:4	0.05	.24	49	—	—	—	0.47	.43	13	-6.66	0.57

Notes and sources: See Appendix 1. Units of G (gold stock) and M (money base) are millions of paper pesos, with G evaluated at parity of 2.27 paper pesos per gold peso. Regression is of ΔM on ΔG, using Ordinary Least Squares, and reporting coefficient b, standard error s.e., and sample size N.

response was to draw down the gold stock and, ipso facto, the money base, given the mechanical rules of the currency board. Thus a deflationary money contraction was an inevitable but undesirable side-effect of the course chosen—at least as long as the Conversion Office played by its own rules.

Monetary Policy

In a pure gold standard regime, expansions and contractions of the nominal quantity of money should be exactly correlated with variations in the gold stock at the Conversion Office. For the 1900–1914 and the 1927–29 gold-standard periods, there was just such a one-to-one and rigid association between money and gold as shown by the data in Table 9.2 and Figure 9.2. More remarkably, there was even strict adherence to the rule from 1914 to 1927 during a long suspension of convertibility.

In this period, many core countries witnessed inflations and hyperinflations, but Argentina maintained a key element of orthodoxy. There was no wild recourse to money printing—for example, to finance spending—even though suspension offered an easy excuse and the exchange rate had drifted away from its anchor. Indeed, drift in the exchange rate was unavoidable as most other countries abandoned their pegs from after 1914 until the mid-1920s. The adherence to orthodoxy was all the more remarkable given the enormous economic contraction in the years 1914–19 already noted.

Argentina unilaterally did what it could to stick to orthodoxy and suspension of convertibility in 1914 was seen as just a temporary measure. After 1914 there were occasional outflows of gold for official purposes but these were still accompanied by a strict application of the gold-for-peso rule. From 1914 to 1927 the Conversion Office worked in a kind of asymmetric fashion: the monetary base augmented automatically when gold reserves increased but gold extractions were rarely allowed. Consequently, in periods of demand pressure in the foreign-exchange market, notably in the recession of 1920–21, adjustment took

Figure 9.2. Changes in Gold Stocks and the Money Base, 1900–1935

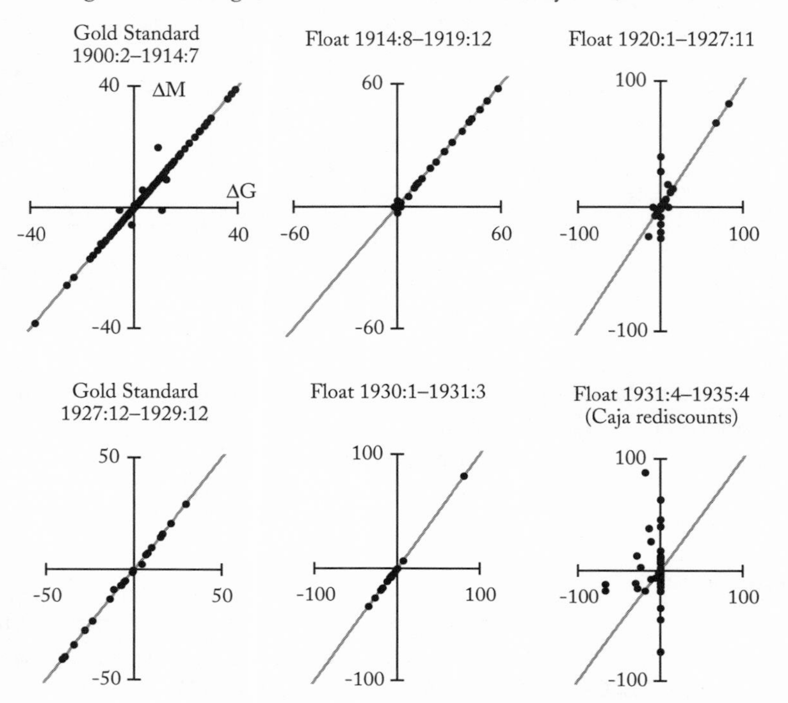

Notes and sources: See Table 9.2. The horizontal axis is always ΔG, the vertical axis is always ΔM. Units for both are millions of paper pesos. The 45 degree line is shown.

another form. The quantity of base money remained unchanged, and there was a depreciation of the exchange rate (Figure 9.3).[22] However, it was the universal belief of policymakers and market players alike that resumption at par was the only possible steady-state solution to the turbulence in the monetary and financial markets. How could this tension be resolved?

A "one-way" gold standard, as this has been called, was still consistent with the long-run goal of resumption at par, for a simple reason. During the boom years of 1900–1914, Argentina had built up a huge gold backing for the currency; from 1914 to the mid-1920s Argentina husbanded that stock carefully via the "one-way" devices of the Conversion Office. By the mid-1920s, resumption still looked credible because this strategy left Argentina with much stronger backing for the currency, at least as compared to many core countries, as the gold-exchange standard was built. Actions were geared to the monetization of

22. Depreciation meant an increase in the paper-gold market exchange rate relative to the par value.

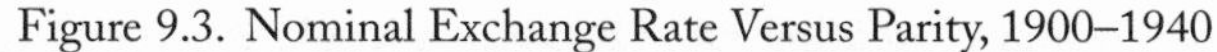
Figure 9.3. Nominal Exchange Rate Versus Parity, 1900–1940

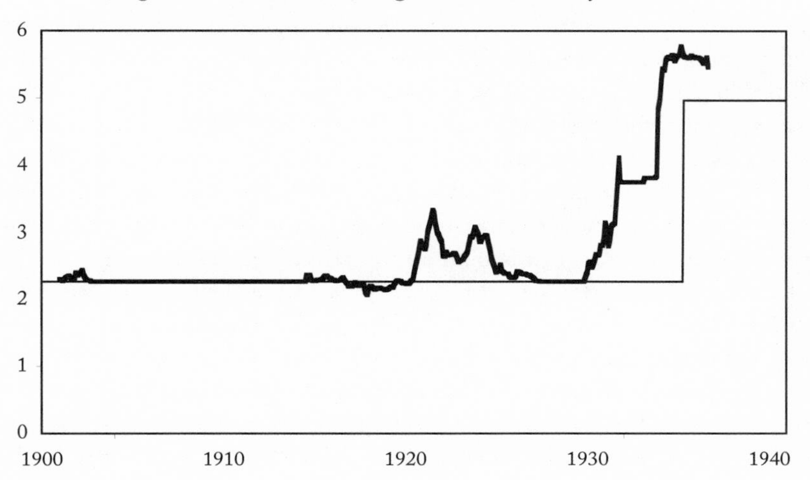

Notes and sources: See Appendix 1. Units are paper pesos per gold peso. The thin line indicates the official parity, 2.27 until April 1935, and 4.96 from May 1935.

gold inflows but officials were strict about keeping the gold-backing of money to a minimum of 78 percent in the turbulent 1920–25 years.[23]

What price did Argentina pay for this curious "one-way" gold standard policy? Did the exchange rate rise well above par making resumption difficult? Not at all. The most dramatic crisis in 1920–21 saw sudden declines in exports and the terms of trade. Even so, the premium over par never went above 33 percent.[24] In contrast, core European countries could only achieve such close convergence to prewar parity by the mid-1920s as they started to resume the gold standard.

Several observers noted that European experiences with floating rates after 1914 were dismal in the absence of a well-understood monetary "straight jacket" to limit expansionary monetary policies, with monetization often deriving from unsustainable fiscal gaps.[25] Conditions in Argentina could not have been more different. More orthodox than the core itself, this peripheral country, from 1914 through to resumption in 1927, in its rhetoric and actions, was intent

23. At the same time, core gold standard countries such as Italy, Netherlands, Norway, or the United States never surpassed a gold-cover ratio of 50 percent of the money base.
24. In the opposite circumstance, of gold inflow pressure, Argentina was even more orthodox than other countries; in the 1918–19 postwar years, the paper peso strengthened well above par before the Conversion Office decided to permit and monetize incipient gold inflows. In 1918 and 1919, the paper peso in terms of the gold peso was quoted at 2.14 and 2.2, well below the 2.27 par value.
25. See the fascinating article by Eichengreen and Temin (1997) that analyzes the policy debates over the resumption of the gold standard in core European and North American countries in the 1920s.

on the idea of resumption at parity. The regime in place was still essentially a metallic monetary regime. The prevailing *mentalité* allowed no room for money issues not fully backed by gold. Historical experience with profligate monetary policies in the 1880s and before, and the inflation and economic chaos that resulted from such actions, lived on in the minds of Argentine policymakers.

Based on legal developments, some might dispute the idea that from 1900 to 1931 the country maintained a metallic regime. We can recall from the previous chapter that emergency laws were passed in August 1914 to overcome the severe financial crisis. The 1914 rediscount law contained two key measures.

The first measure was intended to delegate to the Banco de la Nación, a quasi-public bank, and the largest of all banks, the microeconomic responsibility to forestall liquidity problems in the financial system via the rediscount window. However, the action of rediscounting commercial paper through this first provision in the law could only effect a change in inside money, or banking money (M3), and not in the monetary base (M0) which was controlled by the Conversion Office.

The second provision of the law allowed the Conversion Office to rediscount commercial and government paper so long as gold backing stayed above a lower bound of 40 percent. In the latter we see, as early as 1914, and just 15 years after the 1899 convertibility law, a clear innovation: the design of an institutional capability that would permit the Conversion Office to delink gold and currency movements. Was it used at all? In the period to April 1931 the answer is: almost never. With the exception of three months in the economic crisis of 1925, the monetary authorities never issued fiduciary notes.[26]

The evolution of the money base in Figure 9.4 clearly shows the actions of the monetary authorities during the years of the Conversion Office (January 1900 to April 1935) and the first years of the Central Bank (May 1935 to December 1940). The constancy of the fiduciary issue is immediately apparent as a component of the money base, and above it we see the gold-backed component: the strict gold-money rule applied until April 1931.[27] For this reason we found the very strict correlations between gold and money seen in Figure 9.2.

As we have noted, if gold had to be spent in a fiscal rearguard action, the traditional operations of the Conversion Office would have led to a major adverse monetary shock, unless the rules of the game changed. They did:

26. The conservatism of the Conversion Office contrasts with the more activist behavior of the Banco de la Nación. The bank rediscounted commercial paper in a countercyclical fashion (Salama 1997).

27. Except for a small blip in 1925, and a few other months (where lags kept gold and money slightly out of synchronization) there were no money issues not covered by gold at the Conversion Office. Note that during the First World War, and to a lesser extent in the early 1930s, difficulties in shipping gold out of Europe meant that incipient gold inflows to Argentina were held in European vaults of the diplomatic missions *(legaciones)*, but were the property of the Conversion Office. These were counted as gold backing, and are denoted separately.

Figure 9.4. Composition of the Money Base, 1900–1940

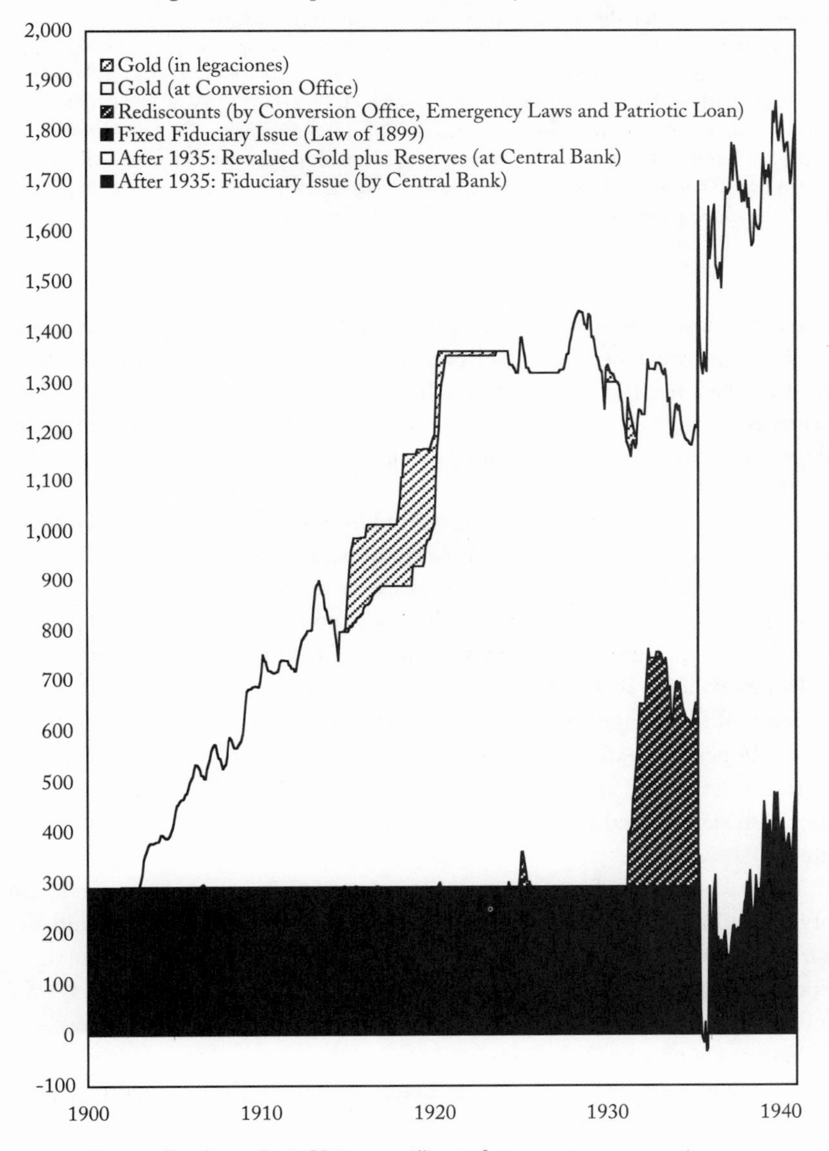

Notes and sources: See Appendix 1. Units are millions of paper pesos.

Maintenance of liquidity was not simply a matter of ending convertibility. On the one hand, even after the abandonment of the gold standard, some countries such as Argentina shipped gold abroad to service the external debt and sold foreign exchange to stem the currency depreciation. On the other hand, as early as 1931 South American monetary authorities began to adopt measures which Professor E. W. Kemmerer and Sir Otto Niemeyer would have found unsound. Thus, the Argentine Caja de Conversión, whose old and only duty was to exchange gold for domestic currency and vice versa, began in 1931 to issue domestic currency in exchange for private commercial paper. By 1931 the old Caja even issued domestic currency against treasury paper.[28]

Gold inflows had long ceased at this point, but subsequent gold outflows for fiscal use were sterilized; and even when there were no gold movements the Conversion Office often unilaterally changed the nominal stock of money via rediscounts.[29] Accordingly, we consider this *the* decisive regime change for Argentine economic policy, certainly during the Great Depression and possibly for the twentieth century as a whole.

The basis of the monetary regime shifted from metallic to fiduciary in 1931. By the end of the year, after just nine months, fiat notes rediscounted by the Conversion Office rose from zero to as much as 30 percent of the monetary base. By 1932 the gold backing had already fallen from the targeted 78 percent in 1929 to 43 percent, a ratio only slightly above the lower limit allowed by law.

In this context, it is instructive to examine expectations as revealed by the behavior of the foreign-exchange market. In 1930, the gold premium was never above 28 percent—still below the 1923 mark. However, after the authorities started to sterilized the fiscal outflow of gold in 1931 by rediscounting, the premium skyrocketed to 81 percent and never reverted to a lower value (Figure 9.3).

The reaction of the foreign exchange market was a (very rapid) manifestation of beliefs that had changed: agents increasingly saw the delinking of gold and currency as a permanent phenomenon. Judging from Figure 9.2 they were right. For the 1931–35 period the average annual change in the gold stock was –6.7 million paper pesos, but the average change in the quantity of money was +0.6 million paper pesos.

We will argue that this precocious heterodox approach by Argentina's policymakers helped avert a severe economic collapse. Yet, it was remarkable that they could effect such a dramatic change in regime given decades of adherence to orthodoxy. Where did their bold ideas originate?

28. Díaz Alejandro (1983, pp. 16–17).
29. The rediscounts began under the auspices of the 1914 law and were augmented by a new series of rediscounts of treasury paper under the "Patriotic Loan" legislation of 1932. These are included in the figure.

The Political Economy of Reflation: A Déja-Vù in 1929?

We recall that the costly effects of deflation on the economy were nothing new in Argentine macroeconomic history. In the aftermath of the 1891 Baring Crisis, Argentine authorities had assured international investors that convertibility would be resumed quickly and at par. It was not to be. As we have noted, there arose a political-economy debate on whether a gold-standard regime should be restored at the original 1881 parity, or if, instead, convertibility should be pursued at the prevailing market rate, thus accommodating the devaluation. We saw that the most important argument denouncing the damaging effects of deflation originated from the little-known Argentine political economist Silvio Gesell (1862–1930) in an article entitled "Monetary Anemia."

The influence of Gesell's ideas on negative expectations and deflationary traps was recognized in the 1930s by Irving Fisher and John Maynard Keynes. In his book *Stamp Scrip,* Fisher acknowledged Gesell's innovative idea:

> Silvio Gesell, who died recently, was a German businessman and quasi-economist.... In 1890, while in Argentina, he proposed essentially that particular substitute for money which now bids fair to sweep [the United States] under the name of Stamp Scrip. Gesell before he died, accumulated a considerable following abroad; but it took the tortures of a depression to bring about any practical efforts to make use of his Stamp Scrip idea.[30]

Keynes went recognized Gesell's influence in the *General Theory:*

> The great puzzle of Effective Demand with which Malthus had wrestled vanished from economic literature. You will not find it mentioned even once in the whole works of Marshall, Edgeworth and Professor Pigou, from whose hands the classical theory has received its most mature imbodiment. It could only live on furtively, below the surface, in the underworlds of Karl Marx, Silvio Gesell or Major Douglas...

In a later chapter Keynes remarked that "it is convenient to mention at this point the strange, unduly neglected prophet Silvio Gesell whose work contains flashes of deep insight..."; he then expended a dozen pages explaining Gesell's contribution to the theory of money and interest.[31]

Gesell's critique of a fixed nominal quantity of money as a suboptimal monetary rule was certainly influential in the 1899 decision to resume convertibility at a new parity. Yet, interestingly enough, he is barely mentioned by the other main influential intellectual figure in our story, Raúl Prebisch. Prebisch was the most influential and respected economist and economic policymaker of the 1930s. He was, perhaps, the only one who could challenge the prevailing *mentalité* and conceive of a policy change to avoid the severe consequences of deflation in line with Gesell's ideas.[32]

30. Fisher (1933b, pp. 17–18).
31. Keynes (1935, pp. 32, 353–58, and 371–79).
32. During the de facto government of General Uriburu, Raúl Prebisch was the Undersecretary of Finance. Already, in 1921, he had written a brilliant article on the problems of the Argentine currency showing that he understood the costly effects of deflation. See Prebisch (1922).

An important task for Prebisch was persuading other policymakers to come around to his position, and his recollection of one such lobbying effort shows how. A crucial figure he had to persuade was Federico Pinedo, a politician and economist who at first viewed deviation from monetary orthodoxy with suspicion. In an interview years later, Prebisch recalled the meeting:

Prebisch: I am going to give you an idea of how Federico Pinedo was converted to the idea of creating a Central Bank. As I have said, when the General Uriburu spoke about the convenience of studying the creation of a central bank, in the report I wrote, Pinedo, in a series of conferences, disputed the idea. And he did it in a harsh manner. At the time, I knew him very little. But during the world depression there was a situation, when I was the Undersecretary of the Treasury, a catastrophic situation. The banking system was on the verge of collapse and we decided—I had the idea—to invoke an old rediscounting law that was never applied. The law was approved during the First World War, in the first week of panic that we experienced, and it allowed the Conversion Office to rediscount banking paper. We made it operational.... We stated that the rediscount law was to be applied.... Then Pinedo, who was in the opposition to the Provisional Government, in spite of having been a revolutionary, enrolled with the Partido Socialista Independiente.... He came to see me, I have now a clear picture of that moment; he said: "Prebisch, what mistake are you going to make?" *(«¿Que barbaridad van a hacer?»)* He was agitated...so nervous that he did not want to sit down.... I explained to him the critical situation of the Banco de la Nación. The Banco de la Nación was the institution that administered the Clearing House. The money that the Banco de la Nación had in the vaults was less than the cash at the Clearing House. That tells you about the gravity of the situation.

Q: In which period did this occur?

Prebisch: This was in the year 1932—no, in the year '31, in the depth of the world depression. I gave him a huge amount of confidential information....

Q: And at issue was the project to create the Central Bank?

Prebisch: No, no, no. It was putting in motion the rediscounting law to allow the Conversion Office to rediscount. And Pinedo believed that we would provoke inflation. I explained to him for two hours. I did not hide any secret....He asked me a few questions and he started to become more calm. After two hours standing up I said: "Ok, Doctor Pinedo, you now know how is the situation. What would you do if you were in my shoes in the cabinet of the Ministry of Finance?" And he had the loyalty of saying, and this is why I admired him so much: "the same thing that you are proposing". He said nothing more. His criticism of the government ceased. For the first time he understood in the dramatic crisis that engulfed the country and the financial system. And he started to support the measures of the government.... He convinced himself that there was no backtrack, that the Argentine monetary system based on the automatic exchange of gold for paper and paper for gold could not function. But this was in the year 1931. Then 1932 and 1933 elapsed and, when he was minister of Finance in 1934 he called me, and he asked me to draft the proposal for the creation of the Central Bank....[33]

With the leadership of Prebisch a consensus was reached by the economic intelligentsia in Argentina in which they clearly understood that the time had

33. Our own translation from Magariños de Mello (1991, pp. 108–109 and 110). We also see here how very careful Prebisch was to distinguish the 1931 change in regime, as he saw it, from his later work in the 1935 creation of the Central Bank.

come to abandon the rigid constraints imposed by a metallic monetary regime. No one was to perceive this as a temporary political economy decision, but as a fundamental break from the past: but could it save the Argentine economy?

Institutional Change: The Impact of Monetary Policy

In the discussion so far we have found strong prima facie evidence that if any policy actions mattered for Argentina's economic recovery from the Great Depression, it was most likely monetary policies and the change of regime that were central. We now try to quantify the impact of these policies on the evolution of the macroeconomy in the 1930s using econometric techniques.

The Model

We construct a three-equation dynamic econometric model of exchange rates, prices, and interest rates. The system is estimated using Ordinary Least Squares on annual data for the period 1884 to 1941 and is used for counterfactual simulations of alternative monetary policies in the 1930s.[34]

The estimated model, shown in Table 9.3, looks reasonable. In the first two equations, exchange rates and prices adjust in accord with PPP as they react to the lagged real exchange rate. There is fast pass through in one period from money to exchange rates (a coefficient of 0.25), but slower pass through to prices (a coefficient of 0.16), a common structure in open economy macromodels, reflecting fast adjustment in financial markets but more nominal rigidities in the

34. The equations of the model are as follows:

$$\begin{aligned}
\Delta \ln E_t &= \alpha_1 + \beta_1(L)(\Delta \ln E_{t-1}, \Delta \ln P_{t-1}) \\
&\quad + \gamma_1(L)(\Delta \ln M_t, \Delta \ln P_t^*) + \delta_1(L) \ln q_{t-1} + \epsilon_{1t}; \\
\Delta \ln P_t &= \alpha_2 + \beta_2(L)(\Delta \ln E_{t-1}, \Delta \ln P_{t-1}) \\
&\quad + \gamma_2(L)(\Delta \ln M_t, \Delta \ln P_t^*) + \delta_2(L) \ln q_{t-1} + \epsilon_{2t}; \\
r_t &= \alpha_3 + \beta_3(L)(\Delta \ln M_t, \Delta \ln Y_t, \Delta \ln P_{t-1}, i_{t-1}) + \epsilon_{3t};
\end{aligned}$$

where E_t is the exchange rate in paper pesos per U.S. dollar, P_t is the price level, M_t is the money base, P_t^* is the U.S. price level, $q_t = \ln(E_t P_t^* / P_t)$ is the log real exchange rate, i_t is the nominal interest rate, $r_t = i_t - \Delta \ln P_t$ is the real interest rate, and Y_t is real output.

The first two equations model adjustments of the real exchange rate as being driven by two forces: endogenous adjustment via the lags of E and P and the error correction term q; and exogenous adjustments via forcing terms M and P^*. We treat the U.S. price level P^* as exogenous to the Argentine economy, and we impose PPP so that q is the relevant error correction term. We also allow monetary policy effects, to the extent that they are orthogonal to q, and any serial correlation terms, to have an impact. This might be viewed as "independent" components of monetary policy; for example, money innovations not, say, predicted via the price-specie-flow rule (that is, via q). Since our sample is 1884 to 1941, the bulk of these years (excluding 1900–1914 and 1927–29) are years of inconvertibility, and the assumption of complete exogeneity of money is reasonable. The final equation is a standard Mishkin interest rate forecasting equation of the type used by Romer in her analysis of the United States. Great Depression. It is used here in a similar form, with three lags found significant using a step down procedure. See Romer (1992); Mishkin (1992).

Cartoon 9.2. *El fenómeno de la Casa Rosada.* (The phenomenon of the Casa Rosada.)
Notes: Federico Pinedo is in command of creating the central bank. On stage, he turns gold into paper. In the box, President Justo and his ministers applaud the performance.
Source: Caras y caretas, vol. 38, no. 1901, March 9, 1935.

economy as a whole. Foreign prices pass through to domestic prices quickly, as one would expect in a small open economy. With noninstantaneous adjustment there is scope for monetary policy to effect real devaluations. In the third equation, the real interest rate is significantly affected by money growth so monetary expansions can temporarily drive down real interest rates.

The Counterfactual

Did monetary policies under a new regime end the Argentine Great Depression? The question contains implicit counterfactuals that needs to be examined: essentially, had the monetary regime not changed, what would have happened? Given the suspension of convertibility in 1929, and the imposition of exchange controls, the fiscal use of gold for debt service implies an exogenous path for the gold stock. This simplifies our analysis greatly as we do not have to model endogenous gold flows in a free market for foreign exchange. We just have to consider counterfactual paths of money, and we study two cases.

The basic counterfactual (CF1) examines what would have happened absent the expansion of domestic credit begun by the Conversion Office in mid-1931. In the counterfactual, the sole movements of gold would have continued to be the fiscal use of gold by the central government to service external debt: the currency board would not break the rules and attempt to sterilize the gold outflows by rediscounting.

In a second and less harsh counterfactual (CF2) we permit the authorities to revalue gold, as actually happened, in 1935. But we allow no other forms of monetary expansion after 1935, and changes in money base are based on the actual path of gold and reserves at the Central Bank. Thus, in CF1, we effectively imagine a world without a Central Bank. In CF2, we effectively imagine a world without the Conversion Office rediscounts, but still allow the Central Bank to revalue gold.

Both counterfactuals imply large shocks to the path of money (see Table 9.1). From 1929 to 1934, M0 held constant at around 1,200 million pesos. Gold stocks fell by almost half, from 954 million, to 561 million; but after 1931 domestic credit expanded from 293 million (its level since 1900) and reached 610 million in 1934, almost exactly offsetting the gold loss. Thus, both counterfactuals would have implied a counterfactual decline in 1934 of about 28 percent in money base—a massive nominal shock.

The two counterfactuals differ in what would have happened after 1935. In CF2 the impacts would have been small, since the revaluation in 1935 added almost a billion pesos to the gold backing, expanding it from 561 million paper pesos to 1,354 million. Arithmetically, this overnight "expansion" of gold was

Table 9.3. *Model of Prices, Exchange Rates, and Interest Rates*

A. VAR Model of Exchange Rates and Prices

Dependent Variable	$\Delta \ln E$	$\Delta \ln P$
Constant	0.11 (0.2)	-0.73 (1.6)
$\Delta \ln E(t\text{-}1)$	0.02 (0.1)	0.30 (1.7)
$\Delta \ln P(t\text{-}1)$	0.04 (0.2)	-0.09 (0.6)
$\Delta \ln M$	0.25 (1.6)	0.16 (1.1)
$\Delta \ln P^*$	-0.51 (1.6)	1.21 (4.2)
$q(t\text{-}1)$	-0.02 (0.2)	0.16 (1.6)
Observations	56	56
R-squared	.15	.35
Mean of Dependent Variable	0.02	0.02
Standard Error of Estimate	0.11	0.10
Regression $F(5,50)$	1.45	4.69

B. Mishkin-Type Forecast of Real Interest Rate

Dependent Variable	r
Constant	9.69 (1.1)
$\Delta \ln M$	-47.24 (3.0)
$\Delta \ln M(t\text{-}1)$	-44.10 (2.6)
$\Delta \ln M(t\text{-}2)$	-48.26 (2.8)
$\Delta \ln Y$	71.73 (2.6)
$\Delta \ln Y(t\text{-}1)$	-4.64 (0.2)
$\Delta \ln Y(t\text{-}2)$	17.02 (0.6)
$i(t\text{-}1)$	-0.27 (0.1)
$i(t\text{-}2)$	3.23 (0.9)
$i(t\text{-}3)$	-3.50 (1.4)
$\Delta \ln P(t\text{-}1)$	9.91 (0.7)
$\Delta \ln P(t\text{-}2)$	25.64 (1.8)
$\Delta \ln P(t\text{-}3)$	23.11 (1.8)
Observations	54
R-squared	.52
Mean of Dependent Variable	3.46
Standard Error of Estimate	10.42
Regression $F(5,50)$	3.20

Notes and sources: See Appendix 1 and text. Sample is annual data 1884–1941. Absolute t-statistics in parentheses.

enough to offset all of the unbacked domestic credit.[35] In CF1, conditions after 1935 would have been tougher. Absent revaluation, the path of reserves after 1935 would have been flat up to 1940. There would never have been a significant expansion of the money base to compensate for the almost one third decline after 1929.

Figure 9.5 shows the paths for prices, exchange rates, and interest rates in the two counterfactuals, using the above estimated model. The results show movements in the various variables that accord with intuition as regards the direction of change.[36]

1. *The price level.* In 1929–33 prices showed a cumulative decline of about 5 to 10 percent. In the counterfactuals Argentina would have suffered a more severe and extended deflation in the early 1930s. Without rediscounting, the price level would have fallen about 40 percent, a scenario which would have prolonged deflationary expectations. In the CF2, prices would have barely regained their 1929 price level after 1935 even with the huge gold revaluation. Significant pass-through of U.S. deflation could only just be offset by the revaluation. Worse still would have been the outcome without a revaluation: CF1 shows a persistent 10 percent decline in prices below the 1929 level, raising the question as to whether deflationary expectations would have ever been erased in the 1930s under the old regime.
2. *The nominal exchange rate.* The exchange rate depreciated markedly after the end of convertibility in 1929, with a more than 50 percent loss of value by 1935. This development seriously undermined the credibility of a resumption at the prevailing par of 2.27. Once par was unilaterally adjusted from 2.27 to 4.96 in May 1935 there was no turning back (Figure 9.3). Absent rediscounting, the exchange rate would have been 15 to 20 percent stronger in 1931–34.[37] It is thus not clear whether, in the counterfactual world, agents would have been sure of a permanent regime shift. Without the revaluation of gold the mild depreciation would have persisted into the late 1930s, and, with it, the prospect of a deflation

35. This followed from the peso's loss of more than half its value relative to the old parity of 2.27. The "new" gold cover allowed the Central Bank to create an apparent reduction in domestic credit from 610 million pesos in December 1934 to just 293 million in December 1935 (see Table 9.1 and Figure 9.4). Note that the money injection was not instantaneous, as can be seen from the monthly data, so, for the first couple of months of the Central Bank's existence domestic credit was actually *negative*—that is, gold and reserve backing at the new parity exceeded the outstanding money base: backing was more than 100 percent. See Figure 9.4.
36. Note that all fitted values are derived using one-step-ahead forecast—i.e., actual lagged values are used. For the counterfactuals, dynamic forecast are used, where current fitted values are saved and used as future lagged values.
37. This should not be dismissed as trivial: the reversibility, via deflation, of a 15 percent depreciation is a lot more plausible than the reversal of a 50 percent depreciation. Indeed, such movements in the paper-gold exchange rate had been reversed in the 1920s to permit resumption in 1927 (see Figure 9.3).

Figure 9.5. Prices, Exchange Rates, and Interest Rates, 1929–41

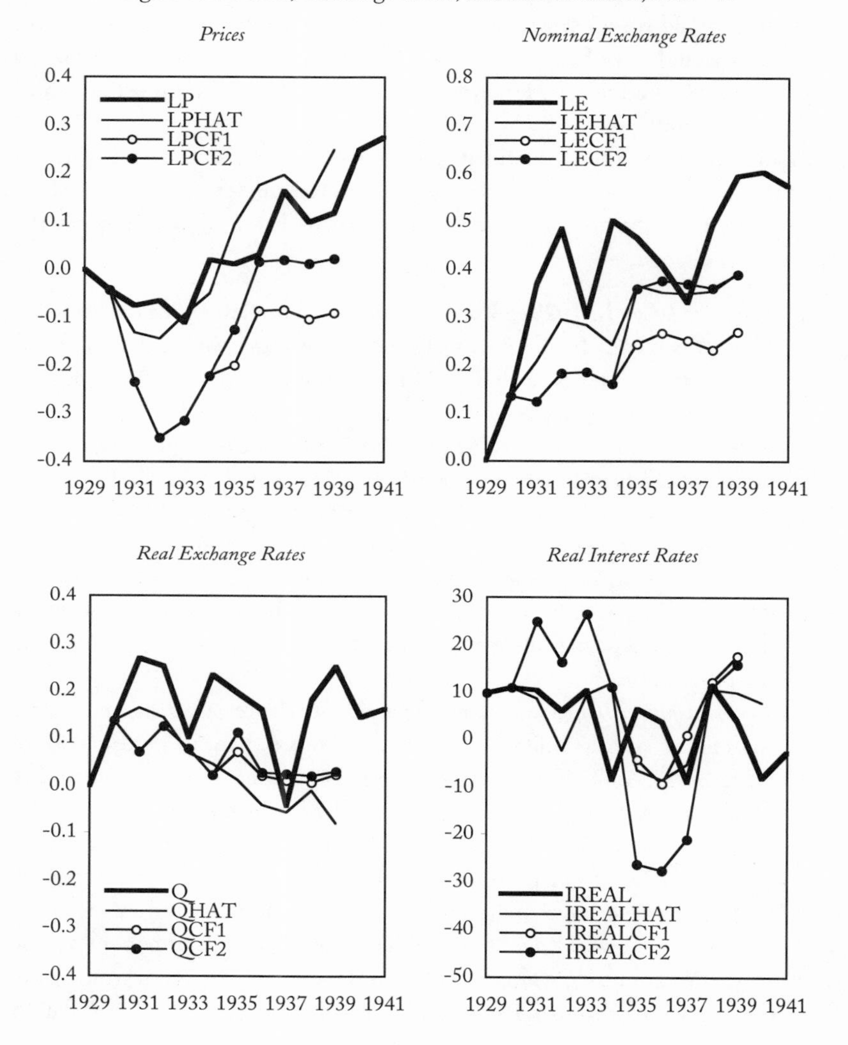

Notes and sources: See Appendix 1, text, and Table 9.3. $LE = \ln E$; $LP = \ln P$; $Q = \ln(EP^*/P)$, IREAL = r; XHAT = fitted value of X; XCF1 = value of X in first counterfactual; XCF2 = value of X in second counterfactual.

to regain the old par, as in the 1920s. In contrast, the actual story for the exchange rate makes clear the regime shift. Once the paper-gold exchange rate had risen into the range of 5 to 6, agents suspected that the government would not embark on a deflationary attack to reactivate the old regime. The costs, political and economic, would have been too high, and the action thus highly implausible. Instead, drawing on their own history, Argentines saw a parallel to the resumption in 1899 after the inflation of the 1890s, when a sufficiently large devaluation of the paper peso relative to gold (from 1.0 to 2.27) required a shift to a new parity to escape the deflation trap.[38]

3. *The real exchange rate.* The real depreciation of 1929–31 is apparent, but the reversion to PPP is also clear in the figure. Further, the impact of monetary policy in the counterfactual experiments appears weak. Certainly, without the rediscounts, there would have been less real depreciation after 1931, but only by 5 to 10 percent. Similarly, after 1935, the real exchange rate would have deviated little from its fitted value. We conclude that the real exchange rate channel was only a weak conduit for the impact of Argentine monetary policy.[39] So, does this imply that recovery was largely external in origin? And did Argentine policymakers have no real impact through their supposedly radical change of regime? We think not—but if the real exchange rate effects were weak, then we are forced to consider an alternative channel.
4. *Real interest rates.* Real interest rates were high in 1929–31, at about 10 percent. Although nominal rates were much lower (Table 9.1), ex post deflation and ex ante expected deflation contributed to high real rates. The fitted real interest rate, an estimate of ex ante real interest rates constructed using the Mishkin regression technique, adds to this sense of a deflationary regime before 1931. The turning point was the start of rediscounts. Absent this action by the Conversion Office the real interest rate would have risen dramatically to between 20 and 30 percent in the years 1931–34, largely as a result of worsening deflation and persistence in the forecasting equation. Such painfully high real interest rates would have had devastating effects on real activity, particularly investment, killing

38. Or in the international context of the 1920s and 1930s, agents could look overseas for comparisons in the event that orthodox thinking should return: at 300–400 pesos a strategy akin to British deflation in the mid-1920s was conceivable, if a reversal of course was to be contemplated. At over 500 pesos to the dollar, agents would see the situation as closer to the French scenario of the mid-1920s, with resumption at a new par or no resumption at all (but certainly no chance of resumption at the old par).
39. This, in part, reflects the counterbalancing impacts of foreign monetary policy in 1929–31. The real and nominal exchange rate effects of Argentina's policy might be expected to be small, as compared to the much bigger effect of U.S. monetary policy on U.S. prices and exchange rates. In this view of the world, mistakes by the U.S. monetary authority helped other countries recover because of their *enrich*-thy-neighbor impact on real activity via the real exchange-rate channel.

Figure 9.6. Real Interest Rates, Consumption, and Investment, 1929–41

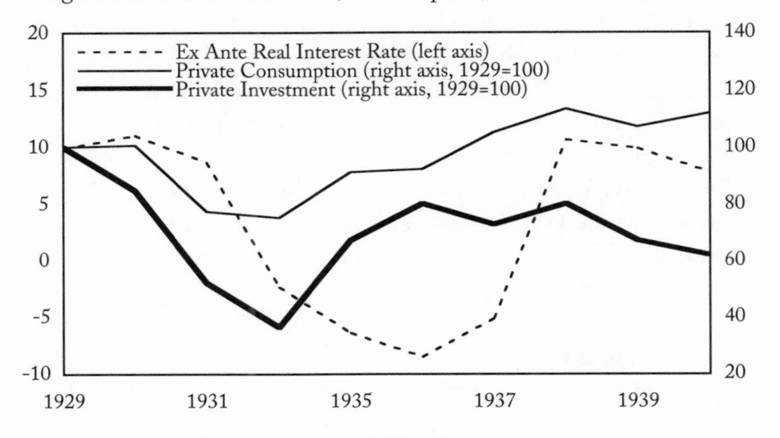

Notes and sources: See Appendix 1, text, and Table 9.3.

any chance of recovery.[40] In actuality investment recovery began in 1932 (Table 9.1) just after real interest rates fell.

Given the evidence from our model, we think the main impact of monetary policy change on recovery was in the years 1931–34, when the collapse of output was reversed and recovery to the 1929 level of activity was secured. This did not result from an explicit policy of real depreciation; movements in Argentine monetary policy were very small relative to changes in foreign (U.S.) monetary policy in this period. Nor was the channel the credit market, and lower nominal interest rates, the so-called "Keynes" effect; after all, nominal rates were low and had little to fall before hitting their floor. Rather, the channel was the elimination of deflationary expectations, or the so-called "Mundell" effect; after 1931, the fear of deflation was gone, expectations changed as the monetary regime shifted, and the institutional change began to look credible and permanent.

Investigating the impact of monetary policies after 1933 in the United States, Romer (1992) found a marked correlation between declines in real interest rates, and recovery in investment and consumption activity. She saw this as confirmation of the transmission mechanism from monetary policy to recovery via real interest rates. In the same fashion, we display in Figure 9.6 the same

40. Of course, under CF2, a large injection of money would still have ensued in 1935, from the gold revaluation plan, and, proportionately this would have been much larger, as a fraction of the level of money base in 1935, than in the actual case, absent the rediscounts of 1931–34. Thus, in CF2, there is one very big change in money base in 1935, enough to temporarily drive real interest rates very low for a year or two. Absent the revaluation, in CF1, this effect disappears and real interest rates stay higher, although they do diminish finally in 1935–36 as a result of temporary gold inflows (see Table 9.1).

variables for the Argentine case. Exactly the same pattern is apparent: after 1931 ex ante real interest rates fell, and, as discussed, all of this movement is attributable to the reversal of deflationary expectations; at the same moment, consumption and investment began to recover, offering more evidence in favor of a "Mundell effect" interpretation.

We think these results show strong support for the idea that the change in macroeconomic regime averted a serious depression in Argentina. However, in support of this hypothesis we might also seek more qualitative evidence that such a regime shift took place.

What Were They Thinking?

In this section we first examine documentary evidence to see what popular opinion in newspapers and other reports has to say about the regime change. We then look back at the trade-off policymakers faced between external default on debts and internal default on convertibility, that is, the choice between fiscal and monetary orthodoxy.

Supporting Evidence: Tracking the Crisis in Contemporary Reports

To better document the perceptions of a change in regime we examined the accounts of contemporaries. Newspapers gave great emphasis to the decrees of December 5, 1929 (the option to rediscount), and December 16, 1929 (suspension of convertibility, referred to as "closure" of the Conversion Office). Reports commented on the impact of gold flows on domestic economy and the inelastic relationship between money and gold. A heated debate about suspension ensued. Some observers considered the rediscount law acceptable, as long as it was not used to monetize deficits and was temporary. Others thought the closure of the Conversion Office illegal. International reaction was not seen as negative since Argentina was able to close on new £5 million loan from Baring and Morgan, despite the suspension.[41]

As the crisis mounted, attention turned to the fiscal problem. Very soon it was appreciated that if the trade balance did not recover and future refinancing

41. "Closure of Caja de Conversión," *Review of the River Plate* (henceforth *RRP*), December 20, 1929, p. 9. Alejandro E. Bunge, "The Rediscounting Faculty," *RRP,* December 20, 1929, p. 11. "The Closure of the Caja de Conversión," *RRP,* December 20, 1929, p. 19. Diego Ortiz Grognet, "Causes and Effects of The Closure of the Caja de Conversión," *RRP,* December 27, 1929, p. 13. Diego Ortiz Grognet, "Results of The Closure of the Caja de Conversión," *RRP,* January 3, 1930, p. 11. Alejandro E. Bunge, "Gold Exports," *RRP,* January 10, 1930, p. 11. Fortunato B. Arzeno, "The Caja de Conversión and the Rediscount Faculty," *RRP,* January 17, 1930, p. 15. "The National Credit," *RRP,* December 27, 1929, p. 19. Guillermo E. Leguizamon, "Illegalidad e inconveniencia de la clausura de la Caja de Conversión," *Revista de Economía Argentina,* June 1931, p. 449.

fell short, then gold would be used to avoid default and it would be desirable to sterilize the outflow:

Everything tends to the belief that the international balance of payments may be unfavorable in 1930.... in consequence, it is of great importance to adopt from now onward, measures tending to reduce imports, to promote the introduction of foreign capital.... In the regrettable event of the foregoing solutions not being adopted in adequate degree, it will be necessary to export more gold, possibly to the equivalent of some 200 million pesos paper.... In the event of this gold going out, it would be desirable to make use of the rediscount facility...[42]

At the same time, pressure came from the banking sector to ease the liquidity crunch. The Banco de la Nación had already made abundant use of its rediscount provision in creating banking money to help other banks in distress. Now it sought relief in the form of high-powered money via the Conversion Office's own, hitherto unused, rediscount facility:

At the moment when the moving of the crops and the usual end-of-year business habitually begin to require a larger quantity of notes in circulation, the private banks would not have been able to contribute adequately to supply them without detriment to their own relatively low supplies.... It was indispensable to give them access to the resources of the Banco de la Nación by means of the rediscount of their commercial portfolios.... Against this however, the situation of the bank itself was an obstacle, as its own cash holdings, reduced by the efflux of gold, could not be strained further.... Hence the necessity of permitting the rediscount of commercial bills at the Caja...and the petition in that sense presented to the Executive Power.[43]

Thus, lobbying began to get the rediscount provision actually used. Still, no action was taken by the Radical government to employ it and nobody was sure the regime change would happen.[44]

Slowly, financial constraints tightened. A new loan of 50 million dollars was secured in April 1930, but only for 6 months. It was a short-term patch of the fiscal gap, and it failed to halt the depreciation.[45] By now pessimism was gathering steam; orthodox views were harder to maintain and the calls for central banking were growing.[46] Observers saw through the gold standard's "asymme-

42. Alejandro E. Bunge, "The Fall in the Peso: Loan Issues Abroad," *RRP,* January 31, 1930, p. 19–23.
43. Banco de la Nación Argentina, "The Financial Year 1929," *RRP,* February 21, 1930, p. 11.
44. Some observers lobbied for a central bank as a solution but this required a long-range plan. Moreover, the Irigoyen administration was distracted, confronting much bigger social and political problems in the year 1930. A rapid reaction was needed as attempts to plug the gap were getting desperate. "The Monetary Question and Possible Answers," *RRP,* March 7, 1930, p. 13. "From Conversion to Centralization? Will Argentina Join the World Movement toward Central Banking?" *RRP,* April 11, 1930, p. 15.
45. *RRP,* April 11, 1930, p. 17. *RRP,* April 18, 1930, p. 7.
46. Alejandro E. Bunge. "Argentine Money, Finance, and Balance of Payments: The Outlook for 1930," *RRP,* June 20, 1930, p. 11. "Central Banking and Currency Control: Gold Movements and Cash Reserves—Their Aplication [sic] to Argentine Conditions," *RRP,* May 9, 1930, p. 15. "Deserting the Gold Standard: Argentina's Attitude toward Gold Movements," *RRP,* May 30, 1930, p. 17.

try" and the adverse consequences of large-scale sterilizations by France and the United States. An early resumption began to seem unlikely and even once-conservative commentators such as the *Review of the River Plate* started to see that reopening the Conversion Office would have disastrous consequences.[47] Around the same time it became apparent that the deflation was having serious effects on business:

If the risk-taking capital and the entrepreneurs' reward are greatly reduced, this being the mainspring of our economic machine, business enterprise is grievously restricted. It is very difficult to get a forward business movement on a *falling* price level. No doubt in the long run just as good business can be done upon one level as another, but it is the transition that works havoc. The object of greater stability is to avoid these dangers.[48]

In September, the Radical government of Irigoyen was deposed amid labor unrest and breakdown in the rule of law. General Uriburu led a new government committed to sound policies to rebuild the economy. But there was still no change in monetary policy: the new Finance Minister thought any "fundamental" change should await a subsequent, democratically elected government.[49]

There was still no use of the rediscount law, and this remained so until April 25, 1931. Contemporary domestic and international reports saw this as the crucial turning point. On the next day the most influential daily *La Nación* led with the story on its front page under the headline "THE REDISCOUNT UP TO 200,000,000 PESOS WAS AUTHORIZED," remarking that

The measure was suggested by the business and commercial corporations to the government. The government affirms that this is not to create new ventures but rather a definite means to regulate credit to avoid the sudden contraction of loans by banks.... Undersecretary Prebisch added that this is an important step that the government has made to overcome the biggest defect in the prevailing monetary system, which is the rigid inelasticity of the volume of money in circulation.

The *Review of the River Plate* reflected the views of international business and led its next issue on May 1 with a story titled "Re-Discount Decreed." A more optimistic outlook came the next week (May 8) in an article "Inflation as a Remedy: Would it Help to Cure Trade Depression?" they cited the "recently granted re-discount facilities" and noted that "needless to say the main interest in connection with the whole idea of inflation is centered upon its possible application to the remedy of the present state of world trade depression..."

International opinions can also be detected in the *Economist* article of May

47. "For while it is true that by opening the Conversion Office tomorrow exchange might be brought to close upon parity, the contraction in Argentine currency which would result might well prove catastrophic in its effects upon the general commercial movement in the country." See "Gold and the Currency: Are Shipments Under Current Conditions Advisable?," *RRP,* August 1, 1930, p. 29.
48. "A Stable Price Level: Are Present Difficulties Really Due to Over-Production?," *RRP,* August 15, 1930, p. 13–15. Emphasis as in the original.
49. "The Government and the Caja," *RRP,* September 19, 1930, p. 9.

23 "Re-Discount Operations in Argentina" where the inflationary essence of the whole plan was applauded:

> Rediscount of commercial paper held by the Banco de la Nación Argentina has already been effected with the Conversion Office.... The backing is ample, and provide that all the safeguards governing the commercial paper are adhered to unflinchingly, the issue of additional money at the present moment will help the local situation. Nevertheless, it is undeniably inflation, and moreover, it undermines, be it by ever so little, the whole principle of Argentina's currency legislation...

We think it is apparent that contemporary observers, domestic and foreign, were in little doubt that Argentina had taken a bold "inflationary" step in April 1931 in defiance of orthodoxy.[50]

Paths Not Taken: Why Not Just Default?

Are our counterfactuals the relevant ones for study? One puzzle not addressed by our analysis is why Argentina did not choose some other counterfactual path. An obvious candidate would be the path chosen by so many other countries in Latin America: default. If Argentina had not used up gold to honor external obligations there would have been no need for sterilizations and the use of the rediscount facility. This would have eased fiscal tensions in the 1930s—and perhaps at a small cost? It has been argued that being a "good debtor" in the 1930s did not do Argentina much good in the long run: in the postwar Argentina was treated no better than "bad debtors" in world markets.[51]

We have two responses to these observations. First, more than any other country in the region, Argentina had bought into the idea of orthodoxy ever since the painful attempt at stabilization during the 1890s Baring Crisis. In that watershed event, the national government suspended any attempt to restore convertibility but stopped short of canceling service on debts, although municipal and corporate issues were in a shameful default and had to be later assumed by the nation. As President Carlos Pellegrini declared during the negotiations:

50. Of course, Prebsich never viewed the policy as inflationary, rather antideflationary, in an attempt to stabilize prices in a specific historical situation. He was always ready to dismiss as academic arguments that the policies might lead to inflation. See his article "La inflación escolastica y la moneda argentina" in the July 1934 issue of *Revista de Economía Argentina.* In the long run, such inflationary tendencies *were* realized, but Prebisch resigned from the Central Bank in 1943 in objection to what he saw as a tendency to excessive money printing.
51. See Lindert and Morton (1989); Jorgensen and Sachs (1989); Eichengreen and Portes (1989). However, the fact that Argentina was not treated better than defaulters in capital markets after 1940 may not be a puzzle after all, because *ceteris paribus* did not apply. Prior to the 1940s Argentina stood out as a bastion of orthodoxy and sound policies in Latin America. With the rise of Perón, and a shift to inward-looking policies and price distortions, Argentina by the 1950s and 1960s looked like one of the worst places in Latin America for foreign investors, not one of the best, based on these objective economic criteria. Potential investors surely did not ignore these more immediate disincentives, whatever the repayment record decades prior. See Taylor (1994; 1998).

Not to have serviced these debts with punctuality, the government would have had to declare the country bankrupt, producing such a terrible reaction in our European creditors that there would not have been limits to the general indignation directed against us, and they would have closed forever those markets, resulting in the shame of our nation and the rapid decadence of our social state.[52]

We think the same *mentalité* persisted in the 1930s, "a conscious internal perception that satisfaction of debts was a necessity."[53] Argentina believed it would be rewarded for good behavior, as Pellegrini believed in the 1890s. It is striking that in the contemporary press the subject of default is almost never raised, and the possibility was dismissed as remote:

A precipitate return to parity is not, apparently, intended and would not be desirable.... The investor must, therefore, wait patiently for the financial and monetary reforms of the Provincial Government to fructify. This should not cause him any distress, since the service of the external debt of the Republic will be promptly effected and default, as far as the present Government is concerned, is unthinkable.[54]

Second, although it is generally agreed that as a "good debtor" Argentina reaped no long-run benefits after the 1940s, the ex post outcome differed from ex ante beliefs. Moreover, beliefs that faithful debt service would be rewarded *were* correct, at least in the short run. In the late 1930s, Argentina obtained much better access to capital markets than defaulting countries. There were several refinancing loans, including 129 million dollar of 35-year external conversion bonds in 1937 and a 25 million dollar 10-year issue in 1938. And the terms of these later loans were good:

The new issues yielded an average 4.7 percent when the U.S. rate on Baa corporate bonds hovered around 5.2 percent.... Thus Argentina's good behavior did seem to earn it some return in easier credit access during the 1930s when capital markets were closed to most Latin American countries.[55]

Sadly, the new loans flowed only briefly after the global crisis abated and before the Second World War. If such large-scale loans had been available in the early 1930s, instead of the small refinancing secured, Argentina might have averted the substantial fiscal use of gold in 1929–35.

The costs of deviating from the gold standard as a "contingent rule" were appreciated, as were the costs of default; capital markets could punish both kinds of deviance with higher costs of borrowing.[56] Argentina understood the tradeoffs and had to make a choice. As in a model of public debt management,

52. Quoted in Fishlow (1989, p. 99).
53. Fishlow (1989, p. 99).
54. *Economist,* March 14, 1931, p. 568.
55. Data on loans and quotation from Jorgensen and Sachs (1989, p. 75). It could be that Argentina gained an increase in reputation by paying in exceptionally harsh external circumstances, giving a "positive surprise" to its creditors. This is argued in a game theoretic model of reputation of capital-market access by Tomz (1998).
56. On the contingent rule, see Bordo and Kydland (1995); Bordo and Rockoff (1996).

the fiscal authority fixed the level of public debt and the monetary authority made the choice as to its composition as between bonds and money:[57]

> Increasing the rediscount limit and at the same time shipping gold to pay for the loan in question, means a reduction of the percentage of the metallic guarantee which Argentina's currency has hitherto enjoyed. It must not be forgotten, however, that even although this is in a sense equivalent to inflation, it has in its favour two very important points; in the first place, an external debt becomes an internal liability, and secondly the actual amount of the currency in the hands of the public suffers, for the time being, little or no change.[58]

The most elegant feature of the Argentine case is that once the country reached a "debt ceiling" the combination of an orthodox fiscal policy and a heterodox monetary policy satisfied the solvency (transversality) condition of the government budget constraint. In an exceptional international crisis, Argentina made a remarkably smooth transition to a fiduciary monetary regime while retaining creditworthiness in external capital markets. Although they had almost no degrees of freedom, such was the technocratic finesse of Prebisch and Pinedo.

57. Sargent (1986).
58. *RRP,* August 28, 1931, p. 17.

Part Five

Postscript

10
Postscript

After decades of monetary anarchy since independence, the enactment of the Monetary Law of 1881, and the subsequent experiments of the 1880s with bimetallism and free banking regimes, marked a moment when Argentina's policymakers started to search for monetary and fiscal stability. In the face of challenges common to all developing countries on the periphery of an integrated global economy, this search was marked by struggles and failures, most notably the spectacular Baring Crisis of 1890–91, which can be seen as the first emerging-market crisis of the modern era.

The lessons of the crisis informed the design of new institutions. From 1891 until the creation of the central bank in 1935, the Caja de Conversión, Argentina's first currency board, unilaterally enforced a hard gold-standard monetary regime in an attempt to provide a firm nominal anchor and restore the confidence of foreign investors. Monetary stability was achieved and economic growth was impressive, at least prior to the First World War. But the system didn't last, and there were signs of increasing vulnerability in the financial sector during the interwar period. The monetary regime prevented any Lender-of-Last-Resort actions, so volatility in world financial markets hit Argentina hard.

Our book has shown that institutional "learning by doing" in the search for macroeconomic stability was a notable feature of Argentina from 1880 to 1935. To invoke an expression of Charles Kindleberger, one senses that Argentine economic history could be summed up as being part of the never-ending struggle of "rules versus men."[1] However, we have shown that the extremely rich political-economy story can be interpreted and rationalized in the light of the modern apparatus of economic analysis. In this way, we have integrated in one approach extremely complex features such as money, public debt, and private finance. Employing such formalism, we seek the advantages of explicitly spelling out the underlying economic models. Though the formal approach requires more effort, it is of the utmost importance in revealing the

1. Kindleberger (2000).

rationales of Argentine policymakers, and why their economic strategy switched back and forth between strict "rules of the game" and broad discretion.

Original Sins: A Tale of Monetary Double Standards

As a concrete example of what we have learned from this approach, recall the chronic use of the inflation tax in the decades after independence, from the 1820s to the early 1860s (Figure 1.3). It should not be perceived as having been just an inefficient tax on domestic money holders but, moreover, as a dispute over the distribution of seigniorage among the different provinces. This was at the heart of the struggle between one of the most powerful economies of the hemisphere, the Province of Buenos Aires, and the other provinces in the Argentine Confederation. It was not only a fight over who would have the power to tax international trade, but also about more subtle ways of financing the governments' public expenditures. As Samuel Amaral has put it, the discovery of inflationary finance in the Province of Buenos Aires "enlightened" the political class and the *caudillos* of the other provinces, and in the issuance of fiduciary money they all saw a most welcome way to enlarge fiscal resources.[2]

Of course, it was here that the first major monetary design problems began for the small open economy of Argentina. Policymakers started thinking that money could function under a double standard: one standard for internal purposes (for this, read "try to extract as much seigniorage as you can"), another standard for external purposes (an internationally accepted standard to promote international finance and trade). The inherent contradictions of this plan did not stand in their way. From the time of independence in 1810, until the creation of the Conversion Office in 1890, domestic and external goals habitually alternated as the focus of Argentina's monetary policy regime, a corollary of alternating political-economy decisions. And, as it later became clear, this was not an easy habit to break.

The first external convertibility plan, from 1868 to 1875, failed. It gave way in the 1880s to a new doctrine that favored a system of plural banks of issue, permitting those banks to issue gold-guaranteed paper notes (wrongly described as a "free banking law"). This system was established alongside the 1881 law that established gold and silver as the bimetallic legal tenders for internal transactions, an attempt to restrict competition between different metallic monies. The new plan was derailed by attempts to deploy activist monetary policy despite the force of the macroeconomic trilemma. This scheme, plus the attempt to limit the use of other metallic monies—which may be seen as a very primitive precursor of capital controls—was a recipe for sure disaster. But it provided a wonderful laboratory for economic historians, namely the Baring Crisis.

2. Amaral (1988).

The First Emerging Market Crisis: Local Causes, Global Effects

We have shown that the Baring Crisis of 1891 was a phenomenon that entirely originated in domestic political-economy choices, namely an acute mismanagement of public debt and serious violations of time consistency in economic policies. It is now well understood that if a sovereign country is to have good standing, or a sound reputation, in its two major liabilities, money and bonds, then the expected solvency of the government should be beyond question.

If a country violates the consistency between monetary and fiscal policies and, hence, the intertemporal government budget constraint is not met, we know that at some point the government will have no option but to choose among several bad outcomes. In other words, if the "promised" values of money and debt cannot be sustained through time because of budget constraint violations, then there is no way out. A government will have to default either to money holders, or to bond holders, or distribute the losses in some particular way in the form of a partial default to both.

The inconsistencies in public debt management were clear in Argentina for the years 1888–91, a time when the government was pursuing an expansionary fiscal policy while simultaneously precommitting to restore a gold-standard regime. For a while, capital inflows could finance the conflicting monetary and fiscal actions, but the policy of sterilization after the balance of payments turned negative only financed an intense process of currency substitution by private agents as the speculative attack loomed. Collapse came about when all the government's specie was virtually depleted.

The specific details of policy inconsistency during the 1880s give us a new perspective on what an old and enduring problem we have in emerging-market crises. We have argued that the Baring Crisis can be seen as the first occurrence of this new breed of crisis. The Argentine policy mix included a fixed exchange-rate commitment (which at times degenerated into a dirty float); the free mobility of capital; a developing economy that for a short time was the darling of the world's financial markets; banks that made dubious loans to cronies (including their provincial overlords); balance sheets that were beset by maturity and currency mismatches (borrowing short in gold, lending long in pesos); no effective prudential banking regulation and oversight; and a monumental crash that brought intervention from a would-be International Lender of Last Resort, the Bank of England.[3]

3. Compare to a typical description of the recent Asian crises: "So what is the underlying cause of financial crises in the 1990s? More often than not, they have been triggered by external financial shocks that are amplified by failed fixed exchange rate regimes. However, the root cause is usually a weak banking system. In many developing countries, undercapitalized and badly supervised banks borrowed too much short-term money abroad and lent it to dubious projects at home. Cronyism and corruption made these weak banks even weaker as they made loans to very risky, unworthy projects owned by their shareholders and managers" (Minton Beddoes 1999).

The Baring Crisis is also one of the first examples of how an ill-fated small open economy can produce devastating spillover effects that radically change the size and direction of international capital flows in the world as a whole. In the early 1890s the London capital markets hastily retreated from investments overseas, after seeing such a massive and unprecedented crisis that almost wiped out a major house. The resulting tightening of capital markets depressed economic activity in many newly settled countries, such as Canada and Australia. The "contagion" thus affected countries that were, initially, very far from the events in Buenos Aires that precipitated the crisis.

Similarly, the recent 1997 Asian crisis developed in relatively small economies but had negative effects for emerging capital markets as a whole, and followed again despite the intervention of a different body seeking to act as International Lender of Last Resort, this time the IMF. After the recent crises in Asia, the ingredients in the Baring Crisis all sound very familiar, and likewise the outcomes. An optimistic reaction is to feel assured that the fundamental features of these crises have not varied so much in the long run, suggesting common economic and institutional problems and potential solutions. A pessimistic reaction is to wonder why, a century later, we are still left trying to figure out what those solutions are.

Curing a Bad Hangover: Good versus Bad Default

One important lesson from the Argentine experience is that when collapse arrives because credibility has totally eroded, even if the government attempts to implement textbook reforms to restore good economic policies, it is probably too late. The transversality condition will only be met by defaulting on some government obligations. This could be interpreted as a discretionary action ex post vis-à-vis what *would have been* the "correct" policy to implement ex ante. Basically you have no choice and you need to reset the initial fiscal conditions that will make credible the future adoption of intertemporally consistent monetary and fiscal policies. Paradoxically, in this state of classic debt overhang, you can only regain reputation for the future through default, by shedding the insolvency created by obligations inherited from the institutionally flawed past.

The Baring Crisis delivers some important lessons for the present. In fact, history seems to have repeated itself with the Argentine hyperinflation of 1989–90 and the convertibility plan devised to end the crisis. In the recent case, in 1990, before the adoption of a currency board and a dollar-exchange standard, the Argentine government had to default in some way. They chose to convert, by decree, all short-run time deposits (on average, seven-day maturity deposits invested in very short-run public bonds by private banks to finance the public sector) into a new ten-year public bond denominated in U.S. dollars called the

Bonex 89 yielding the LIBOR rate.[4] This was one way to smooth out public finance outlays by a forced rescheduling of the debt payments. The lesson again is that, before the highly orthodox convertibility plan could be put in place, the government had to rely on a very heterodox institutional shock to satisfy the transversality condition.

In our historical context, exactly one hundred years prior to the so-called Bonex plan, in 1891 Argentine policymakers chose a similar path. They elected to heavily tax (read, default on) domestic money and deposit balances through a large devaluation and the closure of a large number of domestic financial institutions (more than 40 percent of total financial intermediation). President Carlos Pellegrini's choice was to preserve Argentina's reputation in international debt and capital markets. One detail that is not very well known here is that the Argentine Republic never technically defaulted on its bearer external debt or bonds. This was thanks to the Bank of England, which acted as an International Lender of Last Resort for the benefit of, in essence, the widely dispersed group of bondholders.

The importance of the leadership shown by Pellegrini is clear. He convinced congress that the prospects of the Argentine economy were intimately linked with international markets for goods, labor, and, especially, capital. To have opted to default in that international scenario would have risked condemning Argentina to a long period of autarky, at that time surely a suboptimal strategy of economic development for a capital-scarce economy. Even with a policy of "good behavior" in international capital markets from then on, Argentina had to take the extra step in 1898 of nationalizing all the provincial and municipal external debt—only after that, could it tap fresh funds in the international capital markets.

Escape from a Trap: The Asymmetry of Inflation and Deflation

After the crisis, fresh problems appeared. The drastic monetary, fiscal, and financial reforms of 1891–92 produced a new economic phenomenon. A deflationary scenario set in under a monetary rule that we termed the Gesell-Friedman rule, by which the government switched to a goal of fixing the quantity of monetary base to halt the depreciation of paper money.

There was a protracted deflation of domestic prices and observers like Silvio Gesell, who was later quoted by Irving Fisher and John Maynard Keynes, saw the asymmetric effects of inflationary and deflationary regimes. Gesell's arguments about the disruptive effects of deflation on domestic investment proved convincing. The extremely costly dynamics of monetary policy, aimed at restoration at the old par via a steep deflation, were stopped. Thus, the years

4. LIBOR is the London Inter-Bank Offer Rate, a global interest rate benchmark for safe assets. The Bonex 89 bonds carried no premium, but were floated at a deep discount.

1891–99 provide an extraordinary laboratory to allow us to understand the differences between disinflating an overheated economy, and the danger of going too far and entering a path of deflationary expectations.

As we saw toward the end of the book, deflationary expectations were not avoided during the short-lived 1927–29 Gold Standard period. However, we showed how, under those extreme circumstances, with the use of good economic intuition backed with credibility and a sound monetary and fiscal situation, some very able policymakers were able to put in place a new macroeconomic regime to drastically alter the deflationary expectations prevailing until 1931. We constructed a dynamic model of exchange rates, prices, and interest rates to illustrate how good policy actions mattered for Argentina's recovery from the Great Depression.

The search for price and monetary stability this time took the form of a change in the optimal monetary and exchange rate regime. By using up a relatively abundant and idle government asset, namely international reserves and specie in excess of the legal requirement of the convertibility law, the monetary regime shifted in 1931 toward targeting and anchoring the nominal quantity of money and the level of prices. Only this could convince agents to discard their views as to the likely persistence of deflationary pressures. This, in turn, lowered ex ante real interest rates and boosted recovery in the real sector. The policy was a success in that, by any standard, Argentina was only mildly affected by the Great Depression. This turnaround constituted a classic example of the real effects of changing expectations à la Sargent. It showed how one can use an inflationary regime change to escape a liquidity trap, that is, when one is close to the nominal interest rate floor in a deflationary scenario.

With the so-called "taming of inflation" witnessed in many countries in the 1990s, discussion again has turned to the threat of deflation in the event that central banks err too far on the side of tightening policy. This could be particularly harmful in the event of a major recession coupled with deflationary expectations. It is no wonder then that current events in Japan are prompting such fears, and justifying comparisons to the 1930s and, for those with longer memories, the 1890s. The Argentine experience is highly relevant here, since once the economy stabilized in the late 1890s there began a spectacular period of economic growth and prosperity that is rightly remembered as the Belle Époque. We can only wonder whether some contemporary Japanese equivalent of Silvio Gesell waits in the wings to argue for a radical policy shift to change expectations and restart economic growth in what is, by long-term measures, an economy with still outstanding prospects based on fundamentals.

Local versus Global Finance: Bank Stability in an Open Economy

We noted that previous scholars have curiously neglected the question of the extent of financial deepening in emerging countries during the interwar period. We have shown that Argentine financial intermediation technology was not very strong and could not fill the void left by the downsizing of the London capital market after 1914. Here we found some important features that differentiate the banking experience of Argentina from, say, that in Canada or in the United States. For the latter, it has been said that the absence of a well-diversified branch banking system made financial institutions extremely fragile in the event of a negative idiosyncratic shock to a particular city or region. In the case of Argentina, there was an ongoing process of branch banking and geographic diversification—but the financial system was nevertheless prone to recurrent crises and the banks, especially the domestic ones, were subject to sizeable capital crunches. In particular, there were markedly different lending responses in domestic and foreign banks when subject to shocks.

The volatility of lending by banks in a globalized international capital market is something that deserves close scrutiny. In the Argentine case, while foreign banks brought more efficient and voluminous lending, they also "overreacted" to changes in the fundamentals of this emerging market economy. The issue is obviously relevant today, given the almost unanimous belief that the internationalization of banking is always welfare enhancing for a small open economy.

The usual argument says that if there is an idiosyncratic shock, a well diversified bank (read, an international bank) will basically smooth out the regional shock by reallocating assets or liquid funds to or from world headquarters. However, this assumes that the branches in a particular region, say Argentina, are treated pari passu like any other branch within the country of origin (or in the global network) of the bank in question.

However, our study suggests that in spite of a dramatic internationalization of banking in Argentina, especially between 1895 and 1913, foreign-owned banks still heavily weighed country-specific risk factors in their conduct of banking business in their theoretically multinational enterprise. In practice, we think this meant that there was an in-house segmentation of branches or country networks. If that was (and is) the way banking businesses operate then one might ask if the welfare enhancing effects of the internationalization of banking are truly realized. This is a serious and very open question for countries currently pursuing openness and financial liberalization, and raises the question as to what steps should be taken under a fixed exchange-rate regime to minimize the fugacity of foreign exchange.

A final question regarding financial structure also emerges from the Argentine macroeconomic experience. In particular, we are intrigued by the very different asset structures of foreign banks (a high proportion of very short maturity assets) and domestic private banks (a high proportion of long-maturity assets). What does this mean for the nexus of the financial system and the supply of capital for domestic investment?

Our empirical evidence suggests that the "overreacting" behavior of foreign banks and the "underreacting" behavior of domestic banks were a result of their asset structures. Typically, in bad financial times banks try to call up loans to increase their liquidity cushion. However, not all loans are equally liquid. Foreign banks specialized in commercial short-term and trade finance while domestic banks invested in industrial, venture, and real-estate finance. Domestic banks built a comparative advantage in longer-term lending and local monitoring but they were subject to huge capital crunches in the event of a negative shock because they were doing precisely what a bank is supposed to do, engaging in the transformation of the maturity of assets.

The Dilemma: Internal versus External Convertibility

We saw that domestic banks could not attain high leverage so as to advance large quantities of credit for long-term endeavors. This suggests a clue to understanding the financial fragility (and suboptimality) of small open economies in search of monetary stability. Part of the broader trilemma, we call this the dilemma of internal versus external convertibility, referring to the tension between inside versus outside money.

In the last part of the book we addressed in more detail the role of the financial sector as a possible source of monetary-regime inconsistency. Again, if the money supply is a multiple of the monetary base, we should care about the behavior of the money multiplier. The banking sector creates secondary money by means of the deposits they hold. However, under a fixed exchange-rate regime the monetary authority, the Conversion Office, assumed only a macroeconomic responsibility for preserving the external value of money. It had no instruments to assume the microeconomic responsibility of guaranteeing the stability of the financial system.

This monetary "separation of powers" was the intent, at least; but we showed how, in practice, the banking system did not function without constant bailouts from the state bank and, when that was left insolvent, from the Conversion Office itself. While such an eventual conflict of interest might be held as an institutional failure in the Argentine case, it is a very common confusion. For example, it reveals no more or less inconsistency than was seen the founding charter of the U.S. Federal Reserve Board. The Fed was there authorized to preserve the value of money and also act as a Lender of Last Resort, two fundamentally incompatible goals given a single instrument.[5]

5. This conflict in the U.S. Federal Reserve's charter was highlighted by Sargent (1993).

We can see some quite clear parallels with recent experience here too in many emerging economies, but most clearly so in Argentina. Consider the 1995 shocks following the December 1994 Tequila Crisis in Mexico. The currency board had to sit tight while a run on fractional reserve deposits hit the banking system. An 18 percent fall in deposits in 4 months made for some painful choices. Afterward, the government negotiated alternative fiscal sources for Lender of Last Resort provision, specifically a contingent credit line with various major banks, but at the time it had little power to respond.

Heuristically, we can see the multiple equilibrium possibilities immediately. If you have a bad banking system you can have macroeconomic consistency threatened by a run from deposits to cash to the reserve currency, the "bad equilibrium" where the interest rate defense fails. A "good" equilibrium with strong banks is possible, but here leverage may be very low (because reserves are high), implying less intermediation and weak financial depth.

Steering a course here proved hard for Argentina in the 1920s, just as it has for many emerging markets today seeking to blend private and state-led financing of growth. Argentina's problem was a defective intermediary, a weak link in the chain, the Banco de la Nación. This "too big to fail" state bank unilaterally took on board Lender-of-Last-Resort prerogatives. But even as it did so it completely failed to adhere to sound Lender-of-Last-Resort practices. Instead of offering plentiful liquidity at a penalty rate with good collateral à la Bagehot, the bank offered crony loans at a rate even below the deposit rate, and took on board dubious "lemon loan" paper via rediscounting.[6] These were not principles by which a well-structured banking system could survive, but this lesson is still being rediscovered in the Asian economies after the crises of 1997.

It is at this point worth asking: can countries avoid the dilemma of internal versus external convertibility altogether? We know that two very radical alternatives exist, one or both of which might be followed in the future. One way to avoid runs is via the adoption of a "narrow banking" system, that would make banking deposit insurance redundant, with the major class of retail banks only permitted to be "mutual funds" holding government bonds, thus allowing deposits to be "priced" and eliminating inside money entirely. The other option sidesteps the risk of a run via a unilateral currency union (read, dollarization), eliminating outside money entirely. The overall picture of a chaotic and misdirected evolution in monetary and banking institutions in the Argentine historical case lends considerable appeal to these alternative prescriptions for regime consistency in emerging markets.

Ultimately, unresolved tensions between internal and external convertibility inherent in a small open economy must bring about radical institutional changes, as we saw in the Argentine case. First, in 1931, came the de facto end of the

6. Bagehot (1873).

metallic monetary regime. Then, in 1935, came the creation of the central bank to relieve the still dismal private and public financial situation. Yet can we call these *proactive* institutional changes (in particular the creation of the central bank)? Or were they the *reactive* result of a dynamically inconsistent, ill-conceived monetary and financial structure?

Unsolved political-economy dilemmas (or trilemmas) are the dual of polluted economic institutions in a dynamic context. Thus, as we have said before, in a regime where you have incompatible goals in some bad states of nature, it is just a matter of time before well-conceived institutions fall apart under political or discretionary manipulation. In this case, it was the Great Depression that triggered a radical change. The upside of the post-1931 policies was a rapid macroeconomic recovery; the downside, an unpleasant little secret of the period, was the vast expenditure on bailing out a very large mess in the financial sector. These two events, side by side, show clearly the key dilemma.

Macroeconomic Success: Recovery from the Great Depression

The work of economic historians has led to a new consensus as to the role of the gold standard in fostering deflation and depression in the 1920s and 1930s, and the critical impact of monetary policies as a tool for macroeconomic recovery.[7] Yet evidence is largely restricted, at a detailed level, to the study of the United States, Britain, France, Germany, and other countries in the core. Further research is now needed to see how the same approach can be applied to the World Depression at the periphery.

We argue that Argentine macroeconomic policies in the 1930s did successfully avert a major disaster by subverting, if only marginally, the prevailing orthodox *mentalité* inherited from earlier epochs. Like the core economies, Argentina found itself with little room for maneuver in fiscal matters, a constraint that was made even tighter by the need to service a large external debt. Fiscal orthodoxy was offset, however, by a bold change of monetary regime, from metallic to fiduciary, in an effort to dislodge deflationary expectations.

This plan was the brainchild of Raúl Prebisch, and was a testament to his creativity and brilliance as an economist and policymaker. The actions of the Conversion Office in the Spring of 1931 predated the British departure from gold by a good six months, and United States interventions by almost two years. Events in the history of thought and events in economic history were most clearly intertwined in the Argentine experience. Gesell's insight came in the economic crisis that followed an attempt to pursue rigid metallic rules in the 1890s as a prelude to resumption at the 1881 parity. Thirty-two years of gold standard orthodoxy by the Conversion Office could not diminish the relevance

7. See, *inter alia,* Eichengreen and Sachs (1985); Temin (1989); Eichengreen (1992a; 1992b) ; Romer (1992); and Eichengreen and Temin (1997).

of his ideas in a time of serious deflation. As the prospect of a repeat of the recessions of the 1890s and 1914–19 loomed, the penetrating ideas of Prebisch held sway as those of Gesell had a generation before.

In summing up, though, excessive optimism concerning the change of regime should not be read into our story. In the long run there was rather too much reliance on expansionary monetary policy in subsequent Argentine history, as elsewhere in Latin America. Hyperinflations in many countries brought the need for exactly the opposite kind of regime shift à la Sargent. That shift eventually came to Argentina in an all too familiar form. In 1991 a return to a currency-board rule was instigated with much popular support after all patience had been exhausted with the previous sixty years of floating exchange rates and persistent, often wild, inflations.

The current convertibility law puts Argentina on a dollar-standard rule very similar to, and in some ways stricter than, the gold-standard mechanism used at the Conversion Office from 1899 to 1931. Apart from one tough recession, economic performance has been impressive in the last few years. Though little else would be familiar, one might imagine that a visitor arriving from the 1880s, 1900s, or 1920s, would feel very much at home with today's dollar-peso rule. Yet knowing as they did the pitfalls of a metallic regime, and the crises of the 1890s, 1910s, and 1930s, one cannot be very sure that Silvio Gesell or Raúl Prebisch would so comfortably travel back to the future.

Microeconomic Costs: Institutional Cascades and a Bad Architecture

The 1880–1935 period in Argentina provides a clear example of how economic crises—most of the time more than one!—can induce institutional changes in a cascade fashion. However, the cascade, or, as one might say, the "institutional learning by doing process," ended up polluting the originally well-conceived institutions. Ultimately, a new institution, the central bank, had to be created to clean up the mess dynamically engendered by the polluted trio of the Conversion Office, the Banco de la Nación Argentina, and the private financial system.

The costs of this route were large and not limited solely to the state bank. As early as 1931, with the Conversion Office rediscounting to the Banco de la Nación, and the latter rediscounting to private banks in an exceptionally bad state, the "lemon loans" on state's balance sheet grew large. Moreover, in an idiosyncratic financial structure that coupled a quasi-Lender of Last Resort with no banking regulation, the risky ventures of at least four of the most important Argentine private banks were grossly exacerbated.

This state of affairs led to a clean-up task assigned in 1935 by Congress to a specially created institution, the Instituto Movilizador de Inversiones Bancarias (IMIB). We discuss the precise details of the IMIB bailout operation in Appendix 5, but for now it suffices to note that the costs of this operation were very large by any standard. The main source of funds for the operation were the central bank's seigniorage profits arising from the decision to devalue the peso parity from 2.27 paper pesos per gold peso to 4.96 in 1935. Suddenly, a huge accounting profit of 701 million paper pesos accrued to the government. This was allocated to various uses as follows: to retire some federal floating debt, around 95 million; to augment banking reserves in the central bank, 216 million; and to fund the bailout operation by IMIB, 390 million pesos.

In short, IMIB received 55 percent of the proceeds of the gold revaluation, a sum that in itself represented a 58 percent increase in the quantity of outside money. How costly was this operation to Argentine households? Such a massive seigniorage tax amounted to about 7 percent of 1935 gross domestic product. It is important to note here that the assets bailed out, a total of 553 million pesos, amounted to 16 percent of the loans of the entire financial system (including Banco de la Nación), or 32 percent of the loans of the private banking system. That is, fully one third of the private financial system was rotten, a very large financial crisis by any standard. This upper-bound estimate of the social costs was equal to 5.5 percent of output. A lower-bound estimate of the social costs of the bailout would be the injection of cash to the financial system, amounting to 390 million pesos or 4 percent of output. And it need hardly be said that the main beneficiaries of this action were the principals and investors of the soon-to-fail banks concerned, so the transfer was effectively directing 4 to 5 percent of output to an already wealthy group in society.

Thus, this was a very large banking failure and bailout by any standard. We must, however, be careful with intertemporal comparisons. The costs relative to output hardly do full justice to the scale of the bailout operation because, given the low level of financial development in the early twentieth century, the banking sector was small relative to output.[8] Contemporary emerging market crises may have caused a greater loss of assets as a fraction of output, but rarely (if ever) have we seen the case of a country with as much as one third of its banking sector assets destroyed.[9] And, of course, this static real resource cost understates the long-run costs resulting from the destruction of a (once) clean and well-functioning set of institutions. Thus, we cannot be anything but pessimistic about the potential costs of poor institutional design in emerging market economies; but we can be optimistic to the extent that these illustrations from history can help prevent a repeat of the recent spate of crises.

8. See Goldsmith (1969).

9. "Contemporary conventional wisdom tells us that emerging-market crashes are more frequent and severe than ever before. But even a casual newspaper reader 15 years ago could have very well reached the same conclusion. The truth is, currency crises in emerging economies are nothing new. Judging by how much capital fled, Latin America saw worse crises in the 1980s than in the 1990s. In Asia, however, the late 1990s have brought far worse crises than anything experienced earlier. They have affected a greater share of global gross domestic product. They have also caused substantial recessions, though it seems that economic recovery is occurring more quickly than it did during the 1980s debt crisis" (Minton Beddoes 1999).

Cartoon 10.1. *Justo — Sírvase; están muy bien adobados. Pueblo — Precisamente, por eso les tengo miedo.* ([President] Justo — Help yourself; they are very well marinated. People — Precisely, that's why I am afraid of them.)
Notes: The dishes are the central bank (a turkey), the new banking law (a chicken), and the Instituto Movilizador de Inversiones Bancarias (a pig). There is a double meaning in the word *adobado* (marinated): it can also mean that there is an unclear or nefarious arrangement. In this cartoon the public suspects that what has been cooked up isn't really so good. Moreover, if it had been so tasty, there would have been no need for the waiter, Justo, to insist so much.
Source: Caras y caretas, año 38, no. 1907, April 20, 1935.

Argentina's Legacy: Lessons of History in the Final Balance Sheet

A concise way to sum up Argentina's experience would be to present it as a problem of bad design in the overall financial architecture. Certain elements looked reasonable and stable on their own, but put together the entire edifice could not hold up to the eventual strains.

This observation has some fairly clear implications for how we view recent calls for reform of the world's financial architecture. The Argentine experience shows that—to stretch the metaphor—a little repainting here and there, some new wallpaper, or a rearrangement of the furniture might not suffice to make a structure sound. Rather, what might be needed at the level of a specific country is a tear down, or at least full attention to the whole structure right down to the foundations. Partial reforms of money and banking regimes could be ineffective, and might even be damaging.

In the Argentine case it is clear where the architectural renovations paid off, and where neglect in the design stage came back to haunt everybody. A safe, quasi-narrow bank such as the Banco de la Nación, and a Conversion Office set up as a currency board to maintain a good reputation, were created to solve the 1890s crisis. It was hoped that, unlike their predecessors, they would never descend to soft-budget constraint activities. But external economic forces and internal political manipulations during the interwar period generated a set of challenges and temptations that disturbed the institutional design and pulled it ever so gradually off the rails until there was no possibility of return.

External discipline could not solve all the problems. The Conversion Office was internationally visible, easily monitored and verified; it was a clear and sound adoption of the rules of the game, a well-behaved and consistent institution in this small open economy. Much less visible (internationally and domestically) was the financial system and its workings. In the first phase of its existence (1891–1913) the new Argentine money and banking regime functioned smoothly, faced few shocks, and was little tampered with by policymakers. In its second phase (1913–34), a series of economic shocks polluted first the private banking system and then, despite a seemingly solid design to prevent bailouts and moral hazard, took down the Banco de la Nación and the Conversion Office as the illness spread.

The end result was the creation of an institution—the central bank—that could, with the help of opaque and dubious maneuvers by IMIB, cover up the mess and finally throw in the towel on the idea of external convertibility. Loosening the nominal anchor was to have adverse long-run implications for inflation performance. And having no compelling restraint on the bailouts used to protect internal convertibility, the central bank embraced a Lender-of-Last-Resort function with regard to the private banks that was to invite moral hazard and continuing real resource drains for decades to come.

With banks subject to neither supervision, nor banking laws, nor regulations, and with the mysterious ad hoc evolution of the Banco de la Nación, the system got itself on a path toward inconsistent policies. Instead of a classical Lender-of-Last-Resort system, a free insurance or bailout scheme was the end result. This need not have compromised the Conversion Office and Argentina's commitment to stable macroeconomic policies. But when the 1929 crisis hit, it was so big that the banking system's weakness threatened a disastrous collapse of intermediation absent a rescue, and further real costs. The price was to abolish the Conversion Office and revalue gold, once and for all losing the notion of parity that had endured since the 1899 resumption.

With the loss of a commitment to a stable external value of the currency and, in the longer run, to a stable price level, the genie—money printing—was yet again out of the bottle. We might consider how Sarmiento, Roca, or Pellegrini would have viewed these events. These former Presidents saw Argentina as having an internal tension between progressive sectors of society seeking to create modern institutions with clear rules of the game, and conservative forces seeking to maintain a *status quo* where outcomes usually depended on arbitrary forces and the manipulation of power and influence. Sarmiento's *magnum opus, Facundo [Civilizacion i barbarie],* was devoted to exactly this issue.

The Conversion Office in some sense epitomized the economic attempt at *civilizacion,* by playing to clean rules and meeting externally verifiable standards and monitoring. The more clandestine relationship between private finance and the state, and the capacity of the private and provincial banks to obtain successive bailouts from the Banco de la Nación via political means, were more reminiscent of *barbarie.*

In the end, in the sphere of macroeconomic policy at least, the results seem clear. The Belle Époque was marked by prosperity in incomes, not in institutions. By accident or, we might say, by lack of design, *barbarie* triumphed.

Appendix 1
Historical Statistics

Annual Macroeconomic Statistics, 1884–1940

The following annual data series were collected by della Paolera and Ortiz (1995). The variables and sources are listed here. Full source documentation and the data will be made available online.

1. *Money supply:* money supply in paper, excluding gold, equal to currency in the hands of the public plus checking deposits (private and public) and time deposits (fixed term and savings accounts); definitions vary over time. From della Paolera (1988); Comité Nacional de Geografía (1942–43); Diz (1966).
2. *Banking reserves:* reserves in banks (including banks' deposits at the Banco Central after 1935). From the same sources as money supply.
3. *Currency in the hands of the public:* from the same sources as money supply.
4. *Monetary base:* currency in the hands of the public plus reserves in banks.
5. *Money multiplier:* money supply divided by monetary base.
6. *Banking money* (*secondary expansion*): money supply minus monetary base.
7. *Price level and inflation:* based on an index of wholesale prices. From della Paolera (1988); *Revista de economía argentina* (various issues); Díaz Alejandro (1981).
8. *Exchange rate:* expressed in paper pesos per U.S. gold dollar. Note that the parity was 1.05 Argentine gold pesos per U.S. gold dollar. From Cortés Conde (1979); Alvarez (1929); Organización Techint, *Boletín informativo*.
9. *U.S. and U.K. price levels:* wholesale price levels in the United States and United Kingdom. From Friedman and Schwartz (1982).
10. *Real activity:* gross domestic product at market prices in 1986. From della Paolera (1988); ECLA (1958).
11. *Velocity:* price level times real activity divided by money supply.
12. *International reserves:* 1884–90, gold at banks of emission; 1899–1934, gold at the Conversion Office; post-1935, international reserves at the Banco Central; in paper pesos at market exchange rate. From della Paolera (1988); Cortés Conde (1979); Alvarez (1929); *Memorias de la Caja de Conversión;* Vázquez Presedo (1971).
13. *Domestic interest rate:* 1884–1913, yield of *fondos públicos nacionales;* 1914–34, discount lending rate of banks; 1935–40, interest rate on 90-day fixed-term deposits. From della Paolera (1988); Comité Nacional de Geografía (1941).
14. *Foreign interest rate:* pre-1913, yield on British consols; post-1914, call money interest rate, United States, annual average. From Mitchell (1971); Friedman and Schwartz (1982).
15. *Government revenues, expenditures, and overall deficit:* federal fiscal revenues from taxation, state-owned enterprises, and excluding borrowing; federal fiscal expen-

diture on general uses, state-owned enterprises, and including interest and amorization on debt. From della Paolera (1988); Organización Techint, *Boletín informativo.*

Annual Banking and Financial Statistics, 1884–1914

The following annual macroeconomic and banking series were collected by della Paolera (1988, Appendices C and D). The variables and sources are listed here. Full source documentation and the data will be made available online.

1. *Bank deposits:* Banco de la Nación Argentina (before 1891, Banco Nacional), foreign banks, Banco de la Provincia de Buenos Aires, Banco de la Provincia de Córdoba, private banks, Cara Bassa bank, total private banks, total (three variant series), end-of-year data in millions of paper pesos. From bank balance sheets and other sources.
2. *Bank gold deposits:* Banco de la Nación Argentina (before 1891, Banco Nacional), foreign banks, Banco de la Provincia de Buenos Aires, private banks, total (two variant series), end-of-year data in millions of gold pesos. From bank balance sheets and other sources.
3. *Bank reserves (vault cash):* Banco de la Nación Argentina (before 1891, Banco Nacional), foreign banks, Banco de la Provincia de Buenos Aires, Banco de la Provincia de Córdoba, private banks, Cara Bassa bank, total private banks, total (three variant series), end-of-year data in millions of paper pesos. From bank balance sheets and other sources.
4. *Bank specie:* Banco de la Nación Argentina (before 1891, Banco Nacional), foreign banks, Banco de la Provincia de Buenos Aires, major provincial banks of issue, private banks, total private banks, total mixed banks, and total (two variant series), end-of-year data in millions of gold pesos. From bank balance sheets and other sources.
5. *Money supply:* monetary base, currency in circulation, currency in the hands of the public, bank-created money, end-of-year data in millions of paper pesos. Derived from the above series and other sources.
6. *Specie stock:* specie stock, specie flow, specie held by public, specie at Conversion Office. Derived from the above series and other primary sources, in millions of gold pesos. Public holding of specie derived as a residual.
7. *Yield on internal government bonds:* yield to maturity of *fondos públicos nacionales,* percent per annum, calculated as coupon rate divided by price. From Cortés Conde (1987); *South American Journal; Memorias de la Cámara Sindical de la Bolsa Comercio correspondienta al ejercicio 1888–1920; Review of the River Plate.*
8. *Yield on external government bonds:* yield to maturity of Argentine government bonds in the London market, percent per annum, calculated as coupon rate divided by price. From Cortés Conde (1987); *South American Journal; Memorias de la Cámara Sindical de la Bolsa Comercio correspondienta al ejercicio 1888–1920; Review of the River Plate; The Economist.*
9. *Yield on British Consols:* yield to maturity of British Consols in the London market, percent per annum, calculated as coupon rate divided by price. From Mitchell (1971).
10. *Yield on Rendita Italiana:* yield to maturity of long-term Italian government bond, percent per annum, calculated as coupon rate divided by price. From Fratianni and Spinelli (1984).
11. *Domestic bank lending rate:* annual average, percent per annum. From Comité Nacional de Geografía (1941).
12. *Federal government fiscal expenditures:* total expenditures and components due to

interior, defense, justice/culture/education, finance, and debt service, in millions of paper pesos. From *Memorias de Hacienda* and other sources.

13. *Federal government fiscal revenues:* total revenues and components due to tariffs, export taxes, indirect taxes, direct taxes, services, and state enterprises, in millions of paper pesos. From *Memorias de Hacienda* and other sources.
14. *Federal government deficit and funded debt:* expenditures, revenues, and outstanding debt, in millions of paper pesos. From the above and *Memorias de Hacienda.*
15. *Exports and imports:* corrected and official exports and official imports, in millions of gold pesos. From Diéguez (1972).

Monthly Banking and Financial Statistics, 1908–1935

The following monthly data series were collected by Baiocco (1935), the Banco Central (after 1935), and other sources. The variables and sources are listed here. Full source documentation and the data will be made available online.

1. *Bank capital:* all banks, Banco de la Nación Argentina, other domestic banks, and foreign banks; in millions of paper pesos. From Monthly banking reports, Ministerio de Hacienda.
2. *Bank deposits:* all banks, Banco de la Nación Argentina, other domestic banks, and foreign banks; in millions of paper pesos; excludes cash at the clearing house. From Oficina de Investigaciones Económicas del Banco de la Nación Argentina; *Suplemento estadístico de la Revista Económica,* Banco Central de la República Argentina.
3. *Bank loans:* all banks, Banco de la Nación Argentina, other domestic banks, and foreign banks; in millions of paper pesos. From Monthly banking reports, Ministerio de Hacienda; Oficina de Investigaciones Económicas del Banco de la Nación Argentina; *Suplemento estadístico de la Revista Económica,* Banco Central de la República Argentina.
4. *Bank reserves (vault cash):* all banks, Banco de la Nación Argentina, other domestic banks, and foreign banks; in millions of paper pesos; excludes cash at the clearing house. From Monthly banking reports, Ministerio de Hacienda; Oficina de Investigaciones Económicas del Banco de la Nación Argentina; *Suplemento estadístico de la Revista Económica,* Banco Central de la República Argentina.
5. *Bank checking accounts, savings accounts, fixed term accounts, and other accounts:* all banks; in millions of paper pesos. From Oficina de Investigaciones Económicas del Banco de la Nación Argentina.
6. *Banco de la Nación Argentina short-term loans, advances, loans to the treasury, other loans, and rediscounts to banks:* in millions of paper pesos. From Oficina de Investigaciones Económicas del Banco de la Nación Argentina.
7. *Gold stocks and flows:* at the Conversion Office (after May 1935, Banco Central), at all banks, and total, in millions of gold pesos. From monthly balance sheets of the Caja de Conversión; monthly banking reports, Ministerio de Hacienda.
8. *Gold stocks:* at overseas legations, at the Banco de la Nación Argentina, at other domestic banks, and at foreign banks, in millions of gold pesos; includes cash at the clearing house. From monthly balance sheets of the Caja de Conversión; monthly banking reports, Ministerio de Hacienda.
9. *Money base emission:* total and its components due to gold at the Conversion Office (Law 3871), gold at legations (Law 9480), the 1914 emergency laws (Laws 9479 and 9577), and the Patriotic Loan (Law 11580), in millions of paper pesos. From monthly balance sheets of the Caja de Conversión. After 1935, total money base emission by Banco Central.
10. *Currency in the hands of the public and in banks:* in millions of paper pesos. From monthly balance sheets of the Caja de Conversión; monthly banking reports,

Ministerio de Hacienda; Oficina de Investigaciones Económicas del Banco de la Nación Argentina; *Suplemento estadístico de la Revista Económica,* Banco Central de la República Argentina.

11. *Check clearing:* for Capital Federal, Rosario, Bahía Blanca, Santa Fé, Córdoba, La Plata, Mendoza, Tucumán, Concordia, in millions of paper pesos. From the Cámara Compensadora.
12. *Discount rate of private banks:* Monthly average in percent. From *Boletín Oficial de la Bolsa de Comercio de Buenos Aires.*
13. *Stock price index for bank stocks:* Monthly average price of 100 peso nominal value private bank stocks. From *Boletín Oficial de la Bolsa de Comercio de Buenos Aires.*
14. *Exchange rate:* British pound, French franc, and U.S. dollar spot (cable or demand bill) rates, monthly averages; two variant series plus official, free, buying and selling rates (for the period of multiple exchange rates). From *Boletín Oficial de la Bolsa de Comercio de Buenos Aires; La Prensa; La Nación; La Razón;* Banco Central.
15. *Paper-gold exchange rate:* Paper pesos (*billetes de curso legal* of Law 3871) per 100 gold pesos (*peso moneda nacional de oro* of Law 1130). Official parity of 227.27 at the Conversion Office when open. Based on the market rate of exchange during closures (suspension of convertbility) of the Conversion Office, using the U.S. dollar rate August 9, 1914, to August 25, 1927, and December 16, 1929, to March 5, 1933, and using the French franc rate from March 6, 1933.
16. *Gold-paper exchange rate:* Gold pesos per 100 paper pesos. Official parity of 44 at the Conversion Office when open. Based on the market rate of exchange during closures (suspension of convertbility) of the Conversion Office.
17. *Bankruptcies:* Monthly filings of commercial and civil bankruptcies in millions of paper pesos. From *Revista Económica.*

Appendix 2
The Law of National Guaranteed Banks

At the end of 1887, a new monetary experiment was underway, the Law of National Guaranteed Banks, commonly referred to as the "free banking law." This law allowed any banking organization to issue national paper notes when adequately backed with government gold bonds. The wide use of the term "free banking law" reflects the conventional historical view, one which sees the experiment as a monument to the laissez faire political ideology that was supposed to hold sway in Argentina at that moment.

To temper this view with some empirical evidence, we might observe that, from the time of its inception, the provisions of the new law were for the most part adopted only by government-related (national and provincial) banks. Private financial institutions rarely acquired government bonds as a means to issue notes. This raises the question of whether the technical provisions of the law discriminated among institutions, making the note issue business profitable only for government related banks.

The major provisions of the law are presented in Table A2.1. Under those provisions, the official transactions allowing a banking organization to become a bank of issue operated as follows.

Suppose that a potential bank sought authorization to emit paper peso notes. To receive, say, 100 paper pesos in bank notes, the bank had first to deposit 85 gold pesos at the Banco Nacional in exchange for a 100 gold peso bond. But the bank also had to maintain the equivalent of 10 percent of the received paper notes as specie reserves. The remaining paper notes, only 90 paper pesos, would be issued into circulation in exchange for other assets: to buy more gold to issue more paper, to lend out, to replenish the bank's reserves, and so on. It is important to emphasize here that gold had a 35 percent premium with respect to paper in the market at the time. At that rate of exchange, the potential banker had to surrender the equivalent of 115 paper pesos to put into circulation only 90 paper pesos, net of the required reserves. That is, 25 paper pesos were tied up by such an operation, and would earn no interest. The typical balance sheet of a guaranteed bank was as in Table A2.2.

With this background we can evaluate the profitability of being a bank of issue.[1] Define,

NPV = net present value to a guaranteed bank of the issue;

B = paper peso value of government bonds acquired at the Banco Nacional;

PAR = nominal value of the bonds;

R = yearly interest payments on the bonds;

N = size of issue in paper notes, net of specie requirements;

i = the rate of return on alternative assets.

1. We draw on the seminal work by Cagan (1965) and Rockoff (1972).

Table A2.1. *Provisions of the Law of National Guaranteed Banks*

Date law passed	November 1887
Eligible bonds to secure paper notes	Government bonds specially created for that purpose.
Nature of the financial operation	Each bank had to deposit 85 gold pesos for a 100 gold peso bond and would receive 100 pesos in paper notes.
Capital requirement	Realized capital > 250,000 pesos.
Specie reserve requirements	10% of the received paper notes notes had to be maintained as reserves.
Note volume limitation	For each Bank, notes < 90% of 250,000 pesos. For all banks, total issue < 40 million pesos.
Interest on bonds to the bank	4.5% annual interest and 1% annual amortization at par and payable in gold.
Exceptions to the above provisions	Banks that already had in circulation inconvertible notes at the date of the promulgation of the law could adhere to it by acquiring the public bonds at a specified rate each year.

Sources: Agote (1887, pp. 414–24); Lorini (1902, pp. 431–34).

Note that B is the effective value of the bond. The value of the bank charter is

$$NPV = -B + \sum_{t=1}^{T} \frac{iN + R}{(1+i)^t} + \frac{PAR}{(1+i)^T}.$$

If T is assumed to be large, one arrives at a measure of profitability

$$NPV = -B + (iN + R)/i = (N - B) + (R/i).$$

It follows that the project is profitable, $NPV > 0$, if and only if

$$R/(B - N) > i.$$

The final expression tells us that the rate of return from issuing notes is the ratio of the income from the bonds securing the notes R, to the bank capital tied up $(B - N)$. If this were greater than the average return on alternative assets i then one should expect to see many banks seeking rights to issue paper notes. Only a computation of the rate of return can tell us if this were a likely outcome.

By the provisions of the Argentine law, the capital tied up (defined as the difference between the value of bonds acquired in guarantee and the value of paper notes net of reserves) necessary to obtain 100 pesos in paper notes was 25 pesos. The state gold bonds provided an interest of 4.5 percent a year at par and payable in gold. Assuming, only for the purposes of this exercise, a steady exchange rate of 1.35 paper pesos for one gold peso, the yearly payments on the 100 gold peso bond would amount to 6.1 paper pesos. Thus, the rate of return on note issue may therefore be estimated at 24.4 percent

Table A2.2. *Balance Sheet of a Guaranteed Bank*

Assets		Liabilities and Capital	
Government Bonds	115	Paper Notes	100
Loans	90	Capital	115
Specie Requirements	10		

Notes: See text.

Table A2.3. *Average Bank Profits, 1885–87*

Bank	Dividend as a Percentage of Par Value Capital	Dividend as a Percentage of Percentage of Par Value Capital and Note Issue
Bank of Italy and the River Plate	12.9	12.9
Bank of London and the River Plate	11.0	11.0
Banco Nacional	12.0	4.0
Banco Provincial de Santa Fé	9.4	7.6
English Bank of the River Plate	7.5	7.5
Banco Provincial de Córdoba	7.0	5.3
Banco Provincial de Salta	6.9	5.6
Banco Provincial de Entre Ríos	1.5	1.1
Banco Provincial de Mendoza	1.0	1.0

Source: Agote (1887, pp. 115–340).

(6.1 divided by 25). This would be expected to compare favorably with the average rate of return on capital from all assets of the banks (see Table A2.3).[2]

On the surface, then, the scheme looked extremely profitable for any potential bank of issue because the income provided by the interest earned on the bonds exceeded the opportunity cost of the tied up capital. But, if this were the case, what explains the apparent indifference of the private banks to the project?

One plausible explanation is the private investor's concern with the permanence of law's provisions. Since on this matter there is a lack of historical evidence, the speculations advanced here should be taken as tentative. From the derivation above it is clear that the project's profitability depended both on the government's commitment to honor its bond service obligation and on the legal rights to issue paper notes to endure to a time T that is far in the future. However, there were no guarantees that the scheme would endure over the long run and, simply put, the investor's fear might have been that, once the gold was deposited in the vaults of the Banco Nacional, the government might deviate from its original banking policy. What if, after a while, the government revoked the law and, with it, the property rights to the gold?

Once private investors surrendered their own equity in exchange for bonds, the government could be tempted to tax this capital, repudiation of the law being an extreme taxation scheme. Fears of repudiation were not specious. The Bank of London and the River Plate had suffered a bitter experience with the rights to issue notes in the Province of Santa Fé in the mid-seventies when the provincial government repudiated unilaterally the terms of a concession to issue banking notes.[3]

Expectations about how the law would be enforced were crucial to establish the

2. If return to parity was the expected near future, the rate of return given by the formula $R/(B-N)$ would have been a lower estimate of 18 percent, but still a profitable rate.
3. Joslin (1963) stresses that the Bank of London appealed and lost its case when the federal courts ruled that the provincial government could properly withdraw note-issuing rights.

Table A2.4. *Balance Sheet of a Government-related Wildcat Bank*

Assets		Liabilities and Capital	
Government Bonds	115	Paper Notes	230
Other Assets	230	Capital	115

Notes: See text.

perceived life span of the project. If an abrupt change in the banking regime, or an outright repudiation, were expected in the near future, the negative consequences for expected profits would have been very profound. How profound? That would depend, of course, on the hypothetical timing of the change. To give an extreme example: assume that two years after the law was passed the government revoked the property rights and also repudiated the bond income interest; with an average discount rate of 5 percent it follows (from the first expression above) that the project would have lost 83 percent of capital invested.

A somewhat different explanation is that investors had a less sanguine view about the project, decided to bid for the rights to issue the paper notes, but were denied when the monetary authorities preferentially allotted the rights to government-related banks. There is some evidence that the provincial governments had demanded a banking reform that would allow them to establish banks of issue.[4]

The newly created provincial banks did not invest already-accumulated domestic capital, but rather bought the "theoretical" shares with public debt contracted in the London money market. Thus, the scheme here became an arbitrage operation and to issue paper notes was profitable as long as

$$i^*B < iN + R,$$

where, i^* is interest rate at which the provinces could borrow in the London Market.[5]

In a subsequent, distinctly decadent, stage of the banking experiment, an explosion of "wildcat banking" occurred when the bond requirement of the law was lifted. This change made the expression (N – B) positive, so that the price paid for the rights to issue notes was below the value of the notes. There is evidence that only half of the bonds backing the paper notes issued by the government related banks were ever paid with gold.[6] The official banks overissued well above the law's prescriptions and then the true leverage provided by the notes was severely affected as can be appreciated from the example in Table A2.4.

4. The finance minister reported to Congress that "eight provincial governments are now attempting credit operations for the purpose of founding banks, and thus satisfying necessities which are acutely felt; this pointedly illustrates our present situation and pushes the government to hasten the presentation of the accompanying bill" (Agote 1887, 407).
5. The eight official banks that engaged in arbitrage operation had almost reached the quantitative ceiling prescribed in law by 1888. In addition, newly created private banks were allotted less than 8 percent of the stipulated sum of 40 million (Pillado 1901, 60–61).
6. Williams (1969, 59)

Appendix 3
Money Supply Periodization, 1884–1913

Periodization

One of the more difficult tasks in economic history is the division of an entire period of analysis into several historical subperiods of different economic significance. Monetary historians, usually restricted to annual data, have used a standard rationale for the choice of the subperiods of analysis. Turning points are usually based on changes in several key nominal variables, such as the money supply, the price level or the exchange rate, and usually reflect underlying changes in economic conditions or policies or both. Using this approach we present data on four different periods:

1. The period following the convertibility suspension, 1884–89;
2. The years 1890 and 1891, known as the Baring Crisis years;
3. The period of stabilization and fiscal reform following the crisis, 1892–99;
4. The gold standard with fixed exchange rates, 1900–1913.

We can then subdivide the first period into the period 1884–87 which we call the "return to convertibility scenario" and the period 1887–89, the "banking reform" period. Finally, we also considered as distinct subperiods 1884–99, the "paper standard" period, the "postcrash" period of 1892–13, and the entire period 1884–13.

Definitions

The Monetary Base

The hybrid nature of the monetary standard in 1884–87 creates a problem for choosing a definition for the monetary base. From 1883 the prevailing monetary standard was a mixed bimetallic specie and fiduciary standard in which monetary authorities were issuing specie obligations in the form of gold pesos and fiduciary obligations called "metallic" notes. In principle, gold pesos minted according to the monetary law of 1883 were the monetary base, in the sense that banks held fractional reserve of gold pesos against paper and gold liabilities. Therefore, under this institutional arrangement, the monetary base MB is defined as the sum of specie held by the banks SB plus vault cash held by the commercial banks VC plus hand to hand currency held by the public CU, that is

$MB = SB + VC + CU = RE + CU$, for the years 1884–87,

where $RE = SB + VC$ is reserves of the commercial banks defined as the sum of specie held by banks plus vault cash in paper notes.

The Law of National Guaranteed Banks implied a switch toward a paper-based monetary system. In that institutional arrangement specie and gold were regarded as a source of monetary base and the guaranteed notes were now basically the use of the base. Thus, from 1888 onward we define the monetary base as hand-to-hand currency issued, that is, currency held by the public plus vault-cash held by the commercial banks,

$MB = VC + CU = RE + CU$, for the years 1888 and later,

where now $RE = VC$ is reserves of the commercial banks defined as only vault cash in paper notes.

The Money Supply

The Argentine money supply is defined throughout as hand-to-hand currency plus deposits in commercial banks (including the Banco de la Nación Argentina). No distinction between time and demand deposits is made, so our definition of money is a broad one (equivalent to what is usually termed M2). We have defined the monetary base as

$$MB = CU + RE,$$

and the money stock as

$$M = CU + DE,$$

where

RE = vault reserves at banks;
CU = hand to hand currency held by the public;
DE = commercial banks deposits.

The money multiplier m is defined as the ratio between the money stock and the monetary base

$$m = \frac{M}{MB} = \frac{CU + DE}{CU + RE} = \frac{1}{\frac{CU}{M} + \frac{RE}{M}} = \frac{1}{\frac{CU}{M} + \frac{RE}{DE}\frac{DE}{M}}.$$

It is then straightforward to show that

$$m = \frac{1}{c + r - rc},$$

where

c = CU/M = currency-money ratio of the non-bank public;
r = RE/DE = reserve-deposit ratio of the banking system.

The relationship between the money supply and its determinants is then

$$M = \frac{1}{c + r - rc} MB.$$

Any changes in the money supply M are attributable to changes in the three determinants c, r, and MB. To decompose any given change in M into the change due each of the determinants we can log-differentiate the last expression and obtain

$$\Delta \ln M = \Delta \ln MB - m(1 - c)\Delta r - m(1 - r)\Delta c + \ldots,$$

where we omit higher order terms. Each term on the right-hand side denotes the change in the stock of money that would have occurred if each of the determinants had changed, leaving the others fixed. This decomposition of changes in money supply is used in Table 2.4.[1]

Statistics

Table 2.3 shows, for each of the periods, the total percentage change and the average percentage change per year in several key monetary, real and financial variables. These are: money stock M; monetary base MB; money created by the banks $M - MB$; real output Y; price level P; exchange rate U; and U.K. price level P^*, as a proxy for the rest of the world price level. The table also reports the average level of several other variables: money multiplier M/MB; income velocity of money $V = PY/M$; ratio of gold stock to monetary base G/MB; ratio of specie hoarding by the public to monetary base $GPUB/MB$; and ratio of nonperforming assets to total loans for the principal state banks NA/L.

Table 2.4 shows the proximate determinants of the Argentine money supply for the ten periods under consideration using the decomposition discussed in the previous section. Note that three agents are involved in the determination of the money stock: the monetary authorities (or banks of issue), the (other) commercial banks, and the public. In a fractional reserve banking system, the behavior of the money multiplier should be closely followed since it is affected by two ratios that are largely determined by choices made by the public. The currency-money ratio is determined by the public when they choose between the alternative forms of holding cash-balances, currency in their own hands and deposits in banking institutions. The reserve-deposit ratio may be set at a profit-maximizing level by the banks or may be fixed by legal requirements.

Table 2.4 contains information on several variables derived using this method: percentage change in the proximate determinants of money; fraction of the percentage change in the money stock attributable to its proximate determinants; fraction of change in the money stock consisting of changes in the monetary base and bank credit; fraction of total change in the monetary base attributable to the monetary specie and domestic assets. Figure 2.4 displays the proximate determinants of the money multiplier. Figure 2.5 displays the ratios of fiat currency in hands of the public, bank-created money, and specie hoarding to real output.

1. This is the well-known framework of Friedman and Schwartz (1963) and Cagan (1965).

Appendix 4
Money and Exchange Rates, 1884–1913

In this appendix we briefly discuss the evolution of money supply, exchange rate determination, and money demand during the 1884–1913 period.

Money Supply

As we have already seen (Table 2.4 and Figure 2.3), the 1890–99 stabilization period was characterized by a dramatic change in the source of monetary expansion. Most of the change in the money stock took the form of bank-created money; 58 percent of that change is explained by a fall in the currency-money ratio alone, and 19 percent by change in the the monetary base. In contrast, during the gold-standard 1900–1913, the monetary base explained 82 percent of the growth in the money stock, and this increase in the base was fully backed by specie reserves at the margin. We can also see that the secular decline in the currency and reserve ratios from 1892 onward reflects a slow but continuous process of improved financial intermediation (Figure 2.4).

These changes can be summarized through more formal econometrics. Table A4.1 presents parameter estimates of the long-run determinants of the money stock for the subperiods 1885–99, 1900–1913 and the entire period of study 1885–1913. For the period 1885–99, the currency-money ratio plays a more significant role in the money supply process than during the gold-standard. The lower degree of correlation for the 1885–99 period shows the relative importance of an omitted interaction reflecting a higher degree of volatility in the money multiplier.

Overall, we find the hypothesis that the elasticity of money stock with respect to the monetary base is unity is, again, strongly corroborated.

Exchange Rate Determination

We have already seen that during the flexible exchange-rate regime, the growth in real money stock was sluggish with respect to real output growth (Table 2.4). On the other hand, during the gold-standard, money stock growth exceeded output growth. This result bears great similarity to the experience of countries under the sterling-bloc during the Great Depression of 1870–95 and then, during the boom that followed the new discoveries of gold in Alaska, South Africa, and Colorado.[1]

We will assume that Argentina, a small economy closely integrated into the sterling block, could not sustain in the long run an independent monetary policy. This is a restatement of the classic Mundellian trilemma. Inflating (or deflating) the domestic

1. See Bordo (1986, p. 347)

Table A4.1. *Money Supply Estimation, 1884–1913*

Dependent Variable and Period	$\Delta \ln c$	$\Delta \ln r$	$\Delta \ln MB$	R-squared	SEE
$\Delta \ln m$					
1885–1913	-0.49	-0.38		0.97	0.02
	(0.02)	(0.02)			
1885–99	-0.50	-0.30		0.97	0.03
	(0.03)	(0.03)			
1900–1913	-0.42	-0.45		0.99	0.00
	(0.02)	(0.01)			
$\Delta \ln M$					
1885–1913	-0.48	-0.38	0.97	0.98	0.02
	(0.02)	(0.02)	-0.03		
1885–99	-0.49	-0.36	0.96	0.97	0.03
	(0.03)	(0.03)	-0.05		
1900–1913	-0.42	-0.45	0.99	1.00	0.01
	(0.02)	(0.01)	-0.02		

Notes: See text. Standard errors in parantheses.
Sources: See Appendix 1.

economy at a different pace than the rest of the world would not be sustainable because price or exchange rate adjustments, or both, would take place to restore real exchange rate equilibrium. That is, we are invoking an assumption of long-run purchasing power parity.

We first tested a restricted version of the asset approach to the exchange rate determination for the floating period (1885–99), treating the United Kingdom as the rest of the world.

In equilibrium the existing supply of monetary base must be willingly held, so that

$$MB/P = L,$$

$$MB^*/P^* = L^*,$$

where L is the demand for base money, and an asterisk denotes the U.K. level of each variable in this two-country model.

Purchasing power parity (PPP) is assumed to hold between Argentina and the rest of the world (here proxied by the United Kingdom). For the period 1884–99 we performed a regression test of purchasing power parity in the form $\ln P = \alpha + \beta \ln(EP^*)$. The results were

$$\underset{}{\ln P} = \underset{(0.48)}{0.074} + \underset{(0.09)}{0.915} \ln(EP^*)$$

with $DW = 1.81$, $\rho = 0.64$, Adjusted $R^2 = 0.97$. We take this as evidence in favor of PPP. Hence, we assume $P = EP^*$. Substituting for P and P^* in the equations for money market equilibrium and solving for E, we obtain

$$E = \frac{MB}{MB^*}\frac{L^*}{L}.$$

Taking log first differences and making the money demand a function of real output and the interest rate yields the expression

$$\hat{E} = \alpha + \beta(\hat{MB} - \hat{MB}^*) + \gamma(\hat{Y}^* - \hat{Y}) + \delta(\Delta i - \Delta i^*),$$

Table A4.2. *Exchange Rate Determinants, 1884–1913*

Dependent Variable	$\Delta \ln E$	$\Delta \ln E$	$\Delta \ln E - \Delta \ln (SP/MB)$
$\Delta \ln MB - \Delta \ln MB^*$	0.49	—	—
	(0.23)		
$\Delta \ln MB$	—	1.15	0.99
		(0.18)	(0.31)
$\Delta \ln MB^*$	—	-1.29	-0.97
		(0.54)	(0.84)
$\Delta \ln Y - \Delta \ln Y^*$	1.03	1.38	1.26
	(0.93)	(0.46)	(0.51)
$\Delta i - \Delta i^*$	0.07	-0.03	-0.02
	(0.05)	(0.04)	(0.05)
DW	1.90	2.03	1.85
ρ	0.06	-0.49	0.16
R-squared	0.62	0.86	0.70

Notes: See text. Standard errors in parentheses.
Sources: See Appendix 1.

where the hats denote log differences of the variables ($\hat{x} = \Delta \ln x$) and

E = paper-gold exchange rate;
MB = Argentine monetary base;
MB^* = U.K. monetary base;
Y = Argentine real output;
Y^* = U.K. real output;
Δi = change in internal bond yield;
Δi^* = change in foreign bond yield.

Here, the differential in long-term interest rates is used as a proxy for the anticipated rate of inflation.[2]

In this simple form the money supplies and outputs are restricted to have the same coefficient. We estimated this equation and the regression results were as shown in the first column of Table A4.2.

The explanatory power of this regression satisfactory as a preliminary estimate and all estimated coefficients have the correct sign indicated by the theory.

However, upon more inspection we found that the data reject the hypothesis that the coefficient of the difference in the rate of change in the money supplies is unity. Several factors could account for this:

1. The fact that the respective monetary bases were restricted to have the same coefficient may not be an accurate specification;
2. The sample period under consideration cannot be characterized as a clean float (recall the intervention in the exchange market during 1889–90); and
3. The proxy for the Argentine interest rate is a poor predictor of inflation rates.

Thus, we augmented the equation with two modifications to address for these problems. First, we allowed the monetary variables to have different coefficients. Second, we included a measure of exchange rate pressure to augment the variable E for the years

2. All data from Appendix 1 except MB^* from Bordo (1982) and Y^* from Feinstein (1972).

Table A4.3. *Money Demand Estimation, 1884–1913*

Dependent Variable and Period	ln Y	ln $(1 + \pi)$	ρ	DW	R-squared
1884–91					
ln M/P	2.03	-1.35		2.11	0.76
	(0.44)	(0.37)			
ln M/P (including specie hoarding)	2.13	-0.81		2.61	0.91
	(0.25)	(0.21)			
1891–1900					
ln M/P	1.10	-0.15		1.96	0.87
	(0.17)	(0.11)			
ln M/P (including specie hoarding)	0.73	-0.219		2.17	0.83
	(0.15)	(0.09)			
1884–99					
ln M/P	1.42	-0.21	0.89	1.49	0.95
	(0.52)	(0.21)	(0.10)		
ln M/P (including specie hoarding)	1.28	-0.16	0.80	1.64	0.98
	(0.34)	(0.15)	(0.14)		
1900–1913					
ln M/P	1.28	-0.09	0.48	1.18	0.99
	(0.10)	(0.19)	(0.28)		
ln M/P (including specie hoarding)	1.13	-0.13	0.41	1.15	1.00
	(0.07)	(0.15)	(0.29)		
1884–1913					
ln M/P	1.19	-0.22	0.87	1.45	0.95
	(0.22)	(0.13)	(0.08)		
ln M/P (including specie hoarding)	1.01	-0.20	0.77	1.46	0.97
	(0.12)	(0.10)	(0.11)		

Notes: See text. Standard errors in parantheses.
Sources: See Appendix 1.

when specie reserves shared the brunt of the adjustment in the foreign exchange market, defining a new variable SP/MB equal to the change in specie backing of paper notes divided by the monetary base at the end of the previous year. The augmented results are shown in the final two columns of Table A4.2.

The augmented results provide a better fit, and they reveal that the elasticity of the exchange rate with respect to the domestic stock of paper notes did not differ significantly from unity. The coefficients of the absolute change in interest rates have the expected sign only in the previous regression, but in all cases the coefficients are statistically insignificant.

Money Demand

Finally, we estimated money demand functions. We estimated only the simplest money demand equations because the paucity of the data precludes a more elaborate analysis. Two definitions of money were used: M defined as the sum of currency in the hands of the public plus total deposits (demand plus time deposits); and M defined as above plus the public hoarding of specie.

Two alternative measures of the opportunity cost of holding money were tried. In Table A4.3 we used the ex-post inflation rate π, and estimated an equation of the form

Table A4.4. *Money Demand Estimation, 1884–1913*

Dependent Variable and Period	ln Y	ln (1 + i)	ρ	DW	R-squared
1884–91					
ln *M/P*	2.09	-19.79		1.90	0.58
	(0.61)	(8.36)			
ln *M/P* (including specie hoarding)	2.12	-10.79		2.01	0.81
	(0.39)	(5.32)			
1891–1900					
ln *M/P*	1.31	2.12		1.90	0.83
	(0.36)	(5.95)			
ln *M/P* (including specie hoarding)	0.75	-2.08		1.92	0.70
	(0.37)	(6.18)			
1884–99					
ln *M/P*	1.51	-6.85	0.88	1.73	0.95
	(0.50)	(6.15)	(0.10)		
ln *M/P* (including specie hoarding)	1.36	-3.92	0.81	1.88	0.97
	(0.34)	(4.54)	(0.14)		
1900–1913					
ln *M/P*	1.00	-8.86	0.25	1.58	0.98
	(0.15)	(4.12)	(0.29)		
ln *M/P* (including specie hoarding)	1.00	-4.11	0.32	1.46	0.99
	(0.13)	(3.60)	(0.29)		
1884–1913					
ln *M/P*	1.16	-6.01	0.88	1.73	0.94
	(0.24)	(4.21)	(0.08)		
ln *M/P* (including specie hoarding)	0.95	-2.43	0.72	1.76	0.97
	(0.13)	(3.22)	(0.12)		

Notes: See text. Standard errors in parantheses.
Sources: See Appendix 1.

$$\ln(M/P) = \alpha + \beta \ln Y + \gamma \ln(1 + \pi).$$

In Table A4.4 we used the long-term interest rate proxied by the yield of an internal government bond i, and estimated an equation of the form

$$\ln(M/P) = \alpha + \beta \ln Y + \gamma \ln(1 + i).$$

In most of these regressions the coefficients have the signs predicted by economic theory, but the statistical significance of the opportunity cost coefficients is weak. This may be a data problem: a long-term bond yield could be constructed for most of the period examined; but during the 1892–99 deflationary period, except for two major changes in 1892 and 1896, the long-term yield moved very little while changes in the rate of inflation were considerable. This explains the better performance of the specification using the inflation rate as a measure of the opportunity cost of money.

The relationship between the real money stock and the real income and interest rates appears relatively stable and well defined for the whole period 1884–1913. Breaking the period under consideration into a number of subintervals shows that the estimated parameters are not *perfectly* stable from a statistical point of view. For example, an F-test shows that the 1884–91 and 1891–1900 regression coefficients are significantly different from each other at the 5 percent level. Several statistical and economic factors may have accounted for this structural change.

First, the quality of the data is always a problem. The wholesale price index for 1884–99 is weighted heavily with the prices of primary export products; hence it fluctuates much more widely than an ideal consumer price index, Moreover, since prices for services could not be obtained, our price index may underestimate the inflationary pressures of 1884–91 and overestimate the deflation prevailing up to 1899.

Second, the drastic differences in monetary and financial regimes before and after 1891 could be a very plausible explanation for the observed structural changes. We have seen in Tables 2.3 and 2.4 the extreme volatility of the money multiplier and the dramatic rise of the currency-money ratio for 1890 and 1891, evidence consistent with a lack of confidence in the financial system that could have led to the dramatic fall in the money stock.

Pooling the observations into a 1884–99 money demand regression and comparing it to the 1900–1913 fitted demand, the two regressions are statistically different (at the 5 percent level). In general, for the entire period 1884–1913, the coefficients are within the expected range of magnitude, but the large autocorrelation coefficient suggests that some important variables have been omitted from the specified equation.

A significant conclusion from these simple money demand estimations is our finding of the importance of including the public's hoarding of gold in the definition of money. For the period 1884–91, in which currency substitution was an important phenomenon, the definition of money including specie empirically outperforms the standard definition in terms of a higher variance explained by the simple model.

We also note that money demand sensitivity to changes in the interest rate (or inflation rate) is considerably reduced in the regressions using the definition of money including specie by comparison to the use of the standard definition. This can be largely attributed to the fact that the substitution between paper currency and specie is not captured when using the specie-inclusive definition of money.

Note, however, that the currency substitution phenomenon plays an almost negligible role during the 1900–1913 gold standard years and, therefore, the money definition is rather inconsequential for the empirical estimation of Argentine money demand under the fixed exchange-rate regime.

Appendix 5
Instituto Movilizador de Inversiones Bancarias

In 1935 the Congress approved a specially created institution, the Instituto Movilizador de Inversiones Bancarias (IMIB), to bail out the banking sector. The main source of funds for the operation were seigniorage profits of the Banco Central arising from the decision to devalue the peso parity from 2.27 paper pesos per gold peso to 4.96 in 1935. Suddenly, a huge accouting profit of 701 million paper pesos accrued to the government. This was allocated to various uses as follows: to retire some of the Treasury's floating debt, around 95 million; to augment the banking reserves in the central bank, 216 million; and to supply IMIB with funds for the bailout operation, 390 million pesos.

That is, IMIB received 55 percent of the proceeds of the gold revaluation, which in itself represented a 58 percent increase in the quantity of outside money. How costly was this operation to Argentine households? Such a massive seigniorage tax amounted to about 7 percent of 1935 gross domestic product, around 10 billion paper pesos. If one allows that the retirement of some treasury debt with this operation constituted no change in the net wealth of households, the figure falls to 6 percent of output, still a huge sum.

How did this clean-up operation work? In Table A5.1 we show first the details, starting with the seigniorage operation. IMIB was created to "buy fixed assets, loans, and other investments immobilized or frozen in the banks, and to make good on them gradually" (Article 1). To that end, IMIB performed three big asset swaps to salvage the financial system:

1. It purchased (at book value) the "lemons" at the Banco de la Nación (the rediscounts to private banks) for 301 million pesos, swapping these for 150 million in cash and 151 million in promissory notes;
2. It purchased from four big ailing banks 385 million pesos in assets, and then gave to a newly created merged bank (the Banco Español Limitado) 193 million of these assets, absorbing the remaining 192 million of bad loans in exchange for 129 million in cash and 63 million in promissory notes; [1] and
3. It did a final bailout operation with the private sector by absorbing 61 million pesos of assets in exchange for cash.

1. The bank merger arose because IMIB insisted that the four big banks should be broken up according to function. The newly merged bank took over their traditional commercial banking operations (and the assets and liabilities associated therewith) and the original four banks were left to undertake only investment banking operations or else quit the system.

Table A5.1. *Actions of the Instituto Movilizador de Inversiones Bancarias*

				Public Sector				Private Sector					
								Old Private Banks					New
			House-holds	Treas-ury	BCRA	IMIB	BNA	Esp.	Torn.	Hog.	A-U	Other	Bank
(a)	*Financing of the*	Gold revaluation (seignorage)	-701	95	216	390							
	Scheme	Change in Fiduciary Issue			-216								
		Change in Value of Reserve Backing			216								
	IMIB Rescue of	Private Banks' redisc. from BNA					-301	142	54	40	62		3
	Banco de la	Private Banks' bad assets to BNA					301	-142	-54	-40	-62		-3
	Nación	BNA bad assets taken over by IMIB				301	-301						
		Cash from IMIB to BNA				-150	150						
		Promissory note, IMIB to BNA				-150	150						
	IMIB 1st Bailout	Deposits, Private Banks to IMIB				-385		273	29	55	27		
	of Big 4 Private	Deposits, IMIB to New Bank				385							-385
	Banks	Assets, Private Banks to IMIB				385		-273	-29	-55	-27		
		Assets, IMIB to New Bank				-193							193
		Cash, IMIB to New Bank				-129							129
		Promissory note, IMIB to New Bank				-63							63
	IMIB Second	Cash from IMIB to Old Banks				-61			10			51	
	Bailout	Private Banks' Assets to IMIB				61			-10			-51	
	Total	Net	-701	95	216	390	0	0	0	0	0	0	0
	Transfers	Net, Allowing for Bad Loans	-701	95	216	0	0	390					0
(b)	*Final Balance*		Loans				553	Promissory Notes					-213
	Sheet of IMIB		Cash in Reserve				50	"Liability" of IMIB for Cash					-390
			Assets				603	Liabilities					-603

Notes and sources: See text. Data are from various confidential reports, Ministerio de Hacienda, República Argentina. Units are millions of paper pesos. BCRA = Banco Central de la República Argentina; IMIB = Instituto Movilizador de Inversiones Bancarias; BNA = Banco de la Nación Argentina; Esp. = Banco Español y Rio de la Plata; Torn. = Banco Tornquist Co.; Hog. = El Hogar Argentino; A-U = Banco Argentina-Uruguayo.

Appendix 6
Humor, Politics, and the Economy

by Andrea Matallana[1]

The years of the nation state's organization and subsequent consolidation were rich in terms of political humor. During the peak period of a political press from 1862 to 1890 there were numerous publications that used a humorous "sting" to satirize political and economic situations, albeit from different ideological angles. This is an important point to keep in mind because, although the most effective political humor tends to emanate from those in opposing positions, the satirical press aligned itself with different political groups and used its biting humor against various political actors.

The images included in this volume are taken from satirical publications that delighted the readers of their time. To illustrate the nineteenth century, we have taken cartoons from two publications: *El mosquito* (1863–93), founded by Enrique Stein, a cartoonist and editor of French origin, and *Don Quijote* (1884–1903, founded by Spanish editor Eduardo Sojo. The latter's principal caricaturist was José María Cao, a frequent contributor to many humorous publications in Argentina.

The reader should be aware that these two newspapers held different political positions. *El mosquito* criticized Bartolomé Mitre, Domingo Sarmiento, and Nicolás Avellaneda (the three presidents who preceded Julio A. Roca), and it allied itself with Roca during the period of his first presidency, 1880–86.[2] Conversely, *Don Quijote* was extremely critical of the Roca government (and that of his successor and brother-in-law Miguel Juarez Celman), and it identified itself more with the "Park Civics." The latter group were the allies of Leandro N. Alem and the *Unión Cívica* which was founded in 1890 as the principal opposition group to the Autonomist National Party (Partido Autonomista Nacional).

To illustrate the period between 1900 and 1935, we have used another type of source: general interest magazines that were humorous but not exclusively centered on political satire. *PBT* (1903–18) was founded and edited by Eustaquio Pellicer. *Caras y Caretas* (1898–1939) was founded by writer and journalist José A. Alvarez also known by his nickname Fray Mocho. In these magazines the political content and criticism was less central but no less effective. These extremely popular publications show that satire about economic questions is always in the spotlight during periods of great economic crisis; but, when these crises recede, politics takes center stage with more of a focus on elections, the abstention of radicalism, fraud, and so on.

Humorous publications like these occupied an important place in the press of this

1. Doctoral candidate in History at the Universidad Torcuato Di Tella. I would like to thank the staff of the National Library, especially in the Treasury Room and the Periodicals Department. Translation by Emily Stern.
2. For the reader unfamiliar with Argentine political history, a list of the Argentine presidents and their parties is given in in Table A6.1.

Table A6.1. *Presidents and their Parties, 1862–1938*

1862–1868	Bartolomé Mitre	Partido Nacionalista
1868–1874	Domingo F. Sarmiento	Partido Autonomista
1874–1880	Nicolás Avellaneda	Partido Autonomista Nacional (PAN)
1880–1886	Julio A. Roca	PAN
1886–1890	Miguel Juárez Celman	PAN
1890–1892	Carlos Pellegrini	PAN
1892–1895	Luis Saenz Peña	PAN
1895–1898	José Evaristo Uriburu	PAN
1898–1904	Julio A. Roca	PAN
1904–1906	Manuel Quintana	PAN
1906–1910	José Figueroa Alcorta	PAN
1910–1914	Roque Saenz Peña	PAN
1914–1916	Victorino de la Plaza	PAN
1916–1922	Hipólito Irigoyen	Union Civica Radical (UCR)
1922–1928	Marcelo T. de Alvear	UCR
1928–1930	Hipólito Irigoyen	UCR
1930–1932	José Félix Uriburu	Government *de facto*
1932–1938	Agustín P. Justo	Coalition *(conservadores, antiyrigoyenistas, socialistas independientes)*

era. They criticized, satirized, and, in some cases, even imagined a political direction for the future, an ideal republic to which one might aspire. As Lichtemberg noted, "neither comedy nor satire improves things immediately"; that is, they don't eliminate vice, but they undoubtedly liberate an energy that uncovers certain unspoken elements of a political situation and, thus, expand our horizon of understanding.[3]

3. Lichtenberg (1995).

References

Agote, Pedro. *Informe del Presidente del Crédito Público sobre la deuda pública, bancos y emisiones de papel moneda y acuñacion de monedas de la República Argentina.* 5 vols. Buenos Aires: Crédito Público, 1881–88.

———. *Report on the Public Debt, Banking Institutions, and the Mint.* Buenos Aires: Stiller & Laass, 1887.

Akerlof, George A. The Market for 'Lemons': Quality Uncertainty and the Market Mechanism. *Quarterly Journal of Economics* 84, no. 3 (1970): 488–500.

Alonso, Paula. *Between Revolution and the Ballot Box: The Origins of the Argentine Radical Party in the 1890s.* Cambridge: Cambridge University Press, 2000.

Alvarez, Juan. *Temas de historia económica argentina.* Buenos Aires: El Ateneo, 1929.

Amaral, Samuel. El descubrimiento de la financiación inflacionaria: Buenos Aires, 1790–1830. *Investigaciones y Ensayos* 37 (1988).

Bagehot, Walter. *Lombard Street: A Description of the Money Market.* London: H. S. King & Co., 1873.

Baiocco, Pedro J. *La economía bancaria argentina.* Buenos Aires: Universidad de Buenos Aires, 1937.

Balboa, Manuel. La evolución del balance de pagos de la Republica Argentina, 1913–1950. *Desarrollo Económico* 12, no. 45 (1972): 153–72.

Banco de la Nación Argentina. *El Banco de la Nación Argentina en su Cincuentenario, 1891–1941.* Buenos Aires: Banco de la Nación Argentina, 1941.

Batchelor, Roy A. The Avoidance of Catastrophe: Two Nineteenth-Century Banking Crises. In *Financial Crises and the World Banking System*, edited by Forrest Capie and Geoffrey Edward Wood. London: Macmillan, 1986.

Bernanke, Ben S. Non-Monetary Effects of the Financial Crisis in the Propagation of the Great Depression. *American Economic Review* 73, no. 3 (1983): 257–276.

Bernanke, Ben S., and Harold James. The Gold Standard, Deflation, and Financial Crisis in the Great Depression: An International Comparison. In *Financial Markets and Financial Crises,* edited by R. Glenn Hubbard. Chicago: University of Chicago Press, 1991.

Blanchard, Olivier Jean. Current and Anticipated Deficits, Interest Rates and Economic Activity. *European Economic Review* 25 (1984): 7–27.

Bordo, Michael D., and Lars Jonung. *The Long-Run Behavior of the Velocity of Circulation.* Cambridge: Cambridge University Press, 1987.

Bordo, Michael D., and Finn E. Kydland. The Gold Standard as a Rule: An Essay in Exploration. *Explorations in Economic History* 32, no. 4 (1995): 423–64.

Bordo, Michael D., and Hugh Rockoff. The Gold Standard as a Good Housekeeping Seal of Approval. *Journal of Economic History* 56, no. 2 (1996): 389–428.

Bordo, Michael D., and Carlos A. Végh. What if Alexander Hamilton Had Been Argentinean? A Comparison of the Early Monetary Experiences of Argentina and the United States. Working Paper Series, no. 6862, National Bureau of Economic Research, 1998.

Botana, Natalio. 1986. *El orden conservador: la política Argentina entre 1880–1916.* Buenos Aires: Editorial Sudamericana.

Botana, Natalio, and Ezequiel Gallo. *De la República posible a la República verdadera (1880–1910).* Buenos Aires: Ariel, 1997.

Brown, E. Cary. Fiscal Policy in the Thirties: A Reappraisal. *American Economic Review* 46, no. 5 (1956): 857–79.

Bulmer-Thomas, Victor. The Latin American Economies in the 1930s. In *The Cambridge History of Latin America,* edited by Leslie Bethell. Cambridge: Cambridge University Press, 1996.

Cagan, Phillip. *Determinants and Effects of Changes in the Stock of Money, 1875–1960.* New York: Columbia University Press, 1965.

Calomiris, Charles W. Regulation, Industrial Structure, and Instability in U.S. Banking: An Historical Perspective. In *Structural Change in Banking,* edited by Michael Klausner and Lawrence J. White. Homewood, Ill.: Business One Irwin, 1993.

Calvo, Guillermo. Servicing the Public Debt: The Role of Expectations. *American Economic Review* 78, no. 4 (1988): 647–61.

———. Varieties of Capital-Market Crises. University of Maryland, May 1996. Photocopy.

———. Balance of Payment Crises in Emerging Markets. University of Maryland, March 1998. Photocopy.

Cameron, Rondo, Olga Crisp, Hugh T. Patrick, and Richard Tilly. *Banking in the Early Stages of Industrialization: A Study in Comparative Economic History.* New York: Oxford University Press, 1967.

Campa, José Manuel. Exchange Rates and Economic Recovery in the 1930s: An Extension to Latin America. *Journal of Economic History* 50, no. 3 (1990): 677–82.

Coatsworth, John H. Economic and Institutional Trajectories in Pre-Modern Latin America. In *Latin America and the World Economy Since 1800,* edited by John H. Coatsworth and Alan M. Taylor. Cambridge: Harvard University Press, 1999.

Comité Nacional de Geografía. *Anuario geográfico argentino.* Buenos Aires: Comité Nacional de Geografía, 1941–43.

Corporation of Foreign Bondholders (Great Britain). *Annual Report.* London: Wertheimer, Lea and Co., 1897.

Cortés Conde, Roberto. *El progreso argentino.* Buenos Aires: Editorial Sudamericana, 1979.

———. *Dinero, deuda y crisis: evolución fiscal y monetaria en la Argentina, 1862–1890.* Buenos Aires: Editorial Sudamericana, 1989.

Cuccorese, Horacio Juan. *Historia del Banco de la Provincia de Buenos Aires.* Buenos Aires: Banco de la Provincia de Buenos Aires, 1972.

Davis, Lance E. Capital Immobilities and Finance Capitalism: A Study of Economic Evolution in the United States. *Explorations in Economic History* 1 (1963): 88–105.

De Gregorio, José, and Pablo E. Guidotti. Financial Development and Economic Growth. *World Development* 23, no. 3 (1995): 433–48.

De Long, J. Bradford. Did J. P. Morgan's Men Add Value? An Economist's Perspective on Financial Capitalism. In *Inside the Business Enterprise: Historical Perspectives on the Use of Information,* edited by Peter Temin. Chicago: University of Chicago Press, 1991.

della Paolera, Gerardo. Hacia la crisis de 1866: un análisis de la influencia del gasto público sobre la economía. Fifth Economic History Congress, San Juan, Argentina, 1983. Photocopy.

———. How the Argentine Economy Performed During the International Gold Standard: A Reexamination. Ph. D. dissertation, University of Chicago, 1988.

———. Experimentos monetarios y bancarios en Argentina: 1861–1930. *Revista de Historia Económica* 12, no. 3 (1994): 539–90.

———. Precios de la tierra en la ciudad de Buenos Aires y ciclos económicos: una aproximación. Universidad Torcuato Di Tella, 1999. Photocopy.

della Paolera, Gerardo, and Javier Ortiz. Dinero, intermediación financiera y nivel de actividad en 110 años de historia económica argentina. Documentos de Trabajo, Universidad Torcuato Di Tella, December 1995.

della Paolera, Gerardo, and Alan M. Taylor. Economic Recovery from the Argentine Great Depression: Institutions, Expectations, and the Change of Macroeconomic Regime. *Journal of Economic History* 59, no. 3 (1999a): 567–99.

———. Finance and Development in an Emerging Market: Argentina in the Interwar Period. In *Latin America and the World Economy Since 1800,* edited by John H. Coatsworth and Alan M. Taylor. Cambridge: Harvard University Press, 1999b.

———. Internal versus External Convertibility and Developing-Country Financial Crises: Lessons from the Argentine Bank Bailout of the 1930s. Working Paper Series, no. 7386, National Bureau of Economic Research, October 1999c.

Diamond, Peter A., and Phillip H. Dybvig. Bank Runs, Deposit Insurance, and Liquidity. *Journal of Political Economy* 91, no. 3 (1983): 401–19.

Díaz Alejandro, Carlos F. *Essays on the Economic History of the Argentine Republic.* New Haven, Conn.: Yale University Press, 1970.

———. Tipo de cambio y terminos de intercambio en la República Argentina 1913–1976. Documentos de Trabajo, no. 22, Centro de Estudios Macroeconomicos Argentinos, Marzo 1981.

———. Stories of the 1930s for the 1980s. In *Financial Policies and the World Capital Market: The Problem of Latin American Countries,* edited by Pedro Aspe Armella, Rudiger Dornbusch and Maurice Obstfeld. Chicago: University of Chicago Press, 1983.

———. Latin America in the 1930s. In *Latin America in the 1930s: The Role of the Periphery in World Crisis,* edited by Rosemary Thorp. New York: St. Martin's Press, 1984.

———. Argentina, Australia and Brazil Before 1929. In *Argentina, Australia and Canada: Studies in Comparative Development, 1870–1965,* edited by Guido Di Tella and D. C. M. Platt. London: Macmillan, 1985a.

———. Good-Bye Financial Repression, Hello Financial Crash. *Journal of Development Economics* 19 (1985b): 1–24.

Diéguez, Héctor L. Crecimiento e inestabilidad del valor y el volumen físico de las exportaciones en el período 1864–1963. *Desarrollo Económico* 12 (1972): 333–49.

Diz, Adolfo C. Money and Prices in Argentina 1935–1962. Ph.D. dissertation, University of Chicago, 1966.

Di Tella, Guido, and Manuel Zymelman. *Las etapas del desarrollo económico argentino.* Buenos Aires: Editorial Universitaria de Buenos Aires, 1967.

Dornbusch, Rudiger. Exchange Rate Economics: Where Do We Stand? In *Economic Interdependence and Flexible Exchange Rates,* edited by Jagdeep S. Bhandari, Bluford H. Putnam, and Jay H. Levin. Cambridge, Mass.: MIT Press, 1983.

Dornbusch, Rudiger, Olivier Jean Blanchard, and Willem H. Buiter. Public Debt and Fiscal Responsibility. In *Dollars, Debts, and Deficits.* Cambridge, Mass.: MIT Press, 1986.

Dornbusch, Rudiger, and Jacob A. Frenkel. The Gold Standard and the Bank of England in the Crisis of 1847. In *A Retrospective on the Classical Gold Standard, 1880–1913,* edited by Michael D. Bordo and Anna J. Schwartz. Chicago: University of Chicago Press, 1984.

Duncan, Tim. La política fiscal durante el gobierno de Juárez Celman, 1886–1890: una audaz estrategia financiera internacional. *Desarrollo Económico* 23 (1983): 11–34.

ECLA (United Nations Economic Commission for Latin America). *El desarrollo económico de la Argentina*. 5 vols. Santiago de Chile: ECLA, 1958.
Eichengreen, Barry J. *Golden Fetters: The Gold Standard and The Great Depression, 1919–1939*. Oxford: Oxford University Press, 1992a.
———. The Origins and Nature of the Great Slump Revisited. *Economic History Review* 45, no. 2 (1992b): 212–39.
———. *Globalizing Capital: A History of the International Monetary System*. Princeton, N.J.: Princeton University Press, 1996.
———. Exchange Rate Stability and Financial Stability. *Open Economies Review* 9, no. S1 (1998): 569–607.
———. *Toward a New International Financial Architecture: A Practical Post-Asia Agenda*. Washington, D.C.: Institute for International Economics, 1999.
Eichengreen, Barry J., and Richard Portes. After the Deluge: Default, Negotiation, and Readjustment during the Interwar Years. In *The International Debt Crisis in Historical Perspective,* edited by Barry J. Eichengreen and Peter H. Lindert. Cambridge, Mass.: MIT Press, 1989.
Eichengreen, Barry J., and Jeffrey D. Sachs. Exchange Rates and Economic Recovery in the 1930s. *Journal of Economic History* 45, no. 4 (1985): 925–46.
Eichengreen, Barry J., and Peter Temin. The Gold Standard and the Great Depression. Working Paper Series, no. 6060, National Bureau of Economic Research, June 1997.
Elliott, Graham. Efficient Tests for a Unit Root When the Initial Observation is Drawn from Its Unconditional Distribution. *International Economic Review* 40 (1999).
Elliott, Graham, Thomas J. Rothenberg, and James H. Stock. Efficient Tests for an Autoregressive Unit Root. *Econometrica* 64, no. 4 (1996): 813–36.
Fama, Eugene F. What's Different about Banks? *Journal of Monetary Economics* 15, no. 1 (1985): 29–39.
Feinstein, Charles K. *Statistical Tables of National Income, Expenditure and Output of the U.K.* Cambridge: Cambridge University Press, 1972.
Feldstein, Martin S. A Self-Help Guide for Emerging Markets. *Foreign Affairs* 78, no. 2 (1999).
Fernández López, Manuel. *Convertibilidad: ideas, politicas y reflexiones*. Colegio de Graduados de Ciencias Economicas, Buenos Aires, 1993. Conference presentation.
Ferns, H. S. *The Argentine Republic, 1516–1971*. Newton Abbot: David & Charles, 1973.
Fisher, Irving. The Debt-Deflation Theory of Great Depressions. *Econometrica* 1 (1933a): 337–57.
———. *Stamp Scrip*. New York: Adelphi Company, 1933b.
Fishlow, Albert. Lessons from the Past: Capital Markets during the 19th Century and the Interwar Periods. *International Organization* 39 (1985): 383–416.
———. Conditionality and Willingness to Pay: Some Parallels from the 1890s. In *The International Debt Crisis in Historical Perspective,* edited by Barry J. Eichengreen and Peter H. Lindert. Cambridge, Mass.: MIT Press, 1989.
Ford, Alec G. *The Gold Standard, 1880–1914: Britain and Argentina*. Oxford: Clarendon Press, 1962.
Fratianni, Michele, and Franco Spinelli. The Growth of Government in Italy: Evidence from 1861 to 1979. *Public Choice* 39, no. 2 (1982): 221–43.
———. Italy in the Gold Standard Period, 1861–1914. In *A Retrospective on the Classical Gold Standard, 1821–1931,* edited by Michael D. Bordo and Anna J. Schwartz. Chicago: University of Chicago Press, 1984.
Frenkel, Jacob A. Flexible Exchange Rates, Prices and the Role of 'News': Lessons from the 1970s. *Journal of Political Economy* 89, no. 4 (1981): 665–705.
Frieden, Jeffry A. Sectoral Conflict and U.S. Foreign Economic Policy, 1914–1940. *International Organization* 42 (1988): 59–90.

———. Monetary Populism in Nineteenth-Century America: An Open Economy Interpretation. *Journal of Economic History* 57, no. 2 (1997): 367–95.

Friedman, Milton. *A Program for Monetary Stability*. New York: Fordham University Press, 1959.

Friedman, Milton, and Anna J. Schwartz. *A Monetary History of the United States, 1867–1960, National Bureau of Economic Research. Studies in Business Cycles*. Princeton, N.J.: Princeton University Press, 1963.

———. *Monetary Trends in the United States and United Kingdom: Their Relation to Income, Prices, and Interest Rates, 1867–1975*. Chicago: University of Chicago Press, 1982.

Fry, Maxwell J. *Money, Interest, and Banking in Economic Development*. 2d ed. Baltimore: Johns Hopkins University Press, 1995.

Gallo, Ezequiel. El contexto histórico de la Ley de Convertibilidad de 1899. In *Aspectos analíticos e históricos de la convertibilidad monetaria,* edited by Ana María Martirena Mantel. Buenos Aires: Academia Nacional de Ciencias de Buenos Aires, 1977.

———. *Carlos Pellegrini: orden y reforma*. Buenos Aires: Fondo de Cultura Económico, 1997.

Garber, Peter M. *Famous First Bubbles: The Fundamentals of Early Manias*. Cambridge, Mass.: MIT Press, 2000.

Garrigos, Osvaldo. *El Banco de la Provincia*. Buenos Aires: Imprenta de Pablo Coni, 1873.

Gavin, Michael, and Ricardo Hausmann. The Roots of Banking Crises: The Macroeconomic Context. In *Working Paper*. Inter-American Development Bank, 1996.

Gerschenkron, Alexander. *Economic Backwardness in Historical Perspective*. Cambridge, Mass.: Harvard University Press, 1962.

Gesell, Silvio. La anemia monetaria. Buenos Aires: n.p., 1898 [1909a].

———. La pletora monetaria. Buenos Aires: n.p. 1909b.

Goldsmith, Raymond W. *Financial Structure and Economic Development*. New Haven: Yale University Press, 1969.

Goodhart, Charles A. E. *The Evolution of Central Banks*. Cambridge, Mass.: MIT Press, 1988.

Gurley, John G., and Edward S. Shaw. Financial Aspects of Economic Development. *American Economic Review* 45, no. 4 (1955): 515–38.

Halperín Donghi, Tulio. 1977. *Vida y muerte de la República verdadera (1910–1930)*. Buenos Aires: Ariel.

IEERAL (Instituto de Estudios Económicos sobre la Realidad Argentina y Latinoamericana). Estadísticas de la evolución económica de Argentina 1913–1984. *Estudios* 9, no. 39 (1986): 103–84.

Irigoin, Maria Alejandra. Moneda, impuestos e instituciones en el estado de Buenos Aires 1850–1860. Buenos Aires, 1995. Photocopy.

———. Political Bargaining and Institutional Commitment: The Birth of a Political Market as a Means of Currency Stabilisation in 1850s Buenos Aires. London School of Economics, February 1999. Paper presented at the conference Organizing and Imagining the Market: New Currents in Argentine Economic and Social History.

———. Finance, Politics and Economics in Buenos Aires 1820s–1860s: The Political Economy of Currency Stabilisation. Ph.D. dissertation, London School of Economics, 2000a.

———. Inconvertible Paper Money, Inflation and Economic Performance in Early Nineteenth Century Argentina. *Journal of Latin American Studies* 32 (2000b): 333–59.

James, John A. Public Debt Management Policy and Nineteenth-Century American Economic Growth. *Explorations in Economic History* 21, no. 2 (1984): 192–217.

Jorgensen, Erika, and Jeffrey Sachs. Default and Renegotiation of Latin American Foreign Bonds in the Interwar Period. In *The International Debt Crisis in Historical*

Perspective, edited by Barry J. Eichengreen and Peter H. Lindert. Cambridge, Mass.: MIT Press, 1989.

Joslin, David. *A Century of Banking in Latin America.* London: Oxford University Press, 1963.

Kaminsky, Graciela L., and Carmen M. Reinhart. The Twin Crises: The Causes of Banking and Balance-of-Payments Problems. *American Economic Review* 89, no. 3 (1999): 473–500.

Keynes, John Maynard. *The General Theory of Employment, Interest and Money.* New York: Harcourt Brace, 1935.

Kindleberger, Charles P. *A Financial History of Western Europe.* London: George Allen & Unwin, 1984.

———. *The World in Depression, 1929–1939.* Revised ed. Berkeley: University of California Press, 1986.

———. Rules vs Men: Lessons from a Century of Monetary Policy. In *Comparative Political Economy: A Retrospective.* Cambridge, Mass.: MIT Press, 2000.

King, Robert G., and Ross Levine. Finance and Growth: Schumpeter Might Be Right. *Quarterly Journal of Economics* 108 (1993): 717–38.

Krugman, Paul. A Model of Balance of Payments Crises. *Journal of Money, Credit and Banking* 11, no. 3 (1979): 311–325.

Levine, Ross. Financial Development and Economic Growth: Views and Agenda. In *Policy Research Working Papers.* World Bank, 1996.

Lichtenberg, Georg Christoph. *Aforismos.* Mexico City: Fondo de Cultura Económica, 1995.

Lindert, Peter H., and Peter H. Morton. How Sovereign Debt Has Worked. In *Developing Country Debt and the World Economy,* edited by Jeffrey D. Sachs. Chicago: University of Chicago Press, 1989.

Lizondo, Jose Saul. Foreign Exchange Futures Prices under Fixed Exchange Rates. *Journal of International Economics* 14, no. 1–2 (1983): 69–84.

Lorini, Eteocle. *La Repubblica Argentina e i suoi maggiori problemi di economia e di finanza.* Rome: E. Loescher, 1902.

Luna, Felix. *A Short History of the Argentinians.* Buenos Aires: Editorial Planeta Argentina, 2000.

Mabragaña, Heraclio. *Los mensajes: historia del desenvolvimiento de la nacion argentina, redactada cronologicamente por sus gobernantes, 1810–1910.* 6 vols. Buenos Aires: Talleres Graficos de la Compañia Gral. de Fosforos, 1910.

Maddison, Angus. *Monitoring the World Economy.* Paris: OECD, 1995.

Magariños de Mello, Mateo J. *Diálogos con Raúl Prebisch.* México City: Banco Nacional de Comercio Exterior, Fondo de Cultura Económica, 1991.

Martínez, Alberto B. *Les finances de la République Argentine: budget, dépenses, revenus et dette publique.* Buenos Aires: Compañía Sudamericana de Billetes de Banco, 1898.

Martínez, Alberto B., and Maurice Lewandowski. *The Argentine in the twentieth century.* Translated by Bernard Miall. London: T. F. Unwin, 1911.

McCloskey, Donald N., and J. Richard Zecher. How the Gold Standard Worked, 1880–1913. In *The Monetary Approach to the Balance of Payments,* edited by Jacob A. Frenkel and Harry G. Johnson. London: Allen & Unwin, 1976.

McKinnon, Ronald I. *Money and Capital in Economic Development.* Washington, D.C.: The Brookings Institution, 1973.

———. *Limiting Moral Hazard and Reducing Risk in International Capital Flows: The Choice of Exchange-Rate Regime.* Stanford University, 1999.

Miller, Victoria. Speculative Currency Attacks with Endogenously Induced Commercial Bank Crises. *Journal of International Money and Finance* 15, no. 3 (1996): 383–403.

Minton Beddoes, Zanny. Think Again: The International Financial System. *Foreign Policy* (1999): 16–29.

Mishkin, Frederic S. *The Economics of Money, Banking, and Financial Markets*. Boston: Little Brown, 1986.

———. Is the Fisher Effect for Real? A Reexamination of the Relationship Between Inflation and Interest Rates. *Journal of Monetary Economics* 30, no. 2 (1992): 195–215.

Mitchell, Brian R. *Abstract of British Historical Statistics*. Cambridge: University Press, 1971.

———. *International Historical Statistics: Europe, 1750–1988*. New York: Stockton Press, 1992.

———. *International Historical Statistics: The Americas, 1750–1988*. New York: Stockton Press, 1993.

Moyano Llerena, Carlos. La ley de conversión de 1899. In *n.t.* Buenos Aires: n.p., 1935.

Mulhall, Michael George. *The Dictionary of Statistics*. London: G. Routledge, 1903.

Nakamura, Leonard I., and Carlos E. J. M. Zarazaga. Economic Growth in Argentina in the Period 1905–1930: Some Evidence from Stock Returns. In *Latin America and the World Economy Since 1800,* edited by John H. Coatsworth and Alan M. Taylor. Cambridge: Harvard University Press, 1999.

Obstfeld, Maurice. The Logic of Currency Crises. *Cahiers Économiques et Monetaires* 43 (1994): 189–213.

———. Models of Currency Crises with Self-Fulfilling Features. *European Economic Review* 40 (1996): 1037–47.

Obstfeld, Maurice, and Alan M. Taylor. The Great Depression as a Watershed: International Capital Mobility in the Long Run. In *The Defining Moment: The Great Depression and the American Economy in the Twentieth Century,* edited by Michael D. Bordo, Claudia D. Goldin and Eugene N. White. Chicago: University of Chicago Press, 1998.

———. *Global Capital Markets: Integration, Crisis, and Growth, Japan-U.S. Center Sanwa Monographs on International Financial Markets*. Cambridge: Cambridge University Press, 2002.

Officer, Lawrence H. *Between the Dollar-Sterling Gold Points: Exchange Rates, Parity, and Market Behavior*. Cambridge: Cambridge University Press, 1996.

———. Exchange Rates. In *Historical Statistics of the United States, Millennial Edition,* edited by Susan B. Carter, Scott S. Gartner, Michael Haines, Alan Olmstead, Richard Sutch, and Gavin Wright. Cambridge: Cambridge University Press, Forthcoming 2001.

Ortiz, Javier. *Los bancos centrales en América Latina: sus antecedentes históricos*. Buenos Aires: Editorial Sudamericana, 1998.

Peppers, Larry C. Full-Employment Surplus Analysis and Structural Change: The 1930s. *Explorations in Economic History* 10, no. 2 (1973): 197–210.

Pillado, Jorge. *El papel moneda argentino*. Buenos Aires: Compañía Sudamericana de Billetes de Banco, 1901.

Piñeiro, Norberto. *La moneda, el crédito y los bancos en la Argentina*. Buenos Aires: Jésus Menéndez, Librero Editor, 1921.

Prebisch, Raúl. Anotaciones sobre nuestro medio circulante. *Revista de Ciencias Económicas* (1922).

Pressnell, L. S. Gold Reserves, Banking Reserves, and the Baring Crisis of 1890. In *Essays in Money and Banking in Honour of R. S. Sayers,* edited by Charles R. Whittlesey and John Stuart Gladstone Wilson. Oxford: Clarendon Press, 1968.

Regalsky, Andrés. La evolución de la Banca Privada Nacional en Argentina (1880–1914): una introducción a su estudio. In *La formación de los bancos centrales en España y América Latina (siglos XIX y XX),* edited by Banco de España-Servicio de Estudios. Madrid: Banco de España, 1994.

República Argentina. *Extracto estadístico de la República Argentina correspondiente al año 1915.* Buenos Aires: Compañia Sudamericana de Billetes de Banco, 1916.

———. *Censo bancario de la Republica Argentina 1925.* Buenos Aires, 1926.

Rock, David. 1987. *Argentina, 1516–1987: From Spanish Colonization to Alfonsín.* Berkeley and Los Angeles: University of California Press.

Rockoff, Hugh. The Free Banking Era: A Reexamination. Ph.D. dissertation, University of Chicago, 1972.

Romer, Christina D. What Ended the Great Depression? *Journal of Economic History* 52, no. 4 (1992): 757–84.

Rosa, José María. 1909. *Conversión de la moneda, unidad monetaria, Caja de Conversión.* Buenos Aires: n.p.

Roubini, Nouriel. "The Case Against Currency Boards: Debunking 10 Myths about the Benefits of Currency Boards." n.d.a http://www.stern.nyu.edu/~nroubini/.

———. "What Caused Asia's Economic and Currency Crisis and Its Global Contagion?" n.d.b http://www.stern.nyu.edu/~nroubini/.

Sabsay, Fernando L. *La sociedad argentina: argentina documental (1806–1912).* Buenos Aires: La Ley, 1975.

Salama, Elias. El orden monetario Caja de Conversion - Banco de la Nación. In *Documentos de Seminario.* Universidad Torcuato Di Tella, 1997.

Sargent, Thomas J. The Ends of Four Big Inflations. In *Inflation: Causes and Effects,* edited by Robert E. Hall. Chicago: University of Chicago Press, 1983.

———. *Rational Expectations and Inflation.* New York: Harper & Row, 1986.

———. *Bounded Rationality in Macroeconomics.* Oxford: Oxford University Press, 1993.

Sarmiento, Domingo F. *Facundo [Civilizacion i barbarie: vida de Juan Facundo Qiroga, i aspectos físico, costumbres, i abitos de la Republica Arjentina].* 1st ed. Buenos Aires: Emecé, 1845 [1999].

Schumpeter, Joseph A. *The Theory of Economic Development: An Inquiry Into Profits, Capital, Credit, Interest, and the Business Cycle.* Translated by Redvers Opie. Cambridge, Mass.: Harvard University Press, 1936.

Schwartz, Anna J. Currency Boards: Their Past, Present, and Possible Future Role. *Carnegie Rochester Conference Series on Public Policy* (1993): 147–88.

Shaw, Edward S. *Financial Deepening in Economic Development.* Oxford: Oxford University Press, 1973.

Shepherd, Henry L. *Default and Adjustment of Argentine Foreign Debts, 1890–1906.* Washington D.C.: Government Printing Office, 1933.

Simon, Mathew. The Pattern of New British Portfolio Foreign Investment, 1865–1915. In *The Export of Capital from Britain 1870–1914,* edited by A. R. Hall. London: Methuen, 1968.

Sjaastad, Larry A. International Debt Quagmire: To Whom Do We Owe It? *World Economy* (1983): 305–24.

Taylor, Alan M. External Dependence, Demographic Burdens and Argentine Economic Decline After the Belle Époque. *Journal of Economic History* 52, no. 4 (1992): 907–36.

———. Tres fases del crecimiento económico argentino. *Revista de Historia Económica* 12, no. 3 (1994): 649–83.

———. Argentina and the World Capital Market: Saving, Investment, and International Capital Mobility in the Twentieth Century. *Journal of Development Economics* 57, no. 1 (1998): 147–84.

———. A Century of Purchasing-Power Parity. *Review of Economics and Statistics.* Forthcoming, 2001.

Temin, Peter. *Lessons from The Great Depression.* Cambridge, Mass.: MIT Press, 1989.

Temin, Peter, and Barrie A. Wigmore. The End of One Big Deflation. *Explorations in Economic History* 27, no. 4 (1990): 483–502.

Terry, José Antonio. *La crisis, 1885–1892, sistema bancario*. Buenos Aires: Impr. M. Biedma, 1893.

Timberlake, Richard H. *The Origins of Central Banking in the United States*. Cambridge: Harvard University Press, 1978.

Tomz, Michael. Do Creditors Ignore History? Reputation in International Capital Markets. Harvard University, Department of Government, September 1998. Photocopy.

Tornquist, Ernesto, & Co., Limited. *The Economic Development of the Argentine Republic in the Last Fifty Years*. Buenos Aires: Ernesto Tornquist & Co., Limited, 1919.

Townsend, Robert M. Financial Structure and Economic Activity. *American Economic Review* 73, no. 5 (1983): 895–911.

Twomey, Michael J. The 1930s Depression in Latin America: A Macro Analysis. *Explorations in Economic History* 2, no. 3 (1983): 221–47.

Vázquez-Presedo, Vicente. *Estadísticas historicas argentinas*. 2 vols. Buenos Aires: Ediciones Macchi, 1971–76.

Velasco, Andrés. Financial and Balance-of-Payments Crises. *Journal of Development Economics* 27 (1987): 263–83.

Williams, John H. *Argentine International Trade Under Inconvertible Paper Currency, 1880–1900*. Cambridge: Harvard University Press, 1920.

World Bank. *Global Economic Prospects and the Developing Countries 1998/99*. Washington, D.C.: World Bank, 1999.

Name Index

Agote, Pedro, 46n14, 47n16, 48n17, 50n19, 58, 62n40, 241t, 242t, 243n4
Akerlof, George A., 176n13
Alem, Leandro N., 78c
Alonso, Paula, 100n1, 109n17
Alsina, Adolfo, 51c
Alvarez, Juan, 104f, 236
Amaral, Samuel, 14t, 18n11, 37n1, 222
Avellaneda, Nicolás, 4, 44, 45c, 51c

Bagehot, Walter, 176, 229n6
Baiocco, Pedro J., 147n15, 158n26, 191t, 238
Balboa, Manuel, 147t
Batchelor, Roy A., 67n3
Bernanke, Ben S., 156, 158, 189n4
Blanchard, Olivier, 88n15, 110n19
Bordo, Michael D., 14t, 18n11, 26n18, 37n1, 70n5, 130n16, 148n17, 217n56, 247n1, 249n2
Botana, Natalio, 4n2
Brown, E. Cary, 195n14
Buiter, Willem H., 88n15
Bulmer-Thomas, Victor, 192n11
Bunge, Alejandro E., 214nn42,46

Cagan, Philip, 240n1, 246n1
Calomiris, Charles W., 142n5, 160n28
Calvo, Guillermo, 20n12, 60n36, 77n21, 167n4
Cameron, Rondo, 141
Campa, José Manuel, 189n4, 192n9, 193n13
Carcano, Ramon, 78c
Cavallo, Domingo, 12, 15, 17
Coatsworth, John H., 6
Comité Nacional de Geografía, 93t, 236, 237
Cortés Conde, Roberto, 18n11, 37n1, 39n3, 40t, 41n5, 42n8, 44n12, 76t, 84n7, 113n24, 115t, 139n1, 236, 237
Cortinéz, Santiago, 45c, 51c
Cuccorese, Horacio Juan, 47n16, 51n22, 72n10, 76n19

Davis, Lance E., 141
De Gregorio, José, 147n15, 149n19
de la Plaza, Victorino, 100, 106, 175c
della Paolera, Gerardo, 13f, 14t, 18n11, 26n18, 37n1, 40t, 41n4, 128n13, 139n1, 142n6, 191t, 236
De Long, J. Bradford, 141n4
Diamond, Peter A., 140n2, 168n7
Díaz Alejandro, Carlos F., 3, 139n1, 142n7, 143, 149, 167, 188n1, 190nn5,7, 193n12, 195nn16,19, 196n20, 202n28, 236
Diéguez, Héctor L., 13f, 238
Di Tella, Guido, 139n1, 147t
Diz, Adolfo C., 236
Dornbusch, Rudiger, 88n15, 105n12, 167, 177, 178n15
Duncan, Tim, 58n31, 82n2, 83nn4,5
Dybvig, Phillip H., 140n2, 168n7

ECLA (United Nations Economic Commission for Latin America), 236
The Economist, 90, 106, 169n8, 215–16, 217n54
Eichengreen, Barry, 22n14, 31n23, 114nn25,26, 166n1, 167n4, 168n6, 189nn3,4, 190n7, 193n13, 199n25, 216n51, 230n7

Elliott, Graham, 182n19

Fama, Eugene F., 168
Feinstein, Charles K., 249n2
Feldstein, Martin S., 169n8
Fernández López, Manuel, 120n4
Ferns, H. S., 71n8, 72n10, 73n12, 100n1
Fisher, Irving, 115, 203
Fishlow, Albert, 18n11, 217nn52,53
Ford, Alec G., 18n11, 28n20, 31n23, 52, 53n26, 114n26, 129
Fratianni, Michele, 83n6, 237
Frenkel, Jacob A., 105n12, 167, 177, 178n15
Frieden, Jeffry A., 31n23, 114nn25,26
Friedman, Milton, 127n11, 42n9, 112n21, 113n24, 114n25, 125n9, 148n17, 178n15, 236, 246n1
Fry, Maxwell J., 141n3, 148n17

Gallo, Ezequiel, 4n2, 119n3, 120n5
Garber, Peter M., 58n31, 94n19
Garrigos, Osvaldo, 41
Gavin, Michael, 169n8
Gerschenkron, Alexander, 141
Gesell, Silvio, 31, 115–17, 119, 129, 203, 225
Goldsmith, Raymond W., 141, 232n8
Goodhart, Charles A. E., 33n25
Guidotti, Pablo, 147n15, 149n19
Gurley, John G., 141n3

Halperín Donghi, Tulio, 4n2
Hausmann, Ricardo, 169n8

IEERAL (Instituto de Estudios Económicos sobre la Realidad Argentina y Latinoarmericana), 147t, 191t
Irigoin, Maria Alejandra, 13f, 14t, 18n11
Irigoyen, Hipólito, 145c, 174n10, 194c, 215

James, Harold, 189n4
James, John A., 83n6
Jonung, Lars, 70n5, 148n17
Jorgenson, Dale W., 216n51, 217n55
Joslin, David, 74n15, 242n3
Juarez, Marcos, 78c
Juárez Celman, Miguel, 29, 58n31, 73, 75, 78c, 92, 93–94
Justo, Juan B., 135c, 206c, 233c

Kaminsky, Graciela L., 155n24, 166n2, 167n4
Keynes, John Maynard, 203
Kindleberger, Charles P., 59n34, 95n20, 188n1, 190n7, 221
King, Robert G., 147n15, 148n17, 149n19
Krugman, Paul, 44, 60n35, 87n13, 167n3
Kydland, Finn, 26n18, 130n16, 217n56

Law, John, 58
Lawson, W. R., 16n8, 28n20
Leeson, Nick, 67n1
Levine, Ross, 141, 142n5, 143, 147n15, 148n17, 149n19
Lewandowski, Maurice, 103n10
Lichtenberg, Georg Christoph, 256n3
Lindert, Peter H., 196n21, 216n51
Lizondo, José Saúl, 105n12
López, Vicente Fidel, 69c, 91c, 100
Lorini, Eteocle, 51n20, 241t
Luna, Felix, 4n2

Mabragaña, Heraclio, 100n2
McCloskey, Donald N., 22n15, 124n8
McKinnon, Ronald I., 77, 141n3
Maddison, Angus, 6–7, 8f
Magariños de Mello, Mateo J., 204n33
Martínez, Alberto B., 82n1, 101n3, 103n10, 113n22
Memorias de Hacienda, 29n21, 55n28, 74n14, 82n2, 83n5, 101n3, 102n4, 106n14, 108n15, 174n9, 238
Miller, Victoria, 167n5, 186n21
Minton Beddoes, Zanny, 223n3, 232n9
Mishkin, Frederic S., 93n17, 204n33
Mitchell, Brian R., 110t, 115t, 151f, 190n8, 236, 237
Mitre, Bartolomé, 4, 38, 51c
Morton, Peter H., 196n21, 216n51
Moyano Llerena, Carlos, 119nn1,2,3, 120n6, 121n7
Mulhall, Michael George, 7n5
Mundell, Robert A., 31

Nakamura, Leonard I., 18n11, 147t, 149n18, 156t

Obstfeld, Maurice, 11f, 21n13, 60n36, 70n7, 146n13, 167n3, 189n4
Officer, Lawrence H., 13f

Ortiz, Javier, 236, 18n11, 139n1, 142n6, 191t, 193n12

Palacios, Alfredo, 135c
Pellegrini, Carlos, 28, 29, 69c, 73, 78, 100, 101c, 105, 107c, 216–17, 225
Peppers, Larry C., 195n14
Perón, Juan, 216n51
Pillado, Ricardo, 92, 243n5
Pinedo, Federico, 204, 206c
Piñiero, Norberto, 47n16
Portes, Richard, 216n51
Prebisch, Raúl, 18n11, 189, 203–4, 216n50, 230
Pressnell, L. S., 67n3

Regalsky, Andrés, 18n11
Reinhart, Carmen M., 155n24, 166n2, 167n4
Repetto, Nicolás, 135c
República Argentina, 40t, 159n27, 161n29
Roca, Julio A., 4, 78c, 119
Rock, David, 4n2
Rockoff, Hugh, 26n18, 217n56, 240n1
Romer, Christina D., 189n3, 195n14, 204n33, 212, 230n7
Romero, Juan José, 108–12
Rosa, José María, 120
Rothenberg, Thomas J., 182n19
Roubini, Nouriel, 166n1, 169n8

Sabsay, Fernando L., 94n18, 103nn8,9
Sachs, Jeffrey D., 168n6, 189n4, 193n13, 216n51, 217n55, 230n7
Sáenz Peña, Luis, 108, 109–10
Salaberry, Domingo, 174n10
Salama, Elias, 177n14, 189n2, 200n26
Sargent, Thomas J., 20n12, 31, 88n15, 192n10, 218n57, 228n5
Sarmiento, Domingo F., 4, 42, 51c, 235
Schumpeter, Joseph A., 141
Schwartz, Anna J., 17n10, 42n9, 113n24, 114n25, 125n9, 127n11, 148n17, 178n15, 236, 246n1
Shaw, Edward S., 141n3
Shepherd, Henry L., 109n18, 111n20
Simon, Mathew, 53n26
Sjaastad, Larry, 88n15, 110n19
Spinelli, Franco, 83n6, 237
Stock, James H., 182n19

Taylor, Alan M., 11f, 18n11, 21n13, 22n15, 55n27, 70n7, 139n1, 143n10, 144n12, 146nn13,14, 147t, 150n20, 189n4, 190n6, 216n51
Temin, Peter, 168n6, 189, 190n7, 192n10, 199n25, 230n7
Terry, José, 30n22, 74
Timberlake, Richard H., 127n11
Tomz, Michael, 196n21, 217n55
Tornquist, Ernesto, & Company Limited, 108n15
Townsend, Robert M., 141, 153n22
Twomey, Michael J., 192n11, 195n15

Uriburu, Francisco, 72, 78, 215
Uriburu, José F., 195

Vázquez-Presedo, Vicente, 55n28
Végh, Carlos A., 14t, 18n11, 37n1
Velasco, Andrés, 167n4

Wigmore, Barrie A., 189n3, 192n10
Williams, John H., 18n11, 37n2, 46n15, 53, 59n33, 60n38, 61n39, 72n10, 73n11, 74n14, 75, 83n5, 95n21, 106n13, 108n16, 243n6
World Bank, 166n1

Zarazaga, Carlos E. J. M., 18n11, 147t, 149n18, 156t
Zecher, J. Richard, 22n15, 124n8
Zymelman, Manuel, 139n1, 147t

Subject Index

Avellaneda administration, 44

Balance of payments: with differential treatment of exports and imports, 81–82; at onset of Great Depression, 188
Banco de la Nación Argentina: creation (1891), 106–7, 169; credit restrictions and reserve requirements for, 107–8; as financial agent of government, 33, 143; internal currency convertibility by, 169–86; post-1892 importance, 33; as quasi-Lender of Last Resort (1914), 34, 135–36, 143, 171–72, 183; rediscount service of, 34, 171–77, 183, 200, 214
Banco de la Provincia de Buenos Aires: demise of (1891), 68, 74, 94, 108, 176–77; as fiscal agent of governments, 71–72; management of monetary policy by, 43; paper money as legal tender (1862), 38; run on (1890), 70–72; solvency-liquidity indicators (1886–91), 75–76
Banco Nacional: demise of (1891), 74, 94, 108, 169; run on (1890), 70–72
Banking system: bank money and reserves (1899–1914), 126–27; under Conversion Office regime, 228; domestic and foreign bank presence (1890s–1914), 140; economic shocks polluting (1913–34), 234; effect of Baring Crisis on, 69–79, 144, 176–77; in financial crises (1890–1931), 154–58; during financial crisis (1914), 130–36; fractional reserve system, 21, 177–86; under Law of National Guaranteed Banks (1887), 24–25, 58–60, 103; limits on monetary expansion under Monetary Law (1881), 46–47; post-Baring evolution, 79, 169–77; post-1892 separation from Conversion Office, 33–34; rediscounts from Banco de la Nación Argentina (1914–35), 34, 171–77, 183, 200, 214; runs on (1890–91), 70–74
Bank of England: bridge loan to Argentina (1891), 30, 73–74, 84, 106; as international Lender of Last Resort, 223–25; intervention in Baring Crisis, 67, 73; operation in 1847 crisis, 167–68
Baring Crisis (1890–91): effect on banks in Argentina, 144; effect on economy in Argentina, 68–70; factors provoking, 25; ingredients in, 16; lessons of, 221, 224–25; origin of, 67, 77, 223; timing and intensity of, 70–71
Bimetallic standard: in Argentina (1881), 46–48, 50–51; de jure status only, 51; units of currency under Monetary Law (1881), 46, 50, 222
Bond prices: spreads (1870–1940), 26–29; spreads (1883–1913), 122–24; spreads (1888–89), 89
Bonex 89 plan, Argentina, 224–25
Budget deficit. *See* Public debt

Capital flows: inflows (1868–72), 43; inflows (1884–90), 53, 55, 223; inflows (1891–1902), 30, 77, 105; inflows (1900–1930), 150; at onset

of First World War, 144–46; role of (1881–91), 29–30
Capital markets, international: access with credibility to, 29; after 1913, 29; Argentina's access to (1930s), 217; openness of Argentina to, 77
Central bank, Argentina: Conversion Office reorganized as (1935), 35, 159, 176, 188, 221; emergence of idea of, 34, 176, 204, 231; as Lender of Last Resort in Argentina, 234
Central banks: Bank of England as, 167–68, 223–25; modern conception of, 32; U.S. Federal Reserve Bank as, 228
Conversion Law (1891), 48–49, 120–21, 128
Conversion Office (Caja de Conversión): authority to issue money, 169; as currency board, 49–50; currency contraction policy, 106; defense of currency's external value, 154; emergency powers of, 183; exchange function under Conversion Law, 120; external currency convertibility by, 169–86; foreign exchange reserves held by, 156; gold stocks (1900–1935), 184, 192, 196–99; guaranteed fund deposit at, 108; independence of, 120–21; issuance of domestic currency, 202; as monetary authority, 32, 48–49, 103, 112, 188–89, 228; operation in gold standard regime, 177–86; post-1892 responsibilities, 33; rediscount function of, 34, 200, 202, 214–16; role in economic downturn (1913–14), 134–36; shift from metallic to fiduciary monetary policy (1931), 28, 31, 35, 202–18, 230–31; tenure of (1891–1935), 17–18, 25, 140, 213
Convertibility law (1881). *See* Conversion Law (1891)
Country risk: bond price spreads (1883–1913), 122–24; bond price spreads in Argentina (1870–1940), 26–28; decline in (1888–89), 89; defined, 26. *See also* Bond prices
Coup d'état (1930), 195n18, 215
Currency: bimetallic standard in Argentina (1881), 46–48, 50; Conversion Office exchange policy for, 119–20; under Monetary Law (1881), 46–50; paper pesos assigned to debt service, 82–83; paper-specie mix during Baring Crisis, 70–77; printing of paper pesos as, 87–90; tax payments using paper-gold market rate (1891), 101–2; transactions velocity of, 70; units under bimetallic standard, 46, 50. *See also* Paper currency (paper peso)
Currency boards: adoption in Argentina, 79; present version in Argentina, 18, 231; use in nineteenth century, 17n10
Currency convertibility: Cavallo plan in present-day Argentina, 12, 15, 17–18, 231; under Conversion Office authority (1891–1914), 49, 169; country risk of Argentina with, 26–28; failed plan of Buenos Aires province, 38–45; under Monetary Law (1881), 47–48; second Roca administration policy, 119–20; separation of internal and external functions, 33–34, 41–42, 73, 166–86; suspension in Argentina (1914–27), 197; suspension of, 186–87. *See also* Gold standard convertibility
Currency substitution: effect on inflation tax base, 92; as policy restraint, 24–25; using paper currency to pay off external debt, 90, 92

Debt, external: Bank of England funding loan to service, 30, 73–74, 84–85; burden of servicing (1890), 72; currency mix in payment of (1890–99), 102–3; delinquent provincial and municipal (1897–1900), 85, 225; measured in gold pesos (1883–1913), 84; pay off in paper currency (1889), 90; retirement policy (1906–13), 85; use of gold to service (1930s), 192, 196–97; uses for loans in Argentina (1884–90), 55; value of service in depreciated paper currency, 102–3
de la Plaza-Bank of England agreement. *See* Bank of England; Funding Loan (1891)

Economic performance: in Argentina (1800–1920), 6; in Argentina

(1868–74), 6–7, 42; in Argentina (1899–1914), 9, 126–29; in Argentina (1900–1939), 146–50; in Argentina (1900–1940), 152–54; in Argentina (1880s–1913), 7; comparison of countries (1820–2000), 7–9
Exchange rate: appreciation of real (1899–1914), 128; during Baring Crisis, 70–77; choice of floating or fixed rate system, 21; under Conversion Office, 17; during financial crisis (1914), 130–35; market rate of paper-gold (1899), 117, 119; paper-gold (1883–1902), 103–5; paper-gold (1884–1914), 48–49; paper-gold (1892–99), 113; path (1885–99), 104, 247–52; during recovery (1930s), 205, 207–13. *See also* Currency convertibility
Exchange rate regime: convertible or inconvertible, 22, 24; internal and external convertibility, 34, 41–42, 73, 166–86

Federal Reserve System, United States, 228
Financial crises: Asian (1997), 59, 77, 166n1, 223n3, 224; combined with macroeconomic crisis, 154–58, 166–69; international (1914), 130–35; Mexican (1994), 229; real, 32; recurrences in Argentina (1890–1931), 154–58
Financial intermediation: with collapse of official banks (1891), 94; loss in Argentina of (1890s), 31–32; proxies for, 146–48
Financial systems: comparison of core and peripheral countries (1913–39), 150–54, 162–64; development in Argentina (1900–1939), 146–50; effect of 1914 downturn in Argentina, 130–33. *See also* Banking system
Fiscal deficit. *See* Public debt
Fiscal policy: debt management (1884–90), 5; expansionary (1888–91), 223; during Great Depression, 193–97; related to gold-backed monetary base, 90; resumption of specie standard (1884), 55. *See also* Seigniorage (inflation tax)
Fiscal revenues: gold value of (1892–94), 112; from internal excise taxes (1884–1913), 81, 100–102; from taxes on international trade (1884–1913), 81–82, 102
Fiscal spending: composition of (1884–1913), 81–82; debt service (1884–1913), 81–83
Funding Loan (1891): high interest rates of, 110, 116; syndicated loan to Argentina, 30, 73–74, 84–85, 106

Gold standard, international: adherence in Argentina to (1867–76), 42–43; adjustment in Argentina (1900–1913), 121–30; fractional reserve banks under regime of, 21, 177–86; operation in Argentina (1904–14), 124–25; policies for adequate functioning, 22; public debt of Argentina during adherence to, 85; reentry of Argentina (1899), 50; resumption (1927–29), 186; suspension (1914), 118, 121, 130, 183; suspension in Argentina (1929), 193n13
Gold standard convertibility: restoration and maintenance of (1899–1914), 117–21; support for policy of, 119
Goschen debt conversion (1887), 95
Government, Argentina: intervention in banks runs (1890), 72–73; as Lender of Last Resort, 72–73; merchant banks' Funding Loan to (1891), 106; requirements under Bank of England loan (1891), 73–74
Great Depression: Argentine fiscal policy during, 193–96; experience in Argentina, 188–93
Gresham's Law, 50

Inflation: in Argentina (1820–1935), 13–15; hyperinflation in Argentina (1980s–1990s), 17, 224; median inflation in Argentina (1940–97), 10–12. *See also* Seigniorage (inflation tax)
Instituto Movilizador de Inversiones Bancarias (IMIB): bailout operation of (1935), 231–33

Interest groups: influence on rediscounting to banks, 174–76; influence on trade-related taxes, 82. *See also* Public perception
Interest rates: during Baring Crisis, 92–94; behavior of nominal and real (1891–99), 115–16; effect of inflationary policy on, 92–94; during recovery (1930s), 205, 207–13. *See also* Bond prices
International Monetary Fund (IMF): as international Lender of Last Resort, 224
Irigoyen administration, economic crisis and coup d'état (1930), 215

Juárez Celman administration, 73; bank solvency during, 75; effect of inflationary policies, 92–93; expected duration, 93–94; stabilization of gold value of fiscal revenues, 100

Law of National Guaranteed Banks (1887), 24–25, 58–60, 77, 240–43; debt incurred under, 84; financial deepening during, 126; incentives of, 99; provision for gold-backed paper note issue, 89–90
Lender of Last Resort: Argentine bank as (1914), 134; Conversion Office inability to act as, 154, 221; IMF as, 224
Long Term Capital Management, 67n2

Macroeconomic policy: dilemma of, 21; trilemma of, 16, 21, 70, 99. *See also* Fiscal policy; Monetary policy
Mitre administration, 13–14, 38–39
Monetary base: in Argentina (1899–13), 121–26; composition of (1900–1940), 200–201; increase (1868–72), 42–43; institution to control (1891), 108; rate of growth (1890–91), 68
Monetary Law (1881), 46, 50, 221, 222
Monetary policy: in Argentina (1929–35), 188–89, 197–202, 205, 207–13, 230–31; of Conversion Office, 32, 120–21, 177, 221, 228; experiments in nineteenth century, 38–50; in Funding Loan agreement with Argentina, 106; influence of federal budget on, 83–84; under Law of National Guaranteed Banks (1887), 58; management by Banco de la Provincia, 43; need for reform (1890s), 99; Pelligrini administration reforms, 103; rediscount law (1914), 34, 200; reform of Mitre administration (1862), 38–39; of rigid convertibility under Conversion Office, 17, 34; shift from metallic to fiduciary (1931), 28, 31, 35, 202–18, 230–31. *See also* Banking system; Capital flows; Currency; Currency convertibility; Debt, external; Gold standard, international; Monetization; Paper currency; Sterilization
Monetary standard: for borrower countries, 26; convertible or inconvertible, 22, 24; idea of efficient, 26
Monetization: in Argentina (1820s–1880s), 15–16; combined with convertibility (1868–72), 43–44; to cover budget deficit (1889–91), 90, 92; during interwar period, 143; to service fiscal deficits (1885–93), 87–90. *See also* Seigniorage (inflation tax)
Money base. *See* Monetary base
Money supply: Conversion Office control of (1891–1935), 140; effect of gold reserves on (1904–13), 124–25
Moral hazard: emergence in Argentina, 176–77; of state guarantees to banks, 72–73

Office of Exchange: commitment to international gold standard, 42–43; establishment (1867), 41–42

Paper currency (paper peso): depreciation (1891), 102–4; flight to specie from (1889), 90; investment in assets denominated in, 95; used to payoff external debt (1889), 90
Patriotic Loan law (1932), 35, 202n29
Pellegrini administration: actions to support banking system (1890), 73; acts to preserve Argentina's reputation, 225; new tax measures (1891), 82, 101–2; Romero

Agreement during, 83, 109–10, 112; tax on deposits in foreign-owned banks (1891), 73n12
Public debt: debt instruments in interwar period, 143; levels and service of (1891–99), 100–103; management in Argentina (1881–91), 29–30; measured in gold pesos (1883–1913), 84; paper pesos assigned to service, 82–83, 87–90; post-1890 crash influences on, 84–85; related to insufficient revenue (1885–93), 87–89; service and amortization of (1884–1913), 81–83. *See also* Debt, external
Public debt theory: intertemporal budget constraint in, 20–21
Public perception: of Banco de la Nación Argentina, 106–7; during Baring Crisis, 16; behavior under gold standard (1904–13), 128; of closing of Conversion Office, 213–16; of guaranteed paper peso (1887), 59–62, 68; lack of confidence in convertibility, 50–52, 90–91; of reforms (1890–91), 108–9
Purchasing power parity (PPP), Argentina (1884–1913), 122, 130, 248

Recession, Argentina: effect (1913–14), 171, 190; performance of currency-board system (1913–14), 118
Rediscounting: emergency law about (1913–14), 35, 200; of Banco de la Nación Argentina (1914–35), 35, 171–77, 183, 200, 214; used by Conversion Office (1931), 34, 200, 202, 214–16
Roca administration (second term, 1898–1904), 119–20
Romero Agreement: rescheduling of debt service under, 83, 109–10, 112
Rothschild Committee, 109

Saenz Peña administration (1892), 108
Sarmiento administration, 42
Seigniorage (inflation tax): in Argentina (1820–80), 12–13, 15–16, 19; in Argentina (1820s–1860s), 13f, 222; currency substitution lowers base for, 92; to finance budget deficit (1889–91), 90, 92; with shift to fiduciary regime, 35
Specie reserves: changes in (1885–93), 89t, 90; loss of (1880s), 25; under Monetary Law (1881), 47
Sterilization: of gold outflow (1888–89), 60, 70, 189; of gold outflow by Conversion Office (1931), 202

Uriburu administration, 72